DK SMITHSONIAN

Children's Illustrated

ATLAS

DK | Penguin Random House

This edition
Writer and Consultant Andrew Brooks
Authenticity Consultant Bianca Hezekiah
Editorial Marie Greenwood, John Hort
Design Ann Cannings, Roohi Rais
US Senior Editor Shannon Beatty
US Editor Margaret Parrish
Jacket Designer Ann Cannings
DTP designers Dheeraj Singh, Syed Md Farhan
Production Editor Dragana Puvacic
Production Controller Leanne Burke
Publishing Director Sarah Larter

Previous edition
Writer and Consultant Andrew Brooks
Senior Editor Marie Greenwood
Senior Designer Jim Green

US Editor Margaret Parrish
Map Illustrator Jeongeun Park
Illustrators Maltings Partnership, Daniel Long
Senior Editors Gill Pitts, Cécile Landau
Project Art Editor Hoa Luc
Designer Emma Hobson
Design Assistant Rhea Gaughan
Cartography Ed Merritt, Simon Mumford
Index Helen Peters
Pre-production Dragana Puvacic
Production Srijana Gurung
Managing Editor Laura Gilbert
Managing Art Editor Diane Peyton Jones
Art Director Martin Wilson
Publisher Sarah Larter
Publishing Director Sophie Mitchell

This American Edition, 2023
First American Edition, 2016
Published in the United States by DK Publishing
1745 Broadway, 20th Floor, New York, NY 10019

Copyright © 2016, 2023 Dorling Kindersley Limited
DK, a Division of Penguin Random House LLC
23 24 25 15 14 13 12 11
001–333827–Apr/2023

All rights reserved.
Without limiting the rights under the copyright reserved above, no part of this publication may be reproduced, stored in or introduced into a retrieval system, or transmitted, in any form, or by any means (electronic, mechanical, photocopying, recording, or otherwise), without the prior written permission of the copyright owner.
Published in Great Britain by Dorling Kindersley Limited.

A catalog record for this book is available from the Library of Congress.
ISBN: 978-0-7440-7388-1

DK books are available at special discounts when purchased in bulk for sales promotions, premiums, fund-raising, or educational use. For details, contact: DK Publishing Special Markets, 1745 Broadway, 20th Floor, New York, NY 10019 SpecialSales@dk.com

Printed in the UAE

For the curious
www.dk.com

MIX
Paper | Supporting responsible forestry
FSC™ C018179

This book was made with Forest Stewardship Council™ certified paper – one small step in DK's commitment to a sustainable future. For more information go to www.dk.com/our-green-pledge

CONTENTS

HOW TO READ THE MAPS

A map is a drawing that gives an instant impression of a place. The maps in this book show many of the world's countries plotted with rivers, mountains, forests, and cities.

Picture symbols
You will find picture symbols of a country's produce, industry, sports, and activities plotted on each country map. Look at the key to find what each symbol means

Picture features
Pictures with text pick out a country's special features, including historic sites, animals, and natural wonders

Capital
A country's capital city is marked with a red outline

Bordering countries
Around the edges of the map you can see all the bordering countries

Flag
On every country, you'll find the country's flag

History and culture
These photographs show historical and cultural features that are unique to that country

Places of interest
These photographs zoom in on a city, building, or landscape and show where it is on the map

Produce
Close-up photographs show food, drink, and other goods that a country produces

Page numbers
The circles are color-coded for each continent, so you know which continent you are in

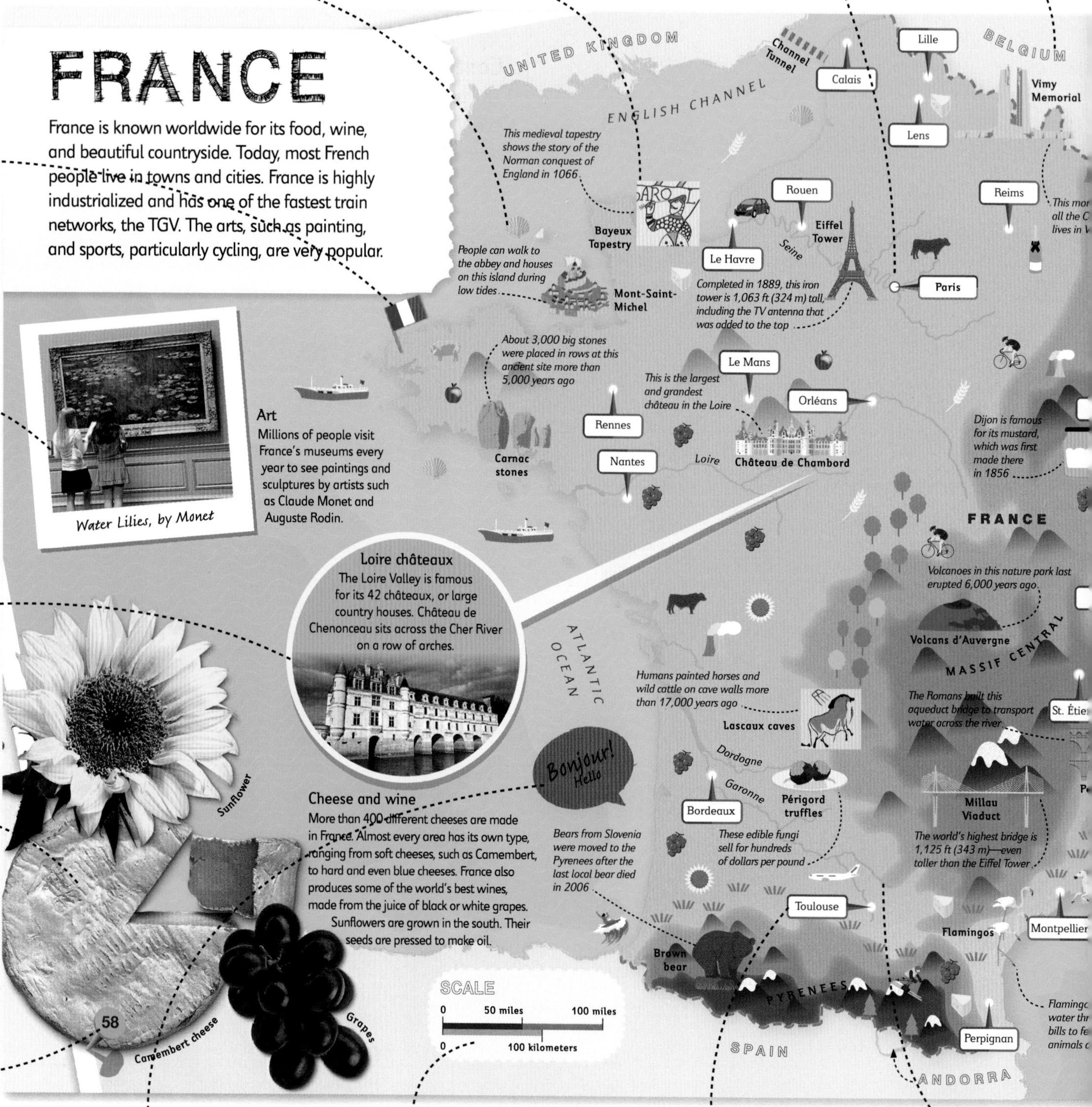

FRANCE
France is known worldwide for its food, wine, and beautiful countryside. Today, most French people live in towns and cities. France is highly industrialized and has one of the fastest train networks, the TGV. The arts, such as painting, and sports, particularly cycling, are very popular.
UNITED KINGDOM
ENGLISH CHANNEL
Channel Tunnel
Calais
Lille
BELGIUM
Vimy Memorial
Lens
This medieval tapestry shows the story of the Norman conquest of England in 1066
Bayeux Tapestry
Rouen
Reims
Eiffel Tower
Le Havre
Seine
Paris
People can walk to the abbey and houses on this island during low tides
Mont-Saint-Michel
Completed in 1889, this iron tower is 1,063 ft (324 m) tall, including the TV antenna that was added to the top
About 3,000 big stones were placed in rows at this ancient site more than 5,000 years ago
Le Mans
This is the largest and grandest château in the Loire
Orléans
Rennes
Nantes
Loire
Château de Chambord
Carnac stones
Dijon is famous for its mustard, which was first made there in 1856
Art
Millions of people visit France's museums every year to see paintings and sculptures by artists such as Claude Monet and Auguste Rodin.
Water Lilies, by Monet
FRANCE
Loire châteaux
The Loire Valley is famous for its 42 châteaux, or large country houses. Château de Chenonceau sits across the Cher River on a row of arches.
Volcanoes in this nature park last erupted 6,000 years ago
Volcans d'Auvergne
MASSIF CENTRAL
ATLANTIC OCEAN
Humans painted horses and wild cattle on cave walls more than 17,000 years ago
Lascaux caves
The Romans built this aqueduct bridge to transport water across the river
Dordogne
Garonne
Bonjour! Hello
Périgord truffles
Millau Viaduct
Bordeaux
Sunflower
Cheese and wine
More than 400 different cheeses are made in France. Almost every area has its own type, ranging from soft cheeses, such as Camembert, to hard and even blue cheeses. France also produces some of the world's best wines, made from the juice of black or white grapes. Sunflowers are grown in the south. Their seeds are pressed to make oil.
Bears from Slovenia were moved to the Pyrenees after the last local bear died in 2006
These edible fungi sell for hundreds of dollars per pound
The world's highest bridge is 1,125 ft (343 m)—even taller than the Eiffel Tower
Toulouse
Flamingos
Montpellier
Brown bear
PYRENEES
SCALE
0 50 miles 100 miles
0 100 kilometers
58
Camembert cheese
Grapes
SPAIN
Perpignan
ANDORRA

Language
You will find speech bubbles that say "Hello" or "Good-bye" in the country's main language

Scale
The scale indicates the size of the country and the distances between different points on the map

Cities
Towns and cities featured on the map are marked with a blue outline

Rivers
A country's most important rivers are shown on each map

Country borders

Borders
The borders between countries are shown with a red line of dashes.

Disputed borders
Some countries disagree about where the border between them should be. These borders are shown with a dotted line.

Compass
The compass always points north (N) in line with the map and also shows the direction of south (S), east (E), and west (W)

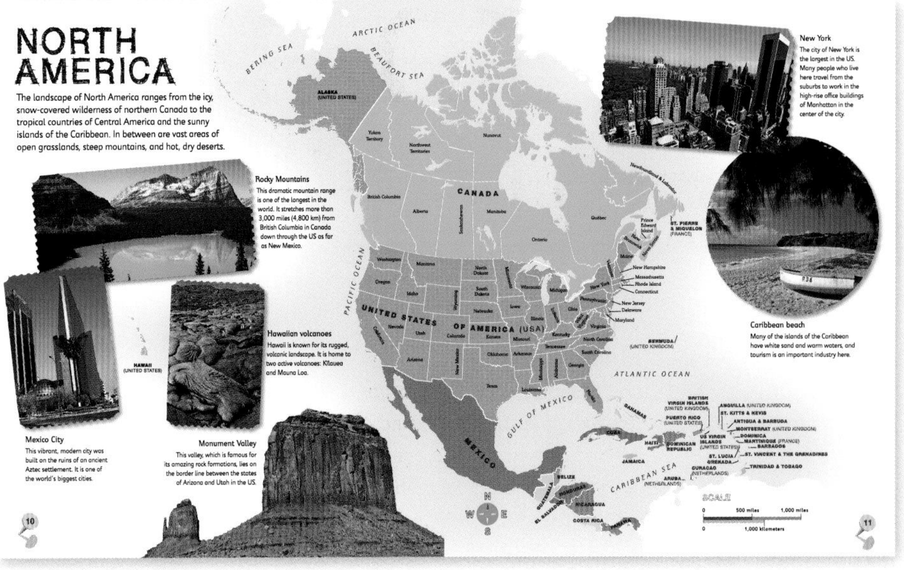

NORTH AMERICA
The landscape of North America ranges from the icy, snow-covered wilderness of northern Canada to the tropical countries of Central America and the sunny islands of the Caribbean. In between are vast areas of open grasslands, steep mountains, and hot, dry deserts.
ARCTIC OCEAN
PACIFIC OCEAN
ATLANTIC OCEAN
CANADA
UNITED STATES OF AMERICA (USA)
MEXICO
GULF OF MEXICO
CARIBBEAN SEA

Continent maps

The continent maps are colored to show every country in each continent. Photographs show the continent's major features.

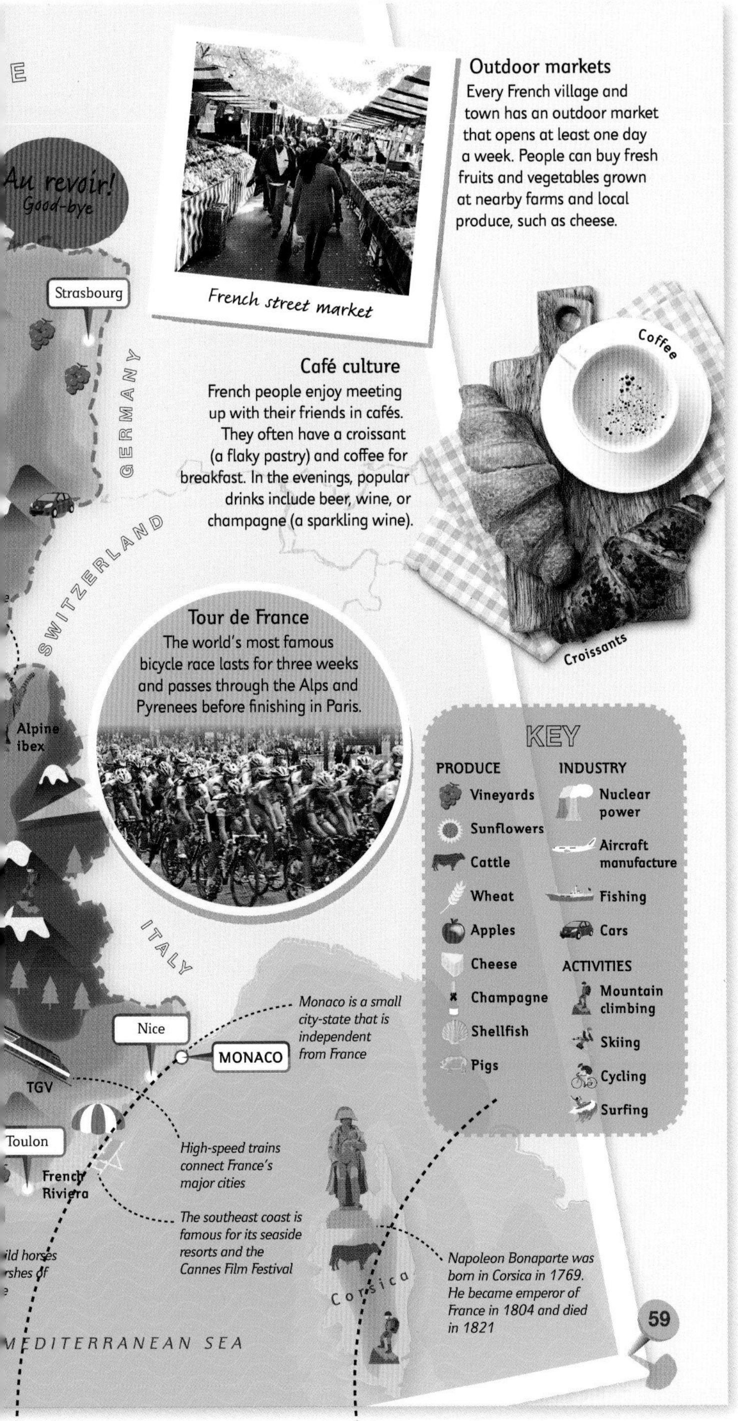

Au revoir!
Good-bye
Strasbourg
GERMANY
SWITZERLAND
ITALY
Outdoor markets
Every French village and town has an outdoor market that opens at least one day a week. People can buy fresh fruits and vegetables grown at nearby farms and local produce, such as cheese.
French street market
Café culture
French people enjoy meeting up with their friends in cafés. They often have a croissant (a flaky pastry) and coffee for breakfast. In the evenings, popular drinks include beer, wine, or champagne (a sparkling wine).
Coffee
Croissants
Tour de France
The world's most famous bicycle race lasts for three weeks and passes through the Alps and Pyrenees before finishing in Paris.
Alpine ibex
KEY
PRODUCE
Vineyards
Sunflowers
Cattle
Wheat
Apples
Cheese
Champagne
Shellfish
Pigs
INDUSTRY
Nuclear power
Aircraft manufacture
Fishing
Cars
ACTIVITIES
Mountain climbing
Skiing
Cycling
Surfing
Nice
MONACO
Monaco is a small city-state that is independent from France
TGV
Toulon
French Riviera
High-speed trains connect France's major cities
The southeast coast is famous for its seaside resorts and the Cannes Film Festival
Napoleon Bonaparte was born in Corsica in 1769. He became emperor of France in 1804 and died in 1821
Corsica
MEDITERRANEAN SEA
59

Independent states
Small independent states, such as Monaco, are shown with a red border and a solid red dot, and the name is in capital letters.

Key
Every country map has a key listing major features, such as produce and industry, that relate to the picture symbols on the map

Habitats

These colors and symbols show the different habitats, or landscapes, of each country.

Hot deserts
Hot deserts are dry and sandy areas and few plants grow here.

Cold deserts
These are dry stretches of land with low temperatures, such as the Gobi in Asia.

Snow and ice
Frozen areas are found high in the mountains and near the North and South poles.

Mountains
High, rugged mountainous areas are often covered with snow.

Oceans and seas
Water surround the seven continents.

Scrubland
Low-lying plants and grasses grow in scrubland areas, such as in southern Spain.

Wetland
Wetlands are marshy, swampy areas, such as the Pantanal in Brazil.

Grassland
Grasslands are flat, grassy plains with few trees, such as the savanna of Africa.

Tropical
Rain forests, such as the Amazon, grow in warm and wet tropical areas.

Deciduous forests
These forests have trees that lose their leaves in the fall and winter.

Coniferous forests
These forests are made up of evergreen trees like pines that keep their leaves in winter.

North America
This huge continent lies wholly in the northern half (hemisphere) of the world. It includes Greenland, which lies above the Arctic Circle.

Equator
This is an imaginary line that goes round the middle of the Earth, dividing it into two halves, called the north and south hemispheres.

South America
This continent lies mainly in the southern hemisphere of the world. North, Central, and South America are together known as the Americas.

THE WORLD

This is a flat map of our round Earth. Land covers about a third of Earth's surface. This land is broken up into seven large blocks called continents. Water makes up the rest of the Earth and is divided into five major areas, called oceans.

Antarctica
This is the most southern of all the continents. It is covered in frozen ice and hardly anybody lives here.

ARCTIC OCEAN
Europe
Europe is the second smallest continent, yet has the third biggest population.
ASIA
EUROPE
Asia
This is the largest continent in the world and the one with the biggest population.
PACIFIC OCEAN
AFRICA
INDIAN OCEAN
AUSTRALASIA
Africa
Africa is the world's second largest continent and the second most populated one.
Australasia
This is the world's smallest continent. It includes the world's biggest island, Australia, and many small islands in the Pacific Ocean.
SOUTHERN OCEAN
ANTARCTICA

2. The merengue is the national dance of which Caribbean country?
3. In which Canadian city is the CN Tower found?
1. Into which mountain is this sculpture carved?
4. In which country would you find this ancient Pyramid of the Sun?

8. Which canal connects the world's two biggest oceans?
7. Who were the first people to settle in northern Canada?
6. Which river flows through the Grand Canyon?
5. In which American city will you see yellow taxis?
You can find all the answers and more quizzes on pages 120–121.

NORTH AMERICA

Canada, the United States of America (USA), Mexico, Central America, and the Caribbean islands make up North America. This vast continent was first settled by Native American people before the arrival of Europeans and people from other parts of the world.

NORTH AMERICA

The landscape of North America ranges from the icy, snow-covered wilderness of northern Canada to the tropical countries of Central America and the sunny islands of the Caribbean. In between are vast areas of open grasslands, steep mountains, and hot, dry deserts.

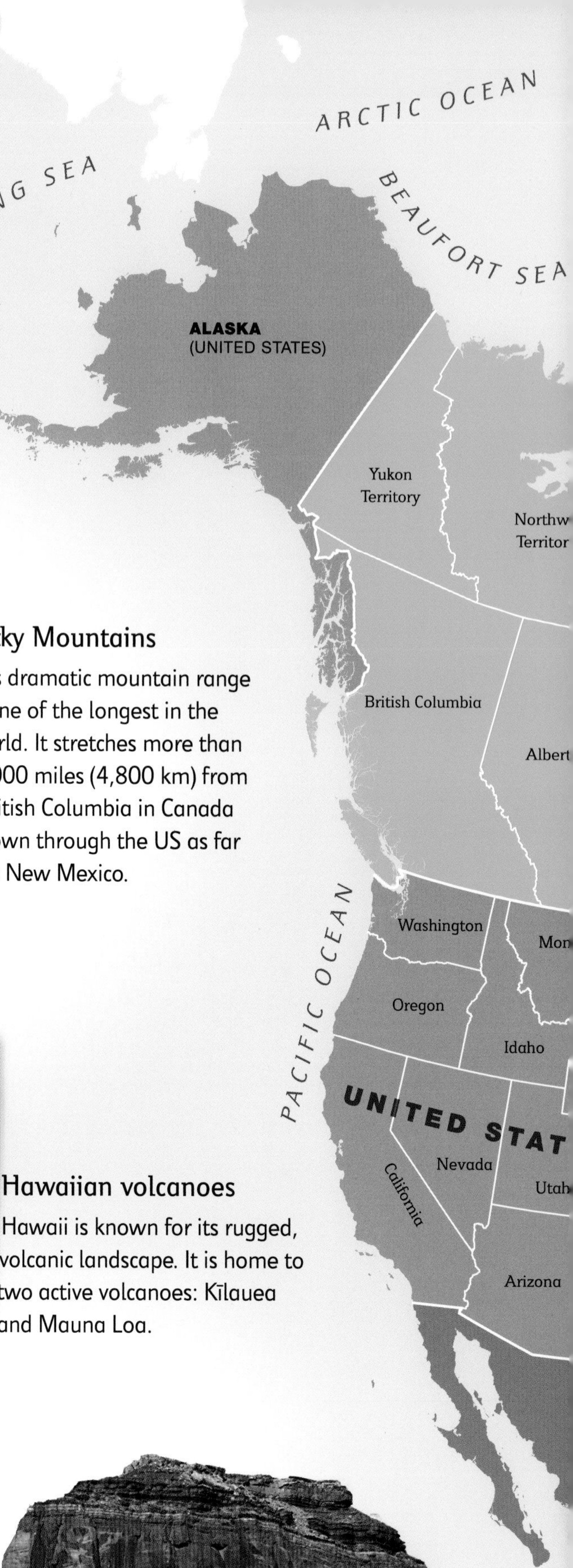
ARCTIC OCEAN
BERING SEA
BEAUFORT SEA
ALASKA
(UNITED STATES)
Yukon Territory
Northw
Territor
British Columbia
Albert
PACIFIC OCEAN
Washington
Mon
Oregon
Idaho
UNITED STAT
Nevada
California
Utah
Arizona

Rocky Mountains

This dramatic mountain range is one of the longest in the world. It stretches more than 3,000 miles (4,800 km) from British Columbia in Canada down through the US as far as New Mexico.

HAWAII
(UNITED STATES)

Hawaiian volcanoes

Hawaii is known for its rugged, volcanic landscape. It is home to two active volcanoes: Kīlauea and Mauna Loa.

Mexico City

This vibrant, modern city was built on the ruins of an ancient Aztec settlement. It is one of the world's biggest cities.

Monument Valley

This valley, which is famous for its amazing rock formations, lies on the border line between the states of Arizona and Utah in the US.

New York

The city of New York is the largest in the US. Many people who live here travel from the suburbs to work in the high-rise office buildings of Manhattan in the center of the city.

Caribbean beach

Many of the islands of the Caribbean have white sand and warm waters, and tourism is an important industry here.

Nunavut
ANADA
Manitoba
Québec
Ontario
Newfoundland & Labrador
Prince Edward Island
New Brunswick
Nova Scotia
ST. PIERRE & MIQUELON (FRANCE)
Maine
Vermont
New Hampshire
Massachusetts
Rhode Island
Connecticut
New York
North Dakota
South Dakota
Minnesota
Wisconsin
Michigan
Pennsylvania
New Jersey
Delaware
Maryland
Nebraska
Iowa
Illinois
Indiana
Ohio
West Virginia
Virginia
AMERICA (USA)
Kansas
Missouri
Kentucky
North Carolina
BERMUDA
(UNITED KINGDOM)
Tennessee
Oklahoma
Arkansas
South Carolina
Mississippi
Alabama
Georgia
ATLANTIC OCEAN
Texas
Louisiana
Florida
GULF OF MEXICO
BAHAMAS
MEXICO
CUBA
HAITI
DOMINICAN REPUBLIC
BRITISH VIRGIN ISLANDS (UNITED KINGDOM)
PUERTO RICO (UNITED STATES)
ANGUILLA (UNITED KINGDOM)
ST. KITTS & NEVIS
ANTIGUA & BARBUDA
MONTSERRAT (UNITED KINGDOM)
US VIRGIN ISLANDS (UNITED STATES)
DOMINICA
MARTINIQUE (FRANCE)
BARBADOS
ST. LUCIA
ST. VINCENT & THE GRENADINES
GRENADA
TRINIDAD & TOBAGO
JAMAICA
CURACAO (NETHERLANDS)
ARUBA (NETHERLANDS)
CARIBBEAN SEA
BELIZE
GUATEMALA
HONDURAS
EL SALVADOR
NICARAGUA
COSTA RICA
PANAMA
N
W
E
S
SCALE
0
500 miles
1,000 miles
0
1,000 kilometers

CANADA AND ALASKA

Canada is the world's second largest country. It has huge mountain ranges, wide and vast forests, and bustling cities. It is also rich in oil and mineral resources, as is Alaska, the biggest state in the US.

Defending the net

Ice hockey
This fast-moving sport is very popular in Canada and can be played on ice rinks or frozen lakes. Both the women's and men's teams have won more Olympic gold medals than any other nation.

ARCTIC OCEAN
BEAUFORT SEA
Oil is carried across Alaska from the north coast to the south by the Trans-Alaska Pipeline
Prudhoe Bay
Trans-Alaska Pipeline
At 20,310 ft (6,190 m) Denali is the highest mountain in North America
Alaska (USA)
Yukon
Mackenzie
The Inuit were the first people to settle in north Canada; they play drums at special events and celebrations
Inuit drummers
Fairbanks
Line fishing
Denali
Anchorage
Valdez
Alaskan rivers are full of trout and other fish
Great Bear Lake
Pelly
ROCKY MOUNTAINS
Yellowknife
The Mounties police force wear red jackets on special occasions
Great Slave Lake
Sea otter
The Alaskan coast is home to groups of sea otters, which rest floating on their backs
Whitehorse
Juneau
COAST MOUNTAINS
Canadian Mountie
More than one million people come to this big rodeo festival every July
Wheelchair basketball is played throug North Americ
PACIFIC OCEAN
The first people of Canada carved wooden totem poles to show their cultural beliefs
Calgary Stampede
Edmonton
Totem pole
Wheelchair basketball
Curling
Dinosa Provinc Park
Victoria
Vancouver
Calgary
This sport is played with sliding stones on a sheet of ice
Well-preserved dinosaur fossils have been found in this park

KEY

PRODUCE
- Wheat
- Dried beans and legumes
- Corn

INDUSTRY
- Gold
- Coal
- Silver
- Oil
- Lumber
- Uranium
- Technology
- Aircraft
- Gas
- Fishing
- Diamonds
- Aluminum
- Paper mills
- Cars

ACTIVITIES
- Hiking
- Skiing

SCALE
0 — 250 miles
0 — 250 kilometers

Grizzly bear
In the rivers of Alaska and western Canada, grizzly bears catch salmon as the fish swim and leap upstream in the fall.

Vancouver coast
Vancouver is an exciting, international city that is surrounded by nature. It is often voted as one of the best places in the world to live.

Haida portrait figures made from wood

Haida figurines

First people
The Haida were among the first people to live in Canada before the arrival of Europeans. "Haida" means "person," and they live on the Pacific Northwest Coast.

Canadian goods

Canada is famous for its maple syrup, which is made from the sap of the sugar maple tree. Canola oil is used for cooking, flax is grown for its seeds and fibers, and lobsters live in the cool waters off the east coast.

Tour de l'Île de Montréal

Every year the French Canadian city of Montréal celebrates the Tour de l'Île de Montréal, a series of major street cycling events.

Niagara Falls

On the border of Canada and the US are the huge Niagara Falls. Water flows over the Horseshoe, American, and Bridal Veil waterfalls.

Flax
Flax seeds
Lobster
Canola oil
Canadian Pure
Maple Syrup
Maple syrup
GREENLAND
BAFFIN BAY
Street cycling
The Arctic Circle marks the edge of the Arctic region
Arctic Circle
CANADA
Iqaluit
N
W
E
S
Beaver
Beavers fell trees and build dams across rivers
Bonjour!
Hello
HUDSON BAY
A male moose's antlers may span 6½ ft (2 m)
Hello!
Moose
This author wrote children's books about Anne of Green Gables, and most were set in Prince Edward Island
St. John's
Lucy Maud Montgomery
This popular sport is similar to football in the US, but played by teams of 12
This grand hotel stands just inside the walls of Old Québec City. It opened in 1893
Château Frontenac
Charlottetown
Prince Edward Island
Fredericton
Halifax
Lacrosse
Canadian football
Québec City
Montréal
Ottawa
Bay of Fundy
Lake Superior
Lake Huron
Winnipeg
This Toronto landmark gives fantastic views of the city
CN Tower
Toronto
London
Lake Erie
Players use a lacrosse stick to catch and hold a rubber ball in this team sport
UNITED STATES OF AMERICA
This bay has the highest tides in the world, which have created amazing rock shapes

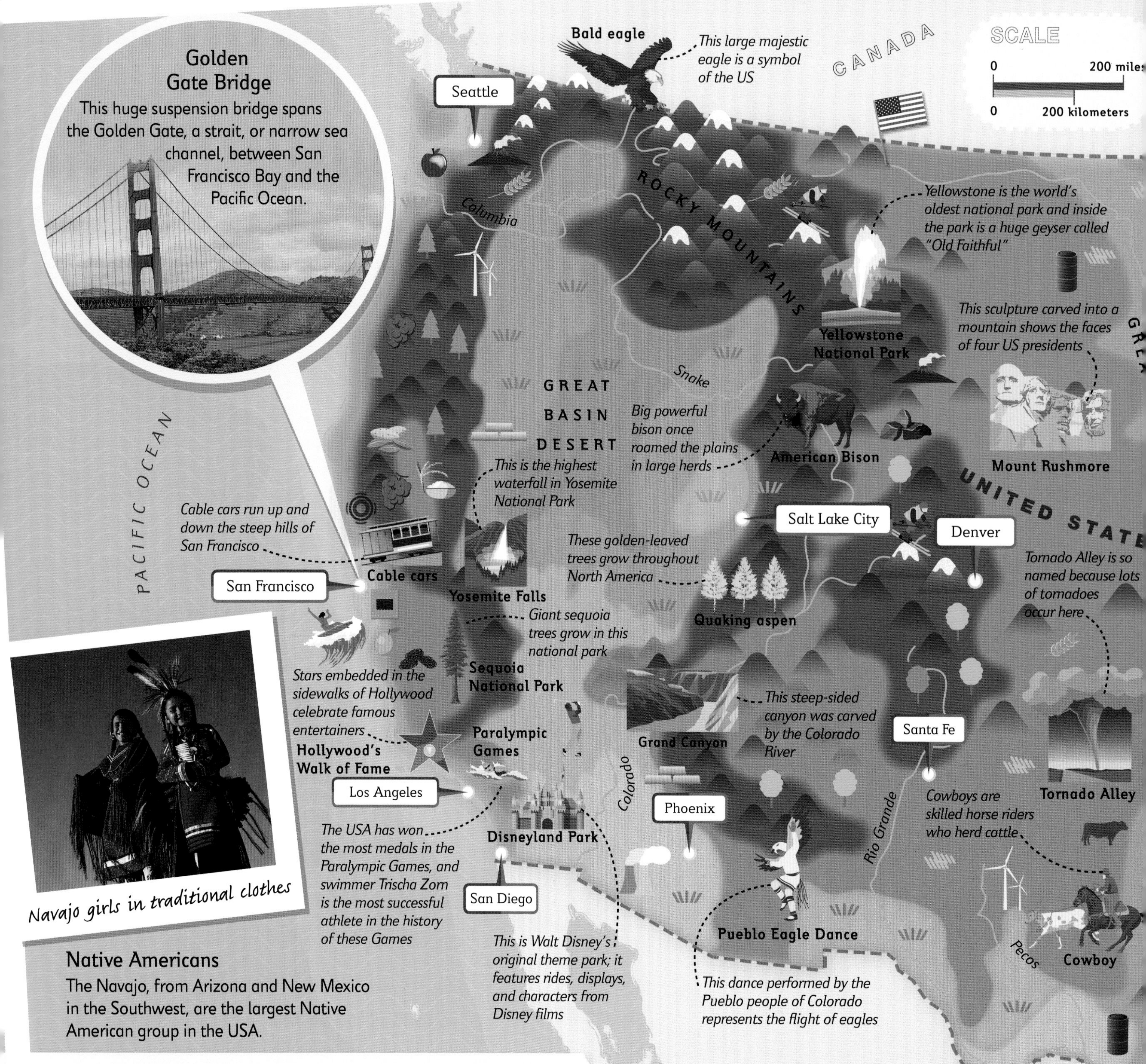
Bald eagle
This large majestic eagle is a symbol of the US
CANADA
SCALE
0 200 miles
0 200 kilometers
Seattle
Columbia
ROCKY MOUNTAINS
Yellowstone is the world's oldest national park and inside the park is a huge geyser called "Old Faithful"
Yellowstone National Park
This sculpture carved into a mountain shows the faces of four US presidents
Mount Rushmore
Snake
GREAT BASIN DESERT
Big powerful bison once roamed the plains in large herds
American Bison
PACIFIC OCEAN
This is the highest waterfall in Yosemite National Park
Cable cars run up and down the steep hills of San Francisco
Cable cars
San Francisco
Yosemite Falls
Salt Lake City
Denver
UNITED STATES
These golden-leaved trees grow throughout North America
Quaking aspen
Tornado Alley is so named because lots of tornadoes occur here
Giant sequoia trees grow in this national park
Sequoia National Park
Stars embedded in the sidewalks of Hollywood celebrate famous entertainers
Hollywood's Walk of Fame
Paralympic Games
Grand Canyon
This steep-sided canyon was carved by the Colorado River
Santa Fe
Tornado Alley
Colorado
Los Angeles
Phoenix
Rio Grande
Cowboys are skilled horse riders who herd cattle
The USA has won the most medals in the Paralympic Games, and swimmer Trischa Zorn is the most successful athlete in the history of these Games
Disneyland Park
San Diego
This is Walt Disney's original theme park; it features rides, displays, and characters from Disney films
Pueblo Eagle Dance
This dance performed by the Pueblo people of Colorado represents the flight of eagles
Pecos
Cowboy
MEXICO

Golden Gate Bridge

This huge suspension bridge spans the Golden Gate, a strait, or narrow sea channel, between San Francisco Bay and the Pacific Ocean.

Navajo girls in traditional clothes

Native Americans

The Navajo, from Arizona and New Mexico in the Southwest, are the largest Native American group in the USA.

USA

The United States of America (USA) is a huge and influential country made up of 50 states. It has wide stretches of wilderness as well as big, modern cities. The landscape is a mix of vast plains, high mountain ranges, deserts, and wetlands. Many people from all over the world have made their home here.

Hawaii
The islands of Hawaii, in the Pacific Ocean, became the 50th US state in 1959
Honolulu
Hawaii
Aloha!
Hello or good-bye

Baseball glove and ball

Independence Day celebrations

Independence Day

The Fourth of July is a holiday that marks the day in 1776 when the US became independent from Britain. People celebrate with firework displays.

Baseball

This is one of the most popular sports in the US. It is played between two teams that take turns batting and fielding.

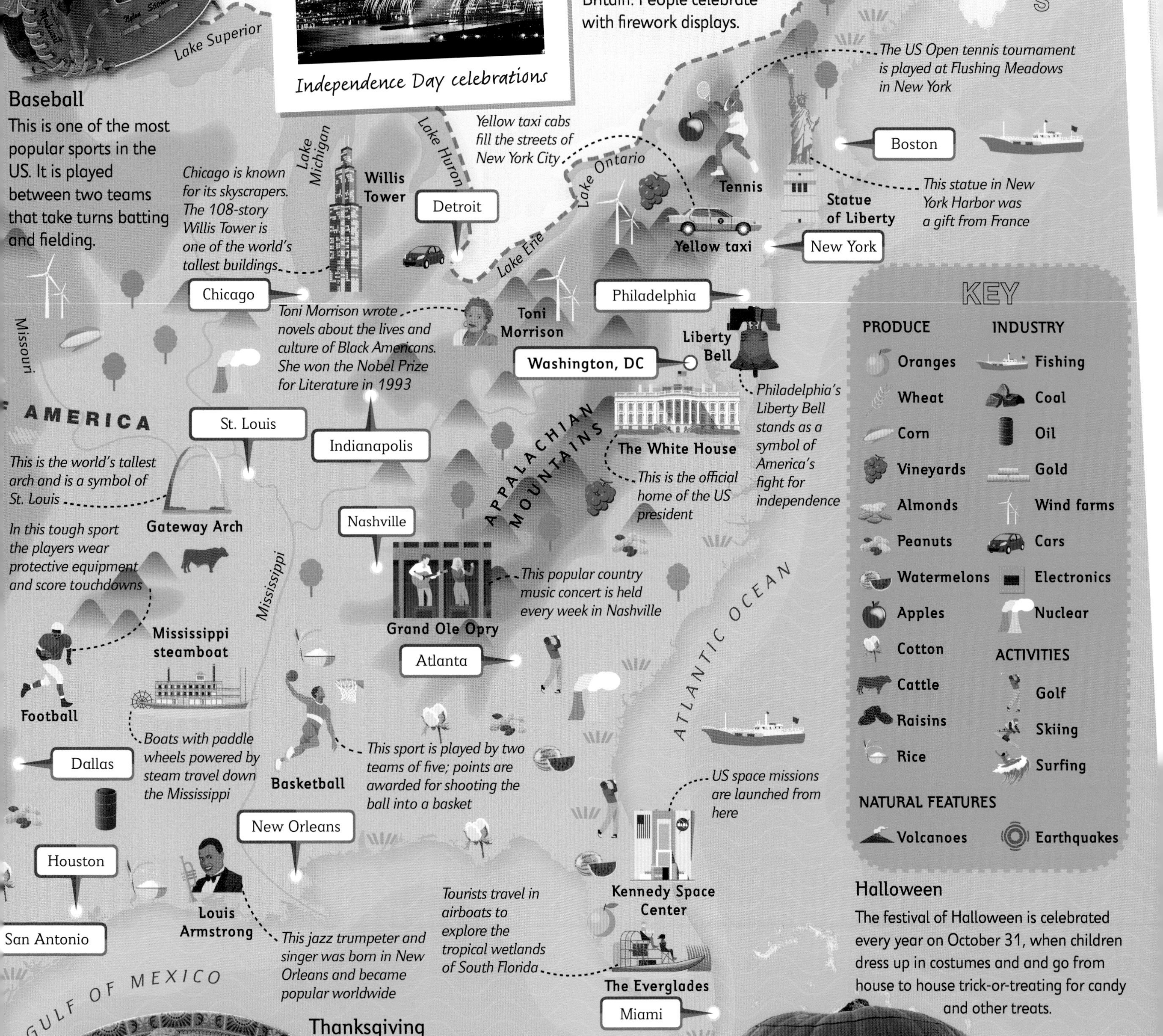
Hello!
N
W
E
S
Lake Superior
Lake Michigan
Lake Huron
Lake Ontario
Lake Erie
Yellow taxi cabs fill the streets of New York City
The US Open tennis tournament is played at Flushing Meadows in New York
Chicago is known for its skyscrapers. The 108-story Willis Tower is one of the world's tallest buildings
Willis Tower
Detroit
Tennis
Statue of Liberty
This statue in New York Harbor was a gift from France
Boston
Yellow taxi
New York
Chicago
Philadelphia
Toni Morrison wrote novels about the lives and culture of Black Americans. She won the Nobel Prize for Literature in 1993
Toni Morrison
Liberty Bell
Washington, DC
Missouri
AMERICA
St. Louis
Indianapolis
APPALACHIAN MOUNTAINS
The White House
This is the official home of the US president
Philadelphia's Liberty Bell stands as a symbol of America's fight for independence
This is the world's tallest arch and is a symbol of St. Louis
Gateway Arch
Nashville
In this tough sport the players wear protective equipment and score touchdowns
Mississippi
This popular country music concert is held every week in Nashville
Grand Ole Opry
ATLANTIC OCEAN
Mississippi steamboat
Atlanta
Football
Boats with paddle wheels powered by steam travel down the Mississippi
This sport is played by two teams of five; points are awarded for shooting the ball into a basket
Basketball
Dallas
US space missions are launched from here
New Orleans
Houston
Kennedy Space Center
Louis Armstrong
Tourists travel in airboats to explore the tropical wetlands of South Florida
This jazz trumpeter and singer was born in New Orleans and became popular worldwide
San Antonio
GULF OF MEXICO
The Everglades
Miami
KEY
PRODUCE
Oranges
Wheat
Corn
Vineyards
Almonds
Peanuts
Watermelons
Apples
Cotton
Cattle
Raisins
Rice
INDUSTRY
Fishing
Coal
Oil
Gold
Wind farms
Cars
Electronics
Nuclear
ACTIVITIES
Golf
Skiing
Surfing
NATURAL FEATURES
Volcanoes
Earthquakes

Thanksgiving

Family and friends gather to give thanks for the blessing of the harvest at Thanksgiving in November.

Turkey is traditionally eaten at Thanksgiving as part of a big meal

Halloween

The festival of Halloween is celebrated every year on October 31, when children dress up in costumes and and go from house to house trick-or-treating for candy and other treats.

Jack-o'-lantern

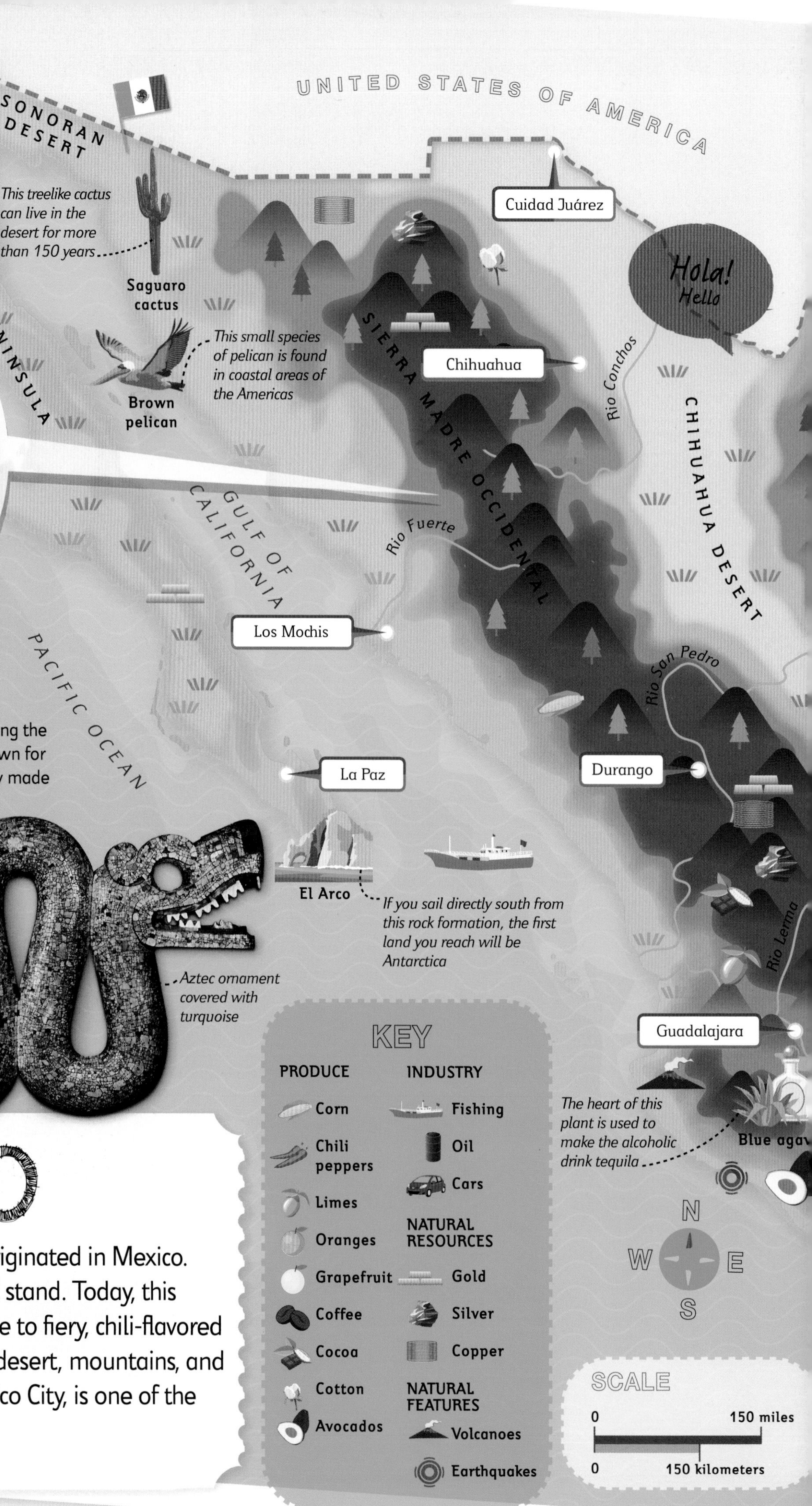

UNITED STATES OF AMERICA
Tijuana
BAJA CALIFORNIA PENINSULA
SONORAN DESERT
This treelike cactus can live in the desert for more than 150 years
Saguaro cactus
This small species of pelican is found in coastal areas of the Americas
Brown pelican
Cuidad Juárez
Hola! Hello
SIERRA MADRE OCCIDENTAL
Chihuahua
Rio Conchos
CHIHUAHUA DESERT
GULF OF CALIFORNIA
Rio Fuerte
Los Mochis
PACIFIC OCEAN
Rio San Pedro
La Paz
Durango
El Arco
If you sail directly south from this rock formation, the first land you reach will be Antarctica
Rio Lerma
Aztec ornament covered with turquoise
Guadalajara
The heart of this plant is used to make the alcoholic drink tequila
Blue agav
KEY
PRODUCE
Corn
Chili peppers
Limes
Oranges
Grapefruit
Coffee
Cocoa
Cotton
Avocados
INDUSTRY
Fishing
Oil
Cars
NATURAL RESOURCES
Gold
Silver
Copper
NATURAL FEATURES
Volcanoes
Earthquakes
N
W
E
S
SCALE
0
150 miles
0
150 kilometers

Copper Canyon

This is a group of deep canyons formed by six rivers. The walls of the canyons are copper- and green-colored, giving them their name.

Aztec ornament

The Aztecs lived in Central Mexico during the 14th to 16th centuries. They were known for their fine art and architecture, and they made beautiful jewelry and ornaments.

MEXICO

The Aztec and Mayan peoples originated in Mexico. The remains of their temples still stand. Today, this Spanish-speaking country is home to fiery, chili-flavored foods. The landscape is a mix of desert, mountains, and tropical forests. The capital, Mexico City, is one of the largest cities in the world.

Butterfly reserve

Every year in the fall, thousands of monarch butterflies migrate (move) from northern North America to Mexico. The Monarch Butterfly Biosphere Reserve, northwest of Mexico City, protects these butterflies during the winter.

Monarch butterflies

Tacos
Limes
Avocados

Spicy food

Mexican food can be very spicy and often includes hot chili peppers. Tacos are a popular dish—they are corn or flour tortillas (a soft or crispy flatbread) filled with beef, chicken, or fish.

Lucha Libre

Lucha Libre, which means "free wrestling," is a special type of wrestling. Fighters wear dramatic costumes, including masks that hide their identities.

Masked wrestlers

Palenque

This abandoned Mayan city in southern Mexico thrived from 500–700 CE. Many of the remains are still covered by jungle.

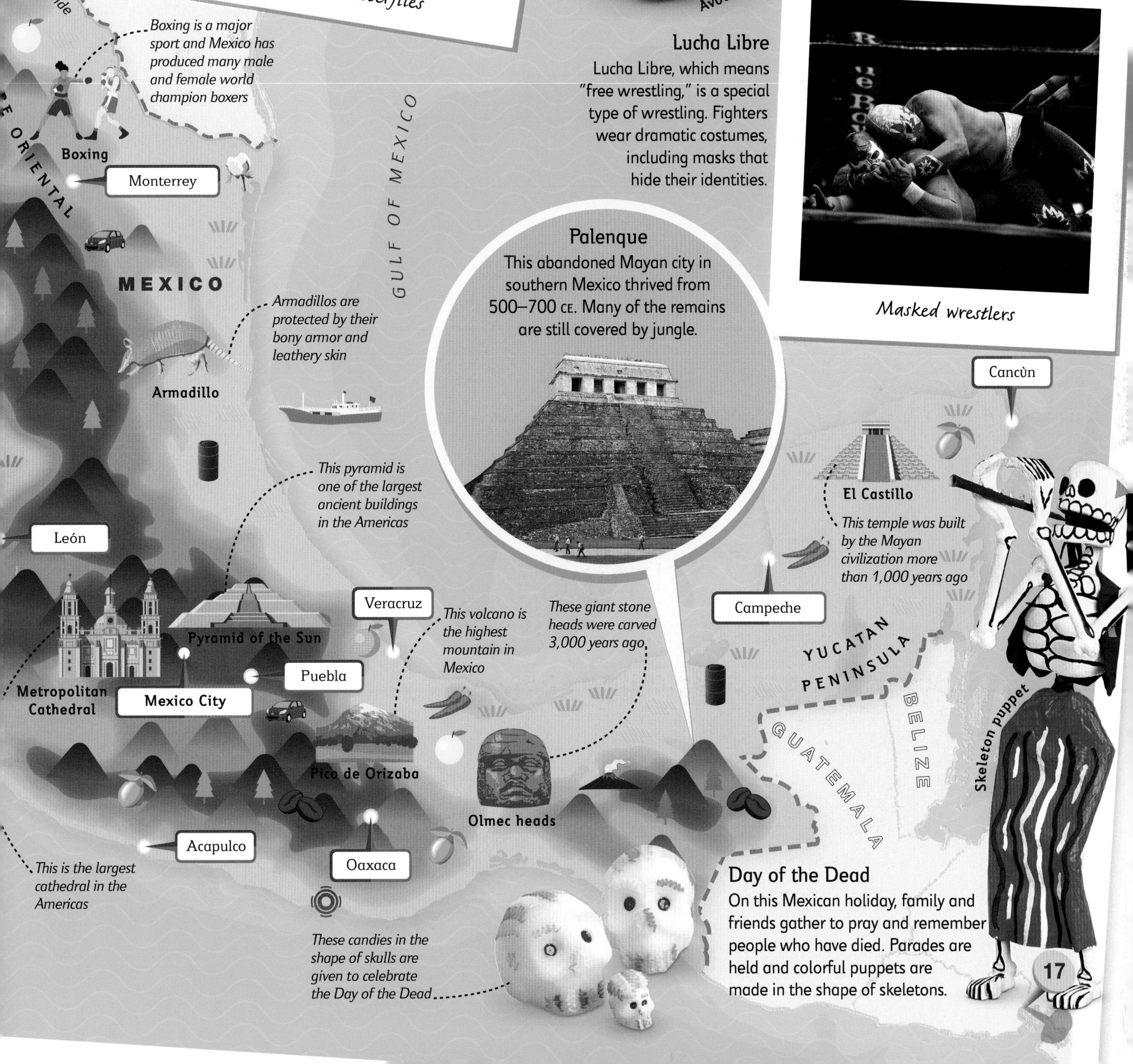
Rio Grande
Boxing is a major sport and Mexico has produced many male and female world champion boxers
Boxing
SIERRA MADRE ORIENTAL
Monterrey
MEXICO
GULF OF MEXICO
Armadillos are protected by their bony armor and leathery skin
Armadillo
This pyramid is one of the largest ancient buildings in the Americas
León
Pyramid of the Sun
Metropolitan Cathedral
Mexico City
Veracruz
Puebla
This volcano is the highest mountain in Mexico
Pico de Orizaba
These giant stone heads were carved 3,000 years ago
Olmec heads
Acapulco
This is the largest cathedral in the Americas
Oaxaca
These candies in the shape of skulls are given to celebrate the Day of the Dead
Cancùn
El Castillo
This temple was built by the Mayan civilization more than 1,000 years ago
Campeche
YUCATAN PENINSULA
BELIZE
GUATEMALA
Skeleton puppet

Day of the Dead

On this Mexican holiday, family and friends gather to pray and remember people who have died. Parades are held and colorful puppets are made in the shape of skeletons.

CENTRAL AMERICA

Central America is a narrow strip of land that links North and South America. The climate is warm and wet, and the lush fertile land is ideal for growing crops, such as bananas and coffee beans. Most of the people in Central America speak Spanish.

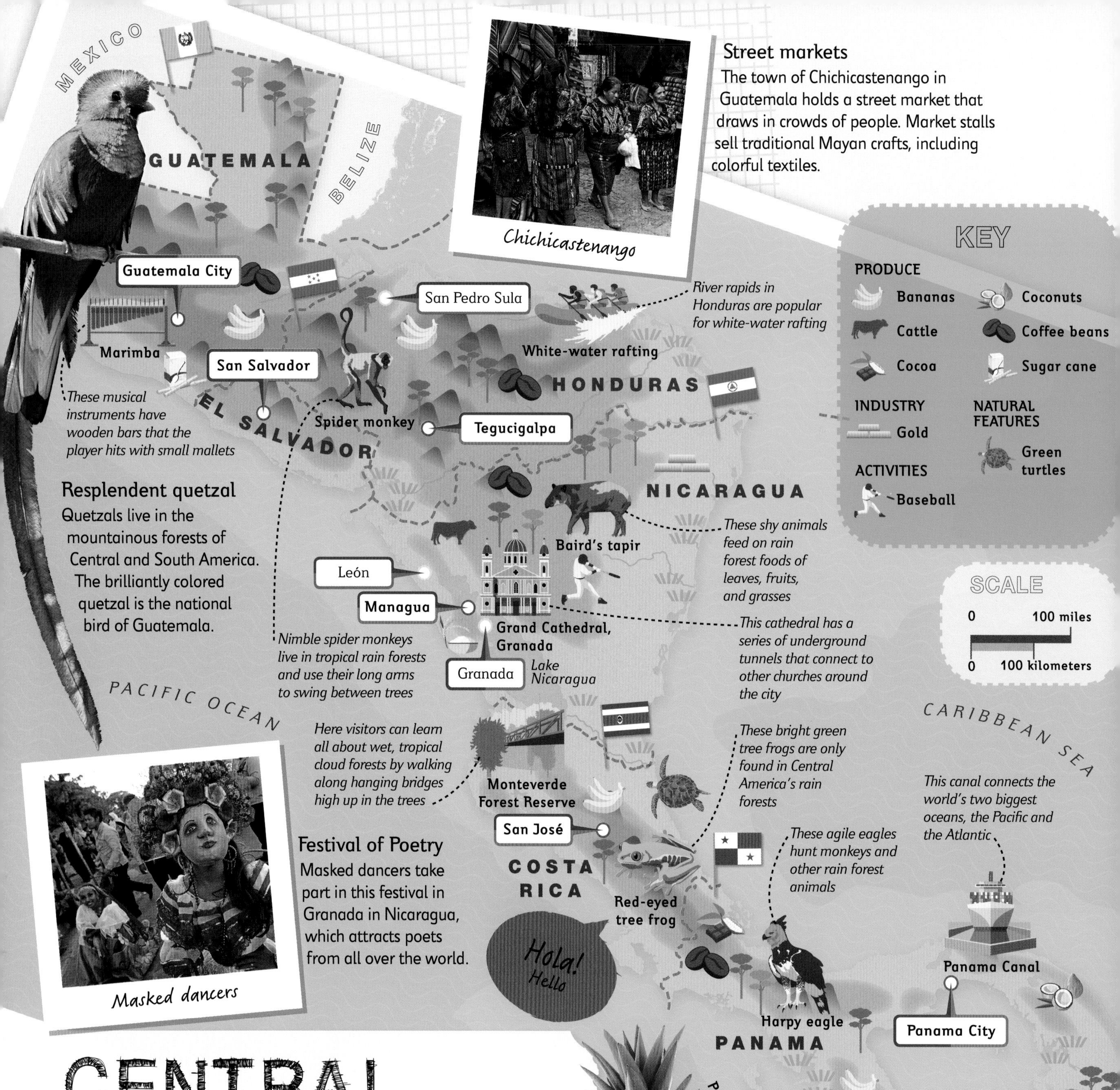
MEXICO
GUATEMALA
BELIZE
Guatemala City
Marimba
These musical instruments have wooden bars that the player hits with small mallets
San Salvador
EL SALVADOR
San Pedro Sula
Spider monkey
Tegucigalpa
White-water rafting
River rapids in Honduras are popular for white-water rafting
HONDURAS
NICARAGUA
Baird's tapir
These shy animals feed on rain forest foods of leaves, fruits, and grasses
León
Managua
Grand Cathedral, Granada
This cathedral has a series of underground tunnels that connect to other churches around the city
Granada
Lake Nicaragua
Nimble spider monkeys live in tropical rain forests and use their long arms to swing between trees
PACIFIC OCEAN
CARIBBEAN SEA
Here visitors can learn all about wet, tropical cloud forests by walking along hanging bridges high up in the trees
Monteverde Forest Reserve
These bright green tree frogs are only found in Central America's rain forests
San José
COSTA RICA
Red-eyed tree frog
These agile eagles hunt monkeys and other rain forest animals
Harpy eagle
Hola! Hello
This canal connects the world's two biggest oceans, the Pacific and the Atlantic
Panama Canal
Panama City
PANAMA
KEY
PRODUCE
Bananas
Coconuts
Cattle
Coffee beans
Cocoa
Sugar cane
INDUSTRY
Gold
NATURAL FEATURES
Green turtles
ACTIVITIES
Baseball
SCALE
0
100 miles
0
100 kilometers
N
W
E
S

Chichicastenango

Street markets

The town of Chichicastenango in Guatemala holds a street market that draws in crowds of people. Market stalls sell traditional Mayan crafts, including colorful textiles.

Resplendent quetzal

Quetzals live in the mountainous forests of Central and South America. The brilliantly colored quetzal is the national bird of Guatemala.

Masked dancers

Festival of Poetry

Masked dancers take part in this festival in Granada in Nicaragua, which attracts poets from all over the world.

Pineapple

Coconut

Fruit and nuts

Large farms, called plantations, are found throughout Central America. They grow tropical fruits and nuts such as juicy pineapples and delicious coconuts.

THE CARIBBEAN

Golden beaches, coral reefs, carnivals, and festivals are all part of life in the Caribbean. This group of small island nations lies between North and South America. The islands have a tropical climate and are surrounded by warm seas.

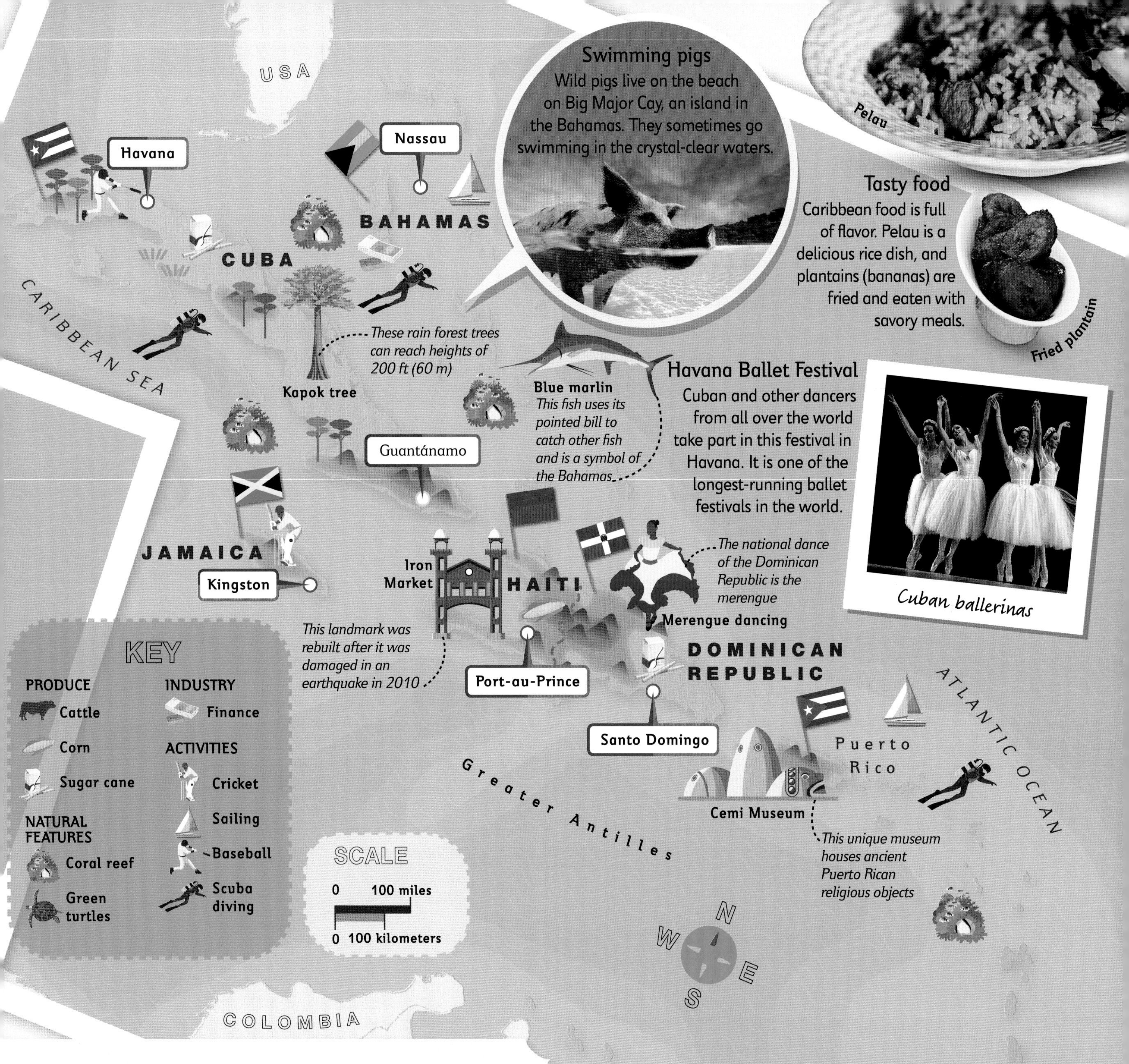

USA
Havana
Nassau
BAHAMAS
CUBA
CARIBBEAN SEA
These rain forest trees can reach heights of 200 ft (60 m)
Kapok tree
Blue marlin
This fish uses its pointed bill to catch other fish and is a symbol of the Bahamas
Guantánamo
JAMAICA
Kingston
Iron Market
HAITI
The national dance of the Dominican Republic is the merengue
Merengue dancing
This landmark was rebuilt after it was damaged in an earthquake in 2010
Port-au-Prince
DOMINICAN REPUBLIC
Santo Domingo
Puerto Rico
ATLANTIC OCEAN
Greater Antilles
Cemi Museum
This unique museum houses ancient Puerto Rican religious objects
KEY
PRODUCE
Cattle
Corn
Sugar cane
NATURAL FEATURES
Coral reef
Green turtles
INDUSTRY
Finance
ACTIVITIES
Cricket
Sailing
Baseball
Scuba diving
SCALE
0 100 miles
0 100 kilometers
N W E S
COLOMBIA
Lesser Antilles
Port-of-Spain
TRINIDAD AND TOBAGO

Swimming pigs

Wild pigs live on the beach on Big Major Cay, an island in the Bahamas. They sometimes go swimming in the crystal-clear waters.

Tasty food

Caribbean food is full of flavor. Pelau is a delicious rice dish, and plantains (bananas) are fried and eaten with savory meals.

Pelau

Fried plantain

Havana Ballet Festival

Cuban and other dancers from all over the world take part in this festival in Havana. It is one of the longest-running ballet festivals in the world.

Cuban ballerinas

Moko Jumbies

Stilt walkers called Moko Jumbies wear colorful costumes and dance in festivals such as the Trinidad and Tobago Carnival.

CLIMATES

The weather that is typical of an area is called a climate. Climates vary around the world. The polar regions at the top and bottom of the Earth are the coldest places. Moving toward the equator, the climate gets warmer. Different animals and plants are suited to different types of climate.

The world is getting warmer. The average temperature has risen by 2°F (1.1°C) since 1880 due to human activity such as burning oil and coal.

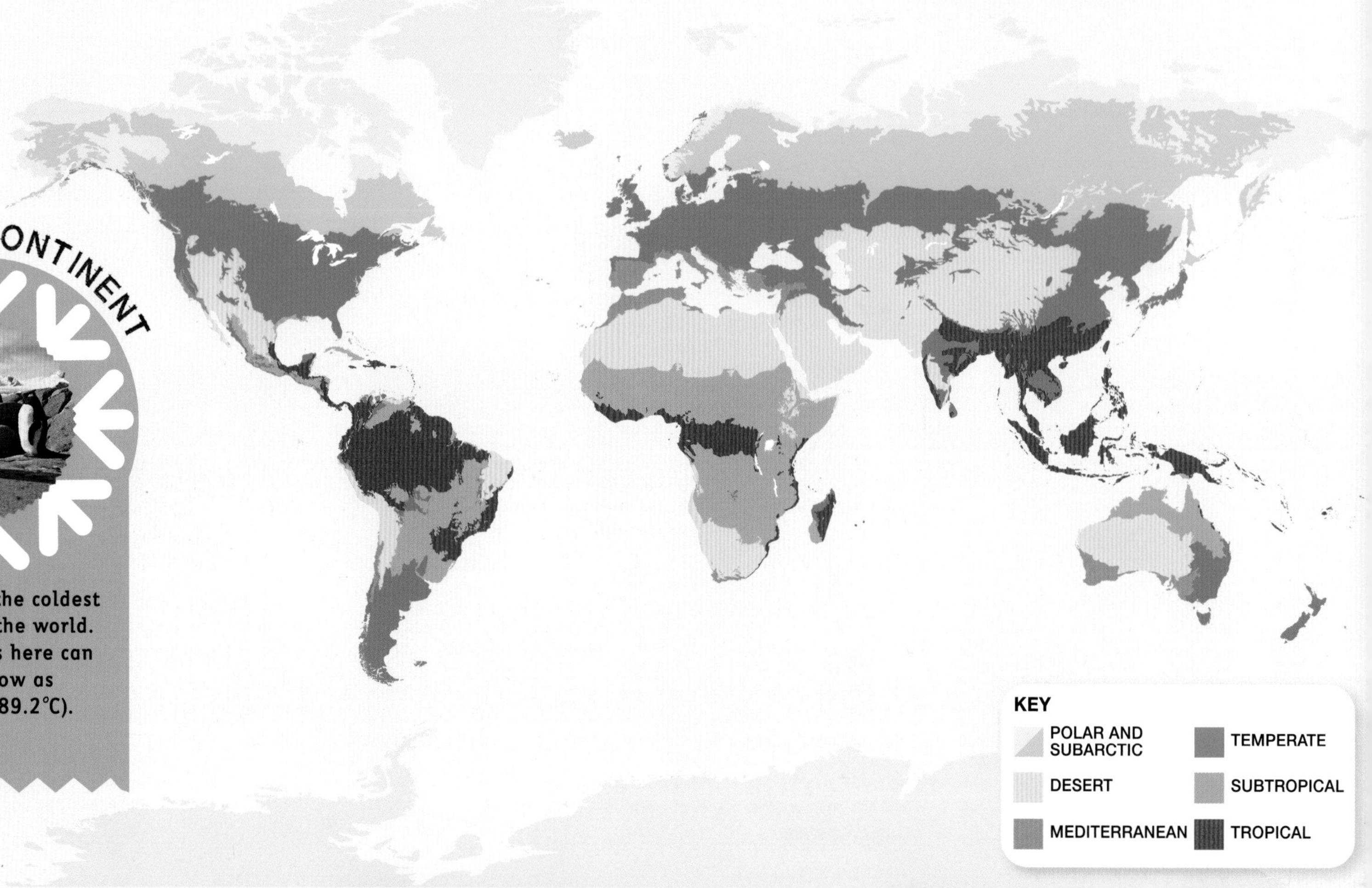
KEY
POLAR AND SUBARCTIC
TEMPERATE
DESERT
SUBTROPICAL
MEDITERRANEAN
TROPICAL

COLDEST CONTINENT

Antarctica is the coldest continent in the world. Temperatures here can drop as low as -128.5°F (-89.2°C).

POLAR AND SUBARCTIC

The climate around the North and South Poles is freezing cold and icy. Subarctic regions lie south of the North Pole, where the climate is a little warmer and some plants can survive.

DESERT

A desert climate is dry, with very little rainfall each year. Many deserts are very hot in the day and cold at night. Only a few plants and animals can survive in this harsh climate.

MEDITERRANEAN

Regions close to the Mediterranean Sea have hot, dry summers and cool, wet winters. This type of climate also describes places with similar weather patterns, such as California.

TEMPERATE

Areas with a temperate climate, such as the British Isles, have warm summers and cool winters. This kind of climate suits deciduous trees, which lose their leaves in winter.

SUBTROPICAL

Hot regions of the world with dry and rainy seasons have a subtropical climate. African savannas, which are large grasslands with few trees, have this kind of climate.

TROPICAL

A tropical climate is hot and rainy. Regions with this kind of climate are near the equator. Dense rain forests grow here. The Amazon rain forest is an example of a tropical region.

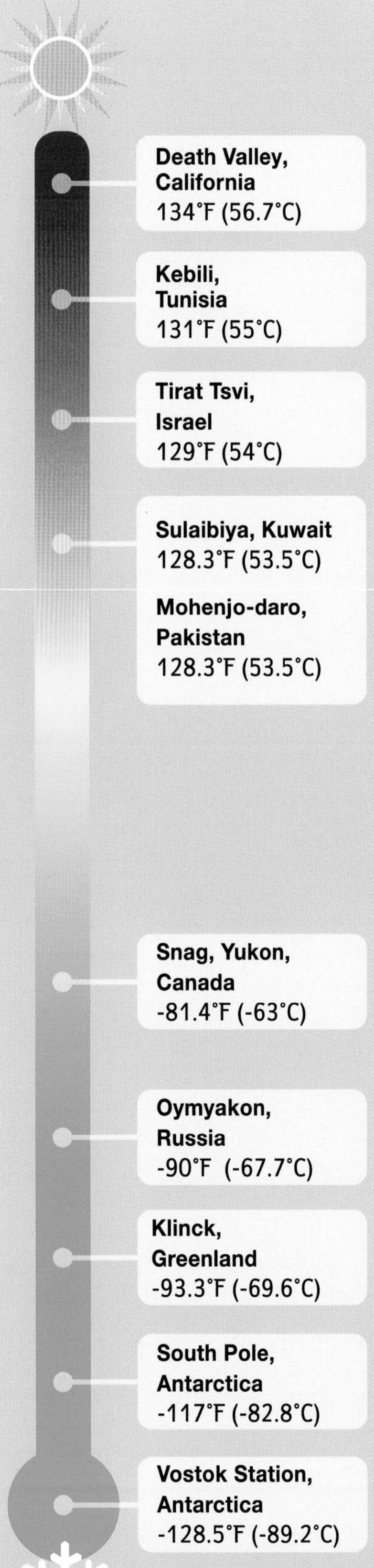
Death Valley, California
134°F (56.7°C)
Kebili, Tunisia
131°F (55°C)
Tirat Tsvi, Israel
129°F (54°C)
Sulaibiya, Kuwait
128.3°F (53.5°C)
Mohenjo-daro, Pakistan
128.3°F (53.5°C)
Snag, Yukon, Canada
-81.4°F (-63°C)
Oymyakon, Russia
-90°F (-67.7°C)
Klinck, Greenland
-93.3°F (-69.6°C)
South Pole, Antarctica
-117°F (-82.8°C)
Vostok Station, Antarctica
-128.5°F (-89.2°C)

Hot and cold places

The hottest places on Earth are in desert regions. They are hotter than tropical areas, because there are no clouds to block the Sun. The coldest places are polar regions. They get less sunlight than other places.

Five rainiest places

A state called Meghalaya in India has the world's highest rainfall each year. Here, seasonal winds called monsoons bring heavy rains. Other very wet places in the world are in rain forests or lush, hilly countryside.

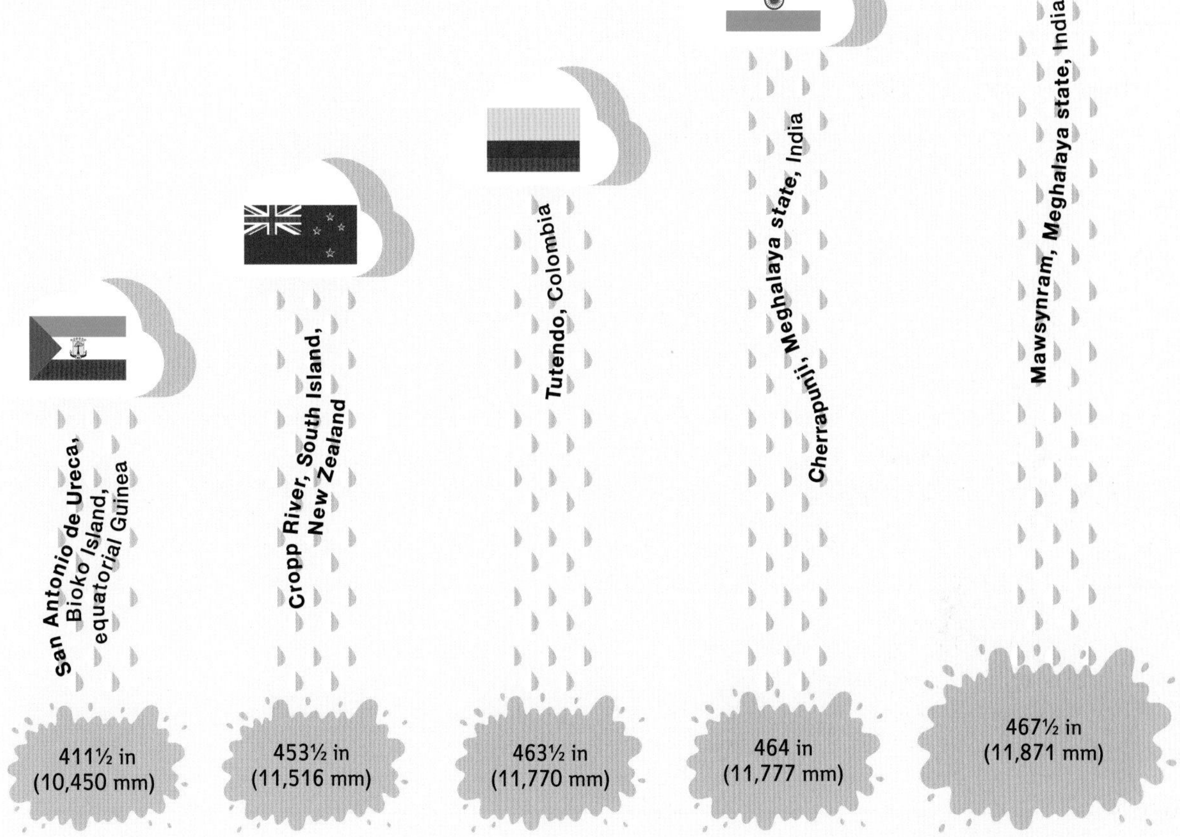
San Antonio de Ureca, Bioko Island, equatorial Guinea
411½ in (10,450 mm)
Cropp River, South Island, New Zealand
453½ in (11,516 mm)
Tutendo, Colombia
463½ in (11,770 mm)
Cherrapunji, Meghalaya state, India
464 in (11,777 mm)
Mawsynram, Meghalaya state, India
467½ in (11,871 mm)

Five driest places

Nothing grows in very dry areas because there is so little rain each year. Antarctica is the driest continent, and it is also the coldest and windiest.

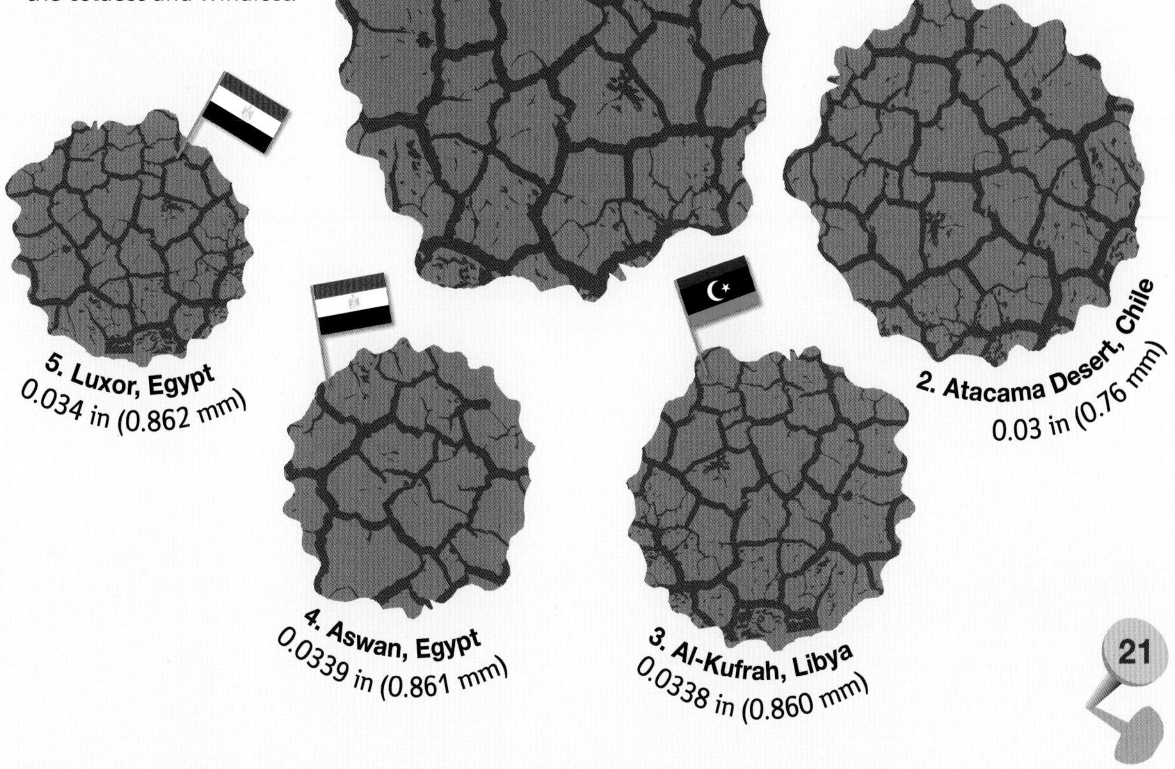
1. Dry Valleys, Antarctica
No rain at all
2. Atacama Desert, Chile
0.03 in (0.76 mm)
3. Al-Kufrah, Libya
0.0338 in (0.860 mm)
4. Aswan, Egypt
0.0339 in (0.861 mm)
5. Luxor, Egypt
0.034 in (0.862 mm)

1. In which city would you find this giant statue?
2. Which range of mountains does this bird soar over?
3. This cathedral is found in which country?
4. Huaso rodeo is very popular in which long, thin country?

5. Which country has won the men's soccer World Cup the most times?

You can find all the answers and more quizzes on pages 120–121.

6. In which country can you see this flightless bird?

SOUTH AMERICA

From the high Andes to the huge Amazon rain forest, South America has a varied and colorful landscape. Here, people are passionate about everything from soccer to carnivals. This continent is a unique blend of Latin culture and the traditions of the Indigenous peoples.

8. Which country is this popular pet a native of?

7. What is the name of this Peruvian bear?

SOUTH AMERICA

South America stretches from the tropical Caribbean Sea in the north to the icy Southern Ocean in the south. The world's largest forest, the Amazon rain forest, covers most of Brazil and the northern part of the continent.

CARIBBEAN SEA
VENEZUE
COLOMBIA
GALÁPAGOS ISLANDS
(ECUADOR)
ECUADOR
PERU
BOLI
PACIFIC OCEAN
CHILE
ARGENTINA
DRAKE PASS

Lake Titicaca

This deep lake, high up in the Andes mountains, sits on the border between Bolivia and Peru. There are several inhabited islands on the lake, including some floating, human-made islands, built from reeds.

Amazon river

This giant river flows through the Amazon rain forest, out into the Atlantic Ocean. It carries more water than any other river in the world.

Andes mountains

This mountain range runs like a spine down the west side of South America. It is about 5,500 miles (8,900 km) long and is the world's longest mountain range, stretching from the north of Colombia to the southern tip of Chile.

SURINAME
FRENCH GUIANA
(FRANCE)
ATLANTIC OCEAN
BRAZIL
N
W
E
S
GUAY
URUGUAY
KLAND ISLANDS
TED KINGDOM)
SCOTIA SEA

São Paulo

More people live in São Paulo than in any other city in South America. It started as a tiny, isolated village, which was founded by Portuguese settlers in the 16th century. After gold was discovered nearby in the 1690s, it grew, and this bustling city is now Brazil's main business center.

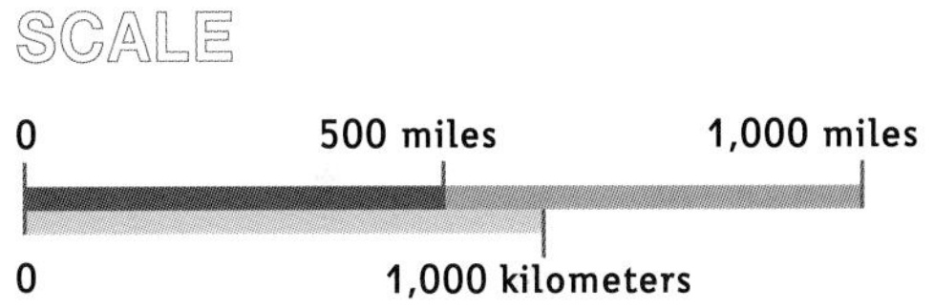
SCALE
0
500 miles
1,000 miles
0
1,000 kilometers

Pampas

This vast, grassy plain stretches over the eastern part of Argentina, most of Uruguay, and the extreme south of Brazil. Parts are now farmed and huge quantities of wheat and vegetables grow here. The grasslands are perfect for rearing animals, including sheep and cattle. Argentine beef is very popular around the world.

COLOMBIA AND VENEZUELA

Colombia and Venezuela lie in the northwest corner of South America. To the north is the Caribbean Sea and to the south is the Amazon rain forest. These Spanish-speaking countries are rich in emeralds, diamonds, and gold.

Scarlet macaw
This large, noisy parrot lives in the rain forests of both Colombia and Venezuela. It eats nuts, seeds, and fruit.

Angel Falls
The Angel Falls is the world's highest waterfall. Water plunges 3,212 ft (979 m) into the rain forest.

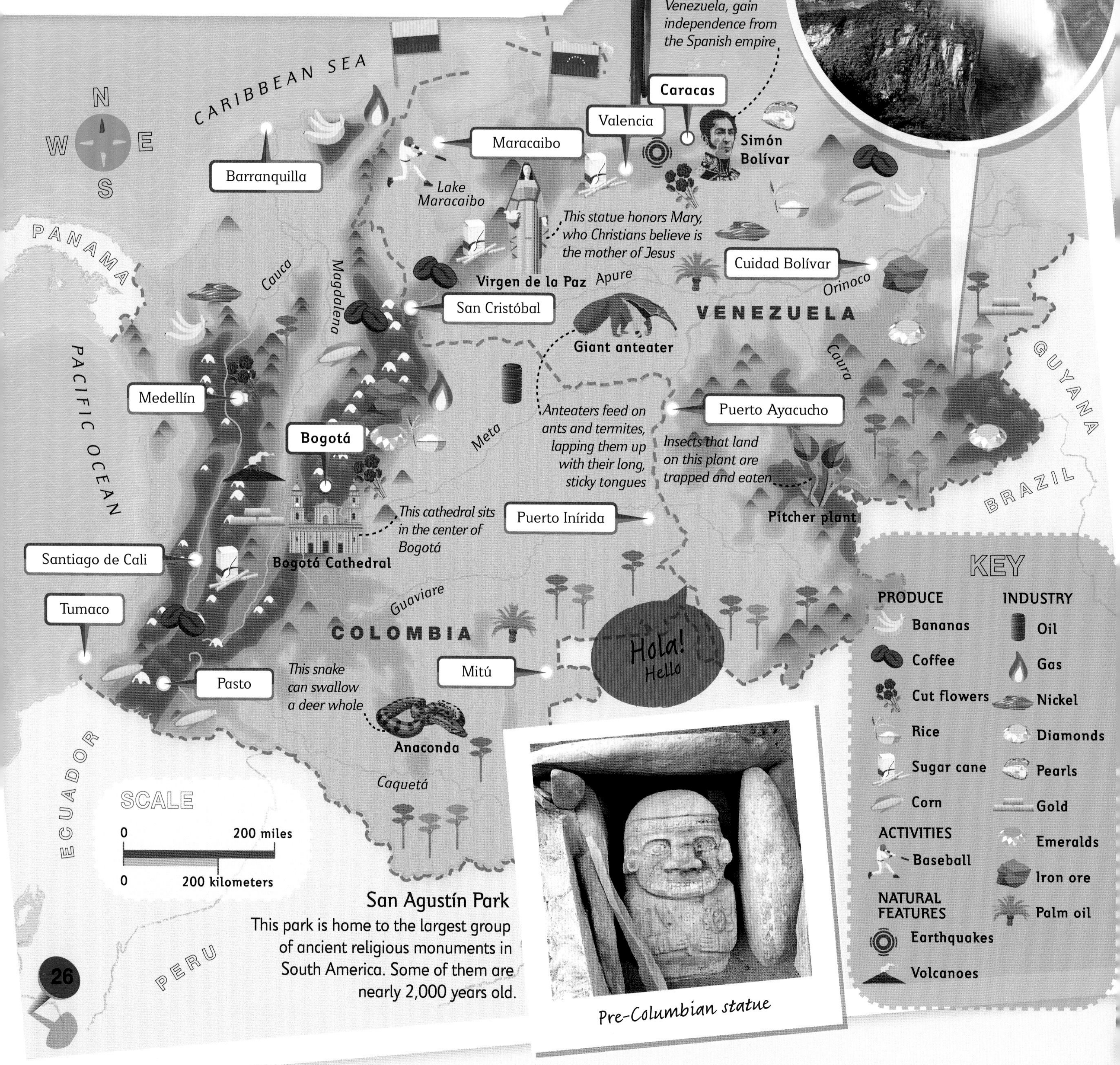

CARIBBEAN SEA
N
W
E
S
Barranquilla
Maracaibo
Lake Maracaibo
Valencia
Caracas
Simón Bolívar
Bolívar helped several South American countries, including his home country of Venezuela, gain independence from the Spanish empire
This statue honors Mary, who Christians believe is the mother of Jesus
Virgen de la Paz
Cuidad Bolívar
Apure
Orinoco
PANAMA
Cauca
Magdalena
San Cristóbal
VENEZUELA
Giant anteater
Anteaters feed on ants and termites, lapping them up with their long, sticky tongues
Caura
GUYANA
PACIFIC OCEAN
Medellín
Bogotá
Meta
Puerto Ayacucho
Insects that land on this plant are trapped and eaten
Pitcher plant
BRAZIL
This cathedral sits in the center of Bogotá
Bogotá Cathedral
Puerto Inírida
Santiago de Cali
Tumaco
Guaviare
COLOMBIA
Hola! Hello
Mitú
Pasto
This snake can swallow a deer whole
Anaconda
Caquetá
ECUADOR
PERU
SCALE
0
200 miles
0
200 kilometers
KEY
PRODUCE
Bananas
Coffee
Cut flowers
Rice
Sugar cane
Corn
ACTIVITIES
Baseball
NATURAL FEATURES
Earthquakes
Volcanoes
INDUSTRY
Oil
Gas
Nickel
Diamonds
Pearls
Gold
Emeralds
Iron ore
Palm oil

San Agustín Park
This park is home to the largest group of ancient religious monuments in South America. Some of them are nearly 2,000 years old.

Pre-Columbian statue

PERU

Peru has some stunning scenery, ranging from dense rain forest to snow-capped peaks. The Andes mountain range runs the length of the country and is a popular destination for hiking. Peru is known for its brightly colored, traditional textiles and its delicious fish and potato dishes.

Quechua textiles

Colorful cloth

Brightly coloured textiles are woven by the Quechua people who live on farms high up in the Andes mountains.

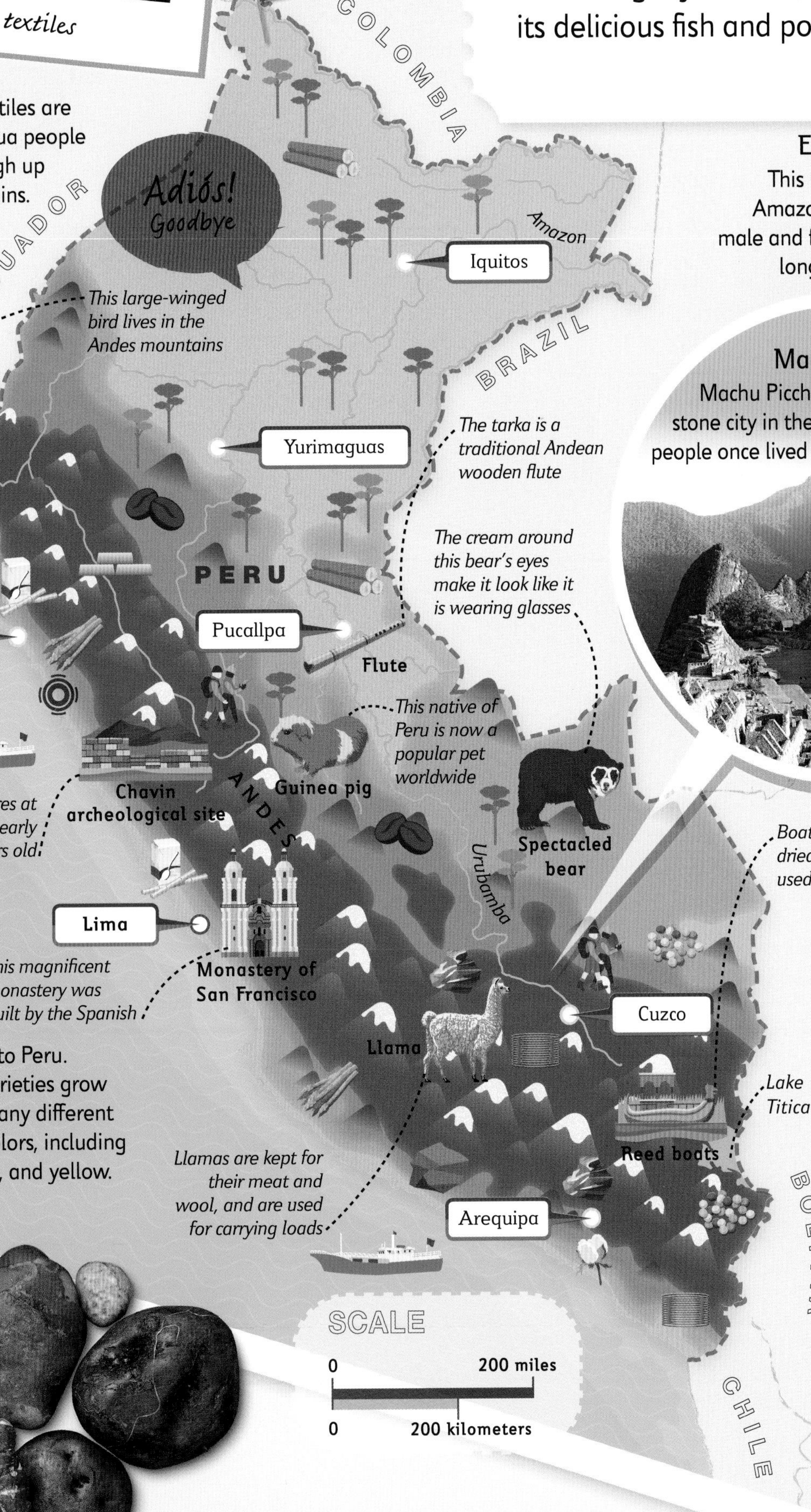

N
W
E
S
COLOMBIA
ECUADOR
BRAZIL
BOLIVIA
CHILE
PACIFIC OCEAN
Adiós!
Goodbye
Amazon
Iquitos
This large-winged bird lives in the Andes mountains
Andean condor
Yurimaguas
The tarka is a traditional Andean wooden flute
Chiclayo
PERU
The cream around this bear's eyes make it look like it is wearing glasses
Trujillo
Pucallpa
Flute
This native of Peru is now a popular pet worldwide
Chavin archeological site
ANDES
Guinea pig
Some structures at this site are nearly 3,000 years old
Spectacled bear
Urubamba
Boats made from dried reeds are used for fishing
Lima
This magnificent monastery was built by the Spanish
Monastery of San Francisco
Cuzco
Llama
Lake Titicaca
Reed boats
Llamas are kept for their meat and wool, and are used for carrying loads
Arequipa
SCALE
0
200 miles
0
200 kilometers

Emperor tamarin

This monkey lives in the Amazon rain forest. Both male and female adults have long, white mustaches.

Machu Picchu

Machu Picchu is an ancient stone city in the Andes. The Inca people once lived here.

KEY

PRODUCE
- Asparagus
- Sugar cane
- Coffee
- Quinoa

INDUSTRY
- Fishing
- Copper
- Lumber
- Cotton
- Gold
- Iron ore
- Silver

ACTIVITIES
- Hiking

NATURAL FEATURES
- Earthquakes

Potatoes

Potatoes are native to Peru. More than 4,000 varieties grow here and come in many different sizes, shapes, and colors, including pink, purple, orange, and yellow.

BRAZIL

Brazil is the largest country in South America and has a great variety of people and cultures. Most Brazilian people live in big, densely populated cities and speak Portuguese, the country's official language, while more than 200 Indigenous groups have their own unique languages.

Oranges

Coffee and oranges

Brazil is the world's largest producer of oranges and coffee beans. About 75 percent of the orange crop is turned into juice and exported. There are about 300,000 coffee farms across the country, and Brazilian people drink half of the coffee they produce.

Coffee beans

Morpho butterfly

The bright blue wings help these large butterflies to see each other in the dark forest

Rain forest life

The vast Amazon rain forest is packed with plant and animal life.

An amazing number of insect species live there—about 2.5 million!

Indigenous peoples

People have lived in the Amazon rain forest for thousands of years. The Yanomami are one of the largest groups. They live in large, circular huts with palm leaf roofs.

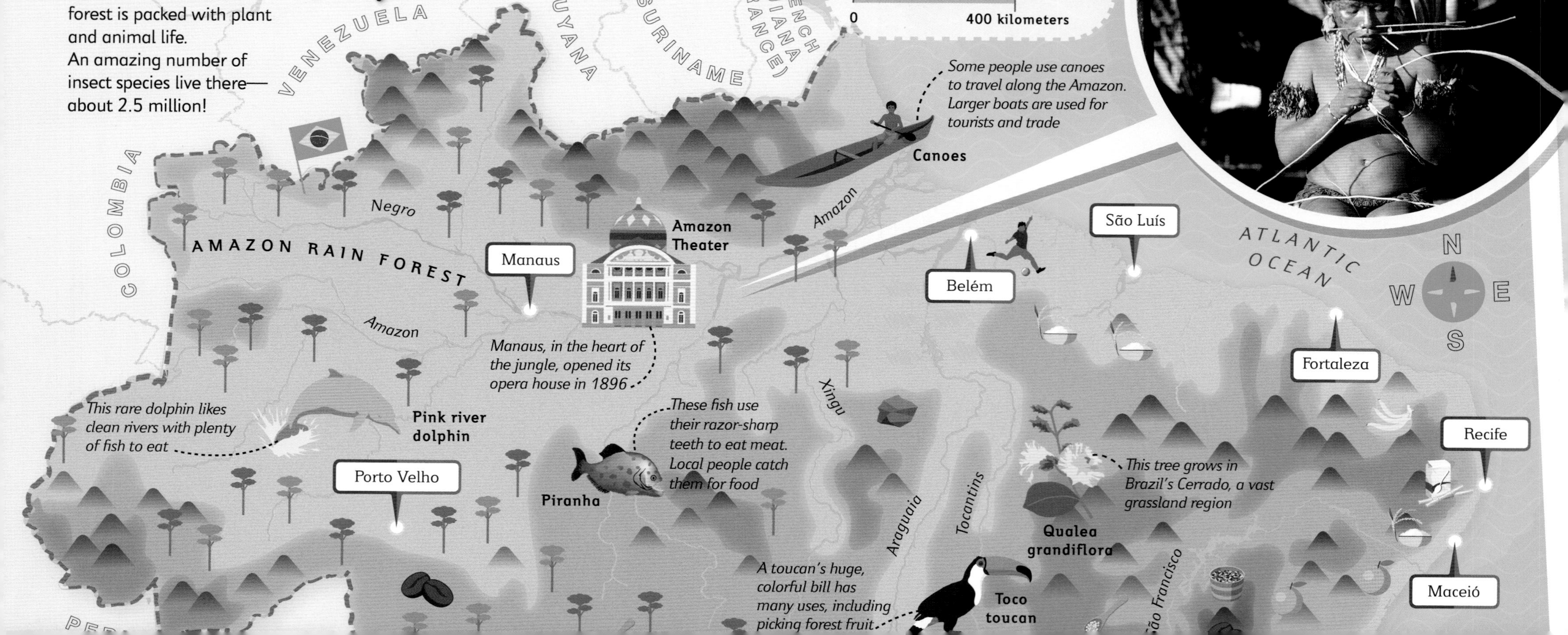
SCALE
0
200 miles
400 miles
0
400 kilometers
VENEZUELA
GUYANA
SURINAME
FRENCH GUIANA (FRANCE)
COLOMBIA
AMAZON RAIN FOREST
Negro
Amazon
Amazon
Manaus
Amazon Theater
Manaus, in the heart of the jungle, opened its opera house in 1896
Canoes
Some people use canoes to travel along the Amazon. Larger boats are used for tourists and trade
São Luís
Belém
ATLANTIC OCEAN
N
W
E
S
Fortaleza
Recife
Maceió
This rare dolphin likes clean rivers with plenty of fish to eat
Pink river dolphin
Porto Velho
Piranha
These fish use their razor-sharp teeth to eat meat. Local people catch them for food
Xingu
Araguaia
Tocantins
Qualea grandiflora
This tree grows in Brazil's Cerrado, a vast grassland region
São Francisco
A toucan's huge, colorful bill has many uses, including picking forest fruit
Toco toucan

Soccer on the beach

Soccer

Brazilian people love soccer. The country has won the men's World Cup more times (five) than any other country. Many great soccer players come from Brazil, including Pelé and Marta.

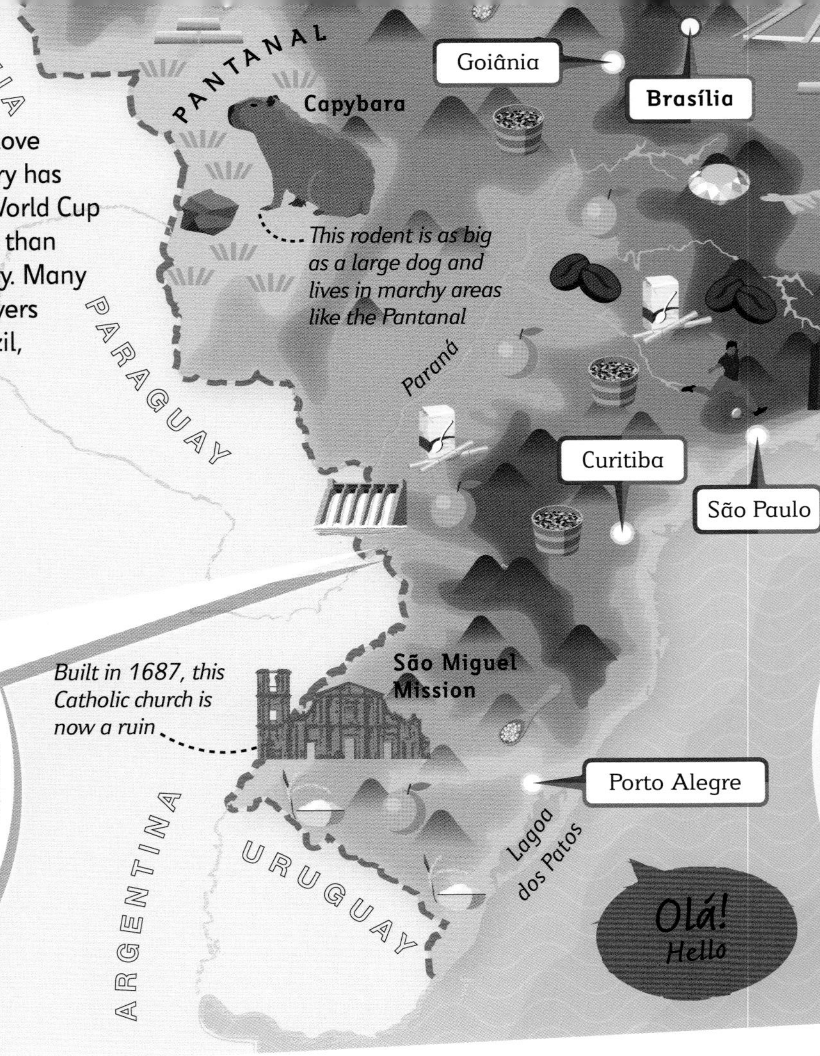

BOLIVIA
PANTANAL
Capybara
This rodent is as big as a large dog and lives in marchy areas like the Pantanal
PARAGUAY
Paraná
Goiânia
Brasília
Brasília replaced Rio as the capital in 1960. The modern cathedral looks like a crown of thorns
Belo Horizonte
Christ the Redeemer
This giant statue overlooks the city and is one of Rio's main landmarks
Rio de Janeiro
ATLANTIC OCEAN
Curitiba
São Paulo
São Miguel Mission
Built in 1687, this Catholic church is now a ruin
Porto Alegre
Lagoa dos Patos
ARGENTINA
URUGUAY
Olá!
Hello

Iguaçu Falls

This spectacular series of waterfalls stretches across the border between Brazil and Argentina. The forests surrounding the falls are protected by two national parks.

Sugar Loaf Mountain

This domed mountain rises above Rio de Janeiro. Stunning views of the city can be enjoyed by people who take a cable car to the top of the mountain.

KEY

PRODUCE
- Coffee
- Oranges
- Bananas
- Soybeans
- Dried beans
- Sugar cane
- Rice

RESOURCES
- Gold
- Iron
- Diamonds
- Oil
- Hydroelectric power

ACTIVITIES
- Soccer

Capoeira

This martial art involves music, dance, and acrobatics. Capoeira was developed in Brazil 500 years ago by people from West Africa, and it is still a popular sport and type of exercise today.

Acrobatic moves

Every jaguar has a unique pattern of spots on its coat

Jaguar

This big cat lives in the Amazon rain forest. Jaguars are strong swimmers and have a powerful bite.

ARGENTINA AND CHILE

These two countries stretch across the southern part of South America. Between them lie the Andes mountains. Argentina's dramatic landscape includes the rugged hills of Patagonia, while Chile is a long, thin country with both desert and fertile farmland.

Tango dancers

Argentine tango

This Latin American style of dance originated in Buenos Aires. Dancers hold one another close and walk together in time to the music, with one partner taking the lead.

Atacama Desert

The Atacama Desert is one of the driest places on Earth. This strip of land between the Pacific Ocean and the Andes mountains receives little rainfall because the mountains block the rain.

Highest vineyard

The highest vineyard in the world lies at 10,200 ft (3,111 m) in the Calchaquí Valley in northern Argentina.

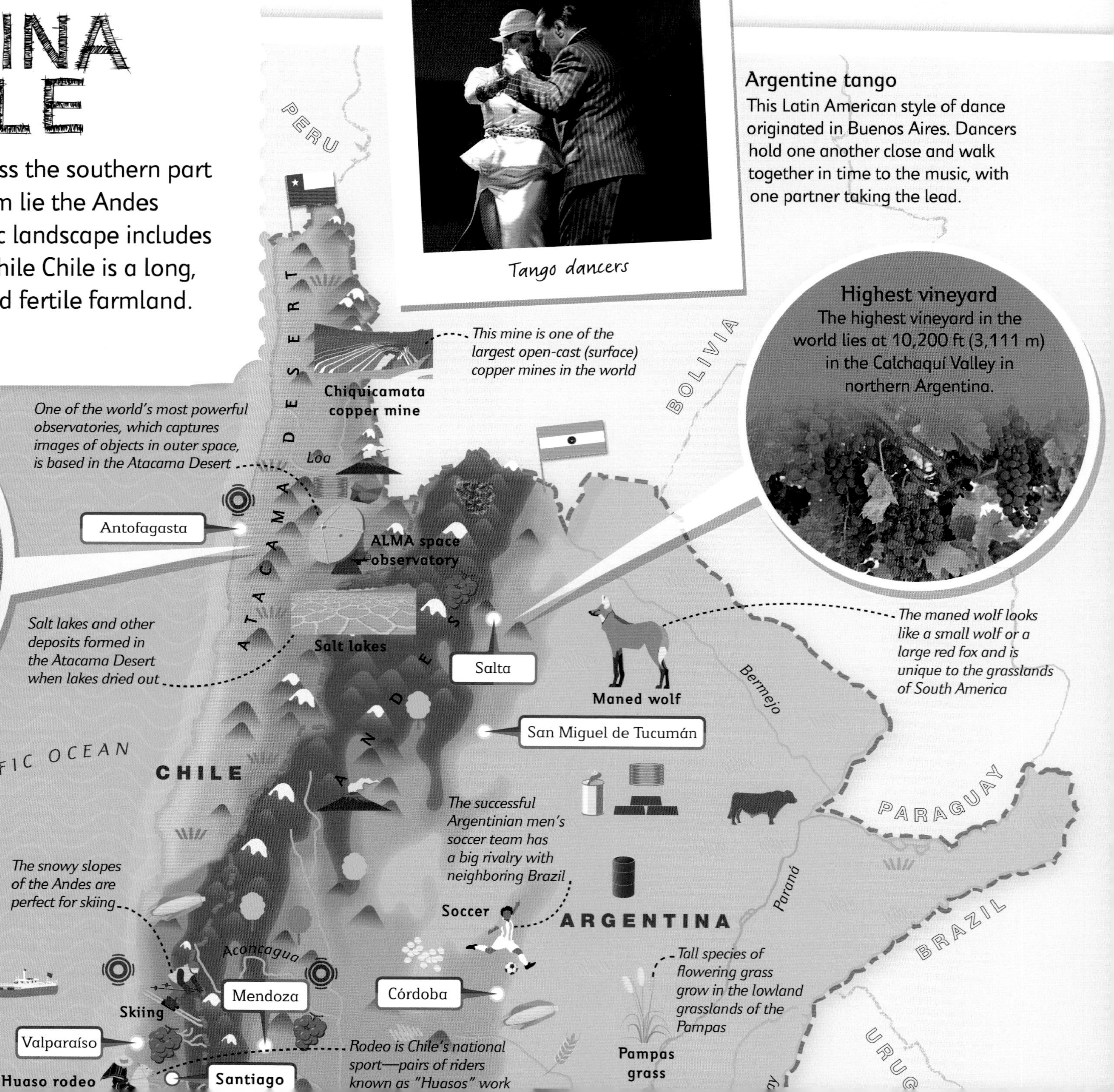

PERU
BOLIVIA
PARAGUAY
BRAZIL
URUG
ATACAMA DESERT
ANDES
PACIFIC OCEAN
CHILE
ARGENTINA
Loa
Bermejo
Paraná
Aconcagua
This mine is one of the largest open-cast (surface) copper mines in the world
Chiquicamata copper mine
One of the world's most powerful observatories, which captures images of objects in outer space, is based in the Atacama Desert
ALMA space observatory
Antofagasta
Salt lakes and other deposits formed in the Atacama Desert when lakes dried out
Salt lakes
Salta
The maned wolf looks like a small wolf or a large red fox and is unique to the grasslands of South America
Maned wolf
San Miguel de Tucumán
The successful Argentinian men's soccer team has a big rivalry with neighboring Brazil
Soccer
The snowy slopes of the Andes are perfect for skiing
Skiing
Mendoza
Córdoba
Valparaíso
Santiago
Huaso rodeo
Rodeo is Chile's national sport—pairs of riders known as "Huasos" work
Tall species of flowering grass grow in the lowland grasslands of the Pampas
Pampas grass

Fertile land

The land of Central Chile is rich and fertile. Here, fruits, such as juicy peaches, are grown in orchards. Grapes also flourish, and Chilean

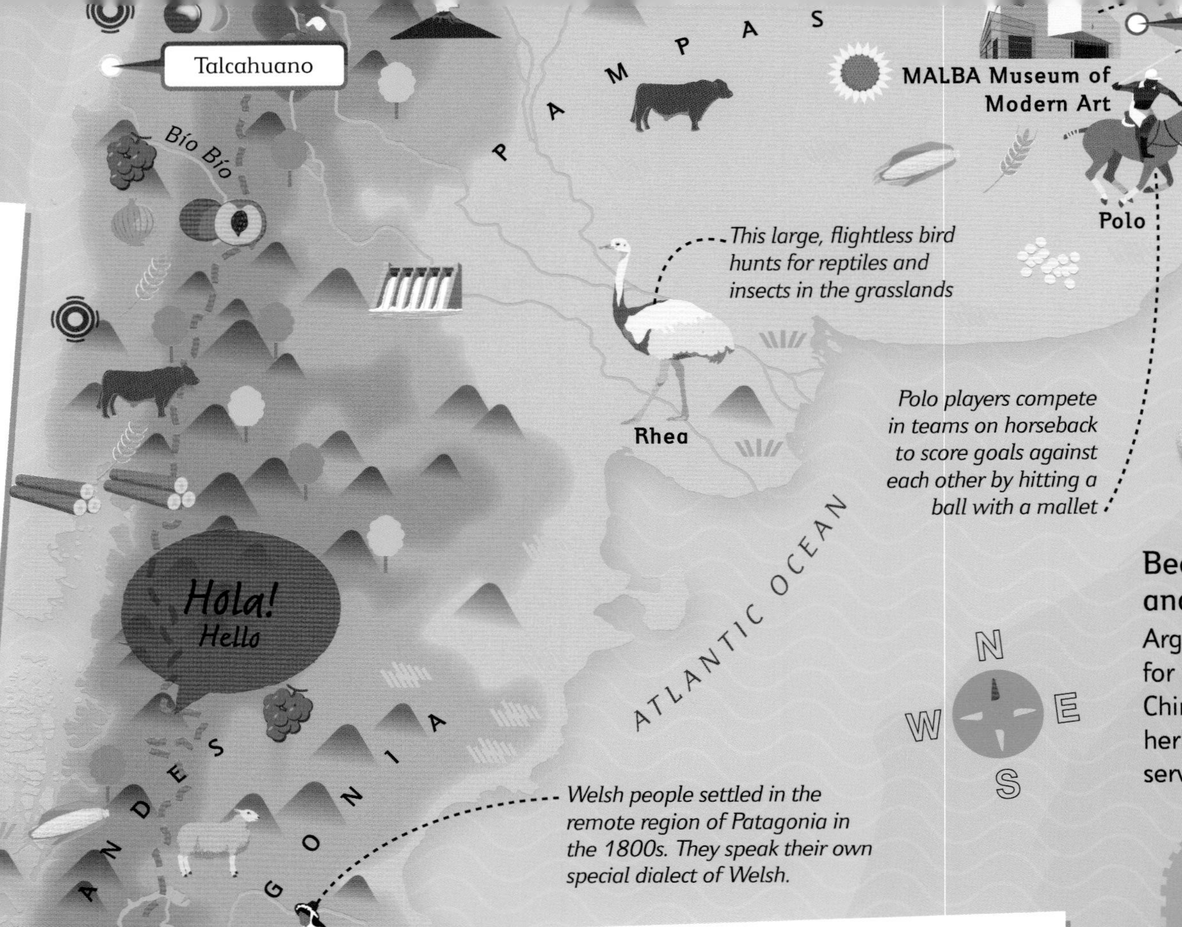
SCALE
0 200 miles
0 200 kilometers
Talcahuano
Bío Bío
PAMPAS
Buenos Aires
MALBA Museum of Modern Art
Río de la Plata
This museum in Buenos Aires features many spectacular art exhibits
Polo
This large, flightless bird hunts for reptiles and insects in the grasslands
Rhea
Polo players compete in teams on horseback to score goals against each other by hitting a ball with a mallet
Hola!
Hello
ATLANTIC OCEAN
N
W
E
S
ANDES
PATAGONIA
Welsh people settled in the remote region of Patagonia in the 1800s. They speak their own special dialect of Welsh.
Patagonian Welsh
Lake Argentino
Perito Moreno Glacier
Ice flows into Lake Argentino from the Perito Moreno Glacier
Magellanic penguins
This is one of seven species of penguin that live in South America
Punta Arenas

Stone heads

Easter Island

This Chilean island lies in the Pacific Ocean, 2,290 miles (3,686 km) west of the mainland. It is known for its huge stone statues, called moai, that were carved by local people hundreds of years ago.

Alpacas

Alpacas are kept in herds high in the mountains of northern Chile. Their thick hair can be woven to make blankets, hats, and sweaters.

Beef steak and sauce

Argentina is well known for producing top-quality beef. Chimichurri sauce, made from fresh herbs, garlic, and olive oil, is often served with steak.

Gaucho herding cattle

Cattle herding

Beef cattle is an important industry on the flat, treeless plains of the Pampas. Argentine cowboys, known as "gauchos," herd the cattle on huge ranches.

KEY

PRODUCE
- Vineyards
- Onions
- Corn
- Beef cattle
- Sunflowers
- Peaches
- Soybeans
- Sheep
- Apples and pears
- Wheat

INDUSTRY
- Hydroelectric power
- Copper
- Lumber
- Zinc
- Lead
- Iron
- Fishing
- Oil
- Tin

NATURAL FEATURES
- Volcanoes
- Earthquakes

POPULATION

The number of people living in the world is growing fast. In 1800, the world's population was about 1 billion. Today, there are more than 7.8 billion people worldwide. More than half of these people live in cities, rather than in the countryside. The population is growing because of healthier eating and better healthcare, which means that people are living longer.

Sparse population

The least densely populated country in the world is Mongolia, with an average of about five people for every square mile (about two people per square kilometer).

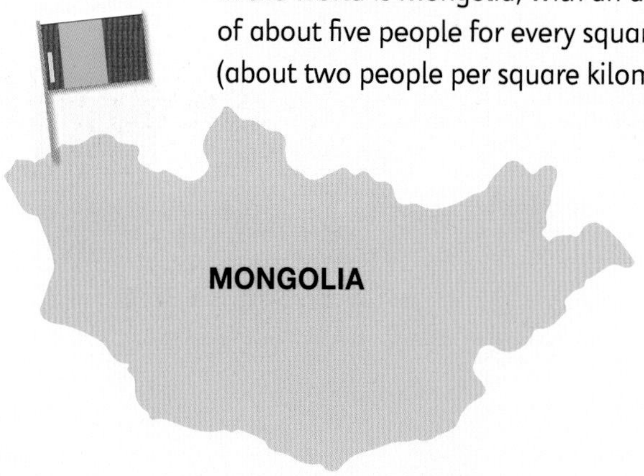
MONGOLIA

Most populated countries

These five countries have some of the biggest populations in the world. They are all large countries with plenty of farmland for growing crops.

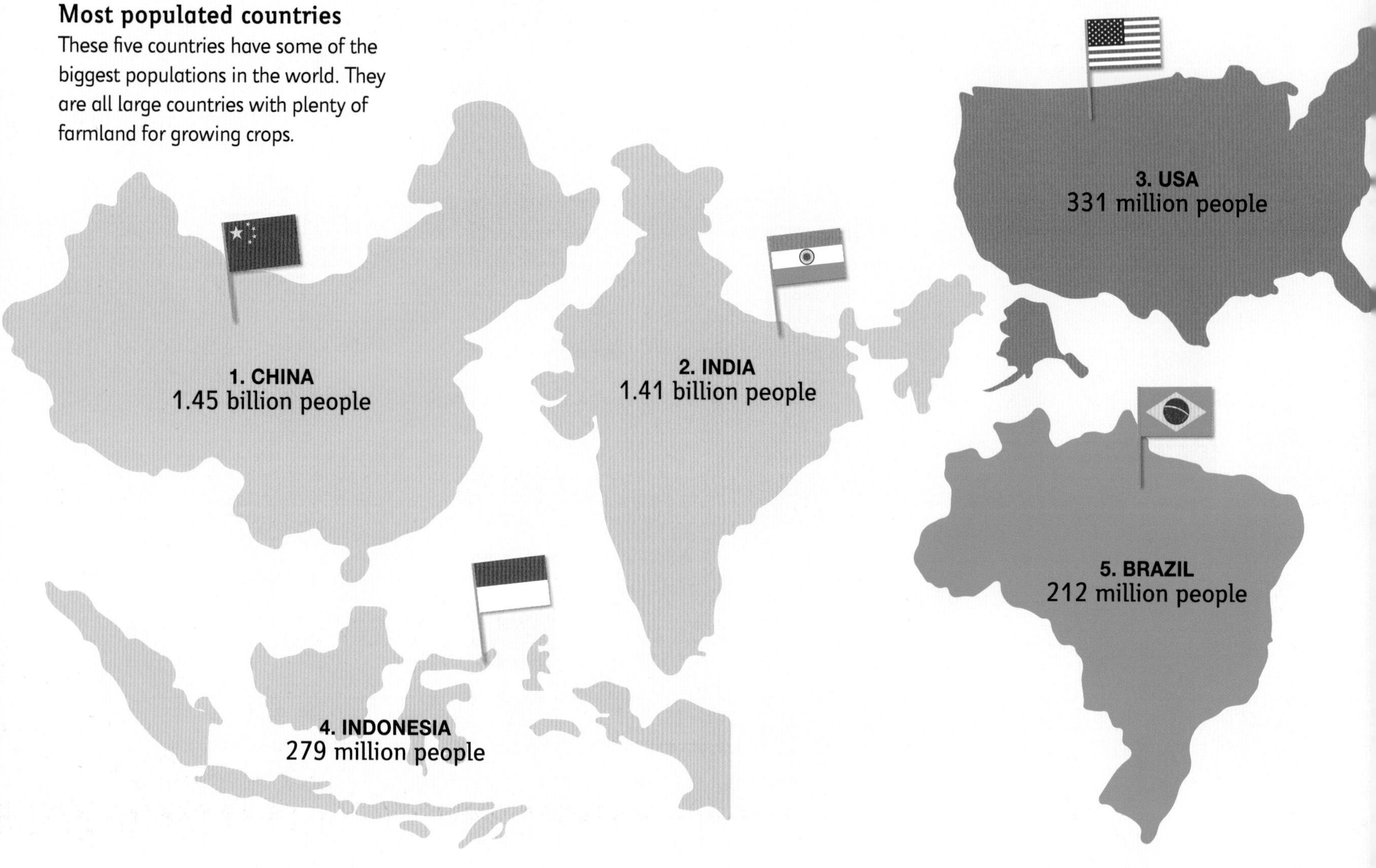
1. CHINA
1.45 billion people
2. INDIA
1.41 billion people
3. USA
331 million people
4. INDONESIA
279 million people
5. BRAZIL
212 million people

Who lives where?

This chart shows the percentage of the world's population in each continent. Asia is by far the world's most populated continent.

ASIA
60%

Most populated cities

The biggest city in most countries is usually, but not always, its capital city. A huge, sprawling city is also known as a metropolis. This chart shows the most populated city in each continent.

The greater Tokyo area has nearly the same population as the whole of Canada!

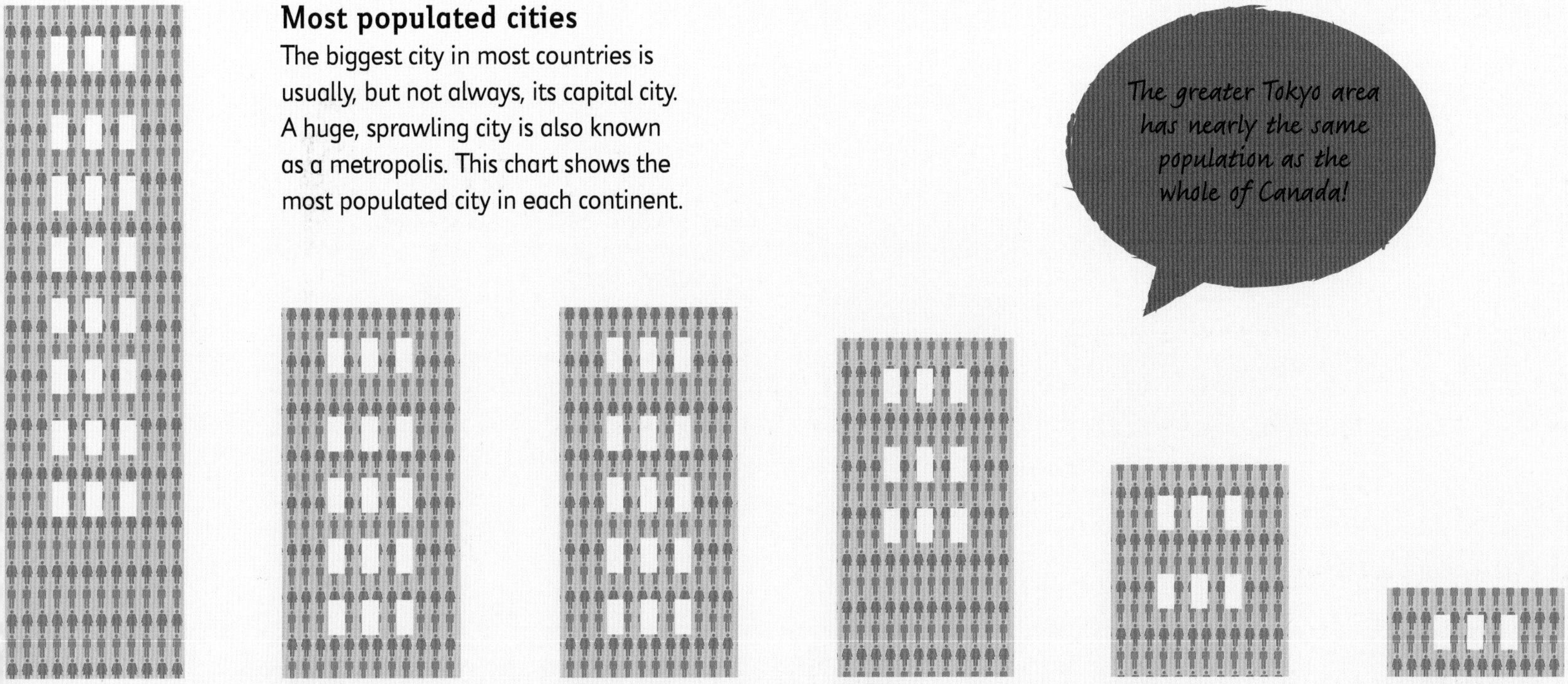

Tokyo, Japan, Asia
37 million people

Mexico City, Mexico, North America
22 million people

São Paulo, Brazil, South America
22 million people

Cairo, Egypt, Africa
21 million people

Moscow, Russia, Europe
12 million people

Melbourne, Australia, Australasia
5 million people

City versus countryside

In many parts of the world, cities are growing fast. People are moving, or migrating, from rural areas (the countryside) into towns and cities. Worldwide, about 56 percent of people live in cities and about 44 percent live in the countryside.

City 48%
Country 52%
Country 29%
City 71%

ASIA **AUSTRALASIA**

City 40%
Country 60%
Country 17%
City 83%
Country 20%
City 80%
Country 26%
City 74%

AFRICA **SOUTH AMERICA** **NORTH AMERICA** **EUROPE**

LARGEST CHILD POPULATION

India is the country with the most children. It has about 450 million children. This is about 40 percent of India's population.

AFRICA 16%

NORTH AMERICA 8%

AUSTRALASIA 1%

EUROPE 10%

SOUTH AMERICA 5%

1. Which North African desert people wear blue robes?
2. From which country do many great long-distance runners come?
3. In which country is the Temple of Zeus found?
4. What are Egypt's white-sailed river boats called?

6. In which country is Kruger National Park?

5. Where might you spot a bonobo?

AFRICA

This vast continent is rich in natural resources, including gold and diamonds. It has magnificent landscapes and bustling cities—from Cairo in Egypt to Cape Town in South Africa. Throughout Africa, there is a large and growing population of young people who are bringing major changes to society.

You can find all the answers and more quizzes on pages 120–121.

8. The baobab is the national tree of which country?

7. In which country would you find a museum of steam trains?

AFRICA

Africa is the world's second largest continent. To the north, the dry countries bordering the Mediterranean Sea are cut off from the rest of Africa by the Sahara Desert. South of the Sahara are grassy plains and tropical rain forests, where many unique wild animals live.

N
W
E
S
TUNISIA
Canary Islands
(SPAIN)
MOROCCO
ALGERIA
WESTERN SAHARA
MAURITANIA
CABO VERDE
NIGER
SENEGAL
MALI
THE GAMBIA
GUINEA-BISSAU
BURKINA FASO
GUINEA
SIERRA LEONE
GHANA
TOGO
BENIN
NIGERIA
IVORY COAST
LIBERIA
ATLANTIC OCEAN
GULF OF GUINEA
Bioco
EQUATORIAL GUINEA
São Tomé & Príncipe
GABO
REPUBLIC THE CO

West African market

Busy markets are found all over West Africa. Many people make a living by traveling to various markets and selling their goods and produce.

Sahara Desert

The Sahara is the world's largest hot desert. It stretches from Mauritania in the west to Sudan in the east. Camels are used to carry goods across the sandy dunes.

RANEAN SEA
BYA
EGYPT
RED SEA
SUDAN
ERITREA
DJIBOUTI
ETHIOPIA
CENTRAL AFRICAN REPUBLIC
SOUTH SUDAN
SOMALIA
DEMOCRATIC REPUBLIC OF THE CONGO
UGANDA
KENYA
INDIAN OCEAN
RWANDA
BURUNDI
TANZANIA
Zanzibar
SEYCHELLES
COMOROS
MALAWI
ZAMBIA
MOZAMBIQUE
MOZAMBIQUE CHANNEL
MADAGASCAR
ZIMBABWE
BOTSWANA
Réunion (FRANCE)
MAURITIUS
ESWATINI
SOUTH AFRICA
LESOTHO
SCALE
0
500 miles
1,000 miles
0
1,000 kilometers

Nile River

This is the world's longest river. It flows north through 11 countries, from Tanzania to Egypt's Mediterranean coast. Many early civilizations flourished along the Nile's banks, using its waters to grow crops and as a trading route.

Table Mountain

This magnificent mountain overlooks the city of Cape Town in South Africa. Its large, flat top makes it look like a table, and it is often covered by white clouds, which are nicknamed "the tablecloth."

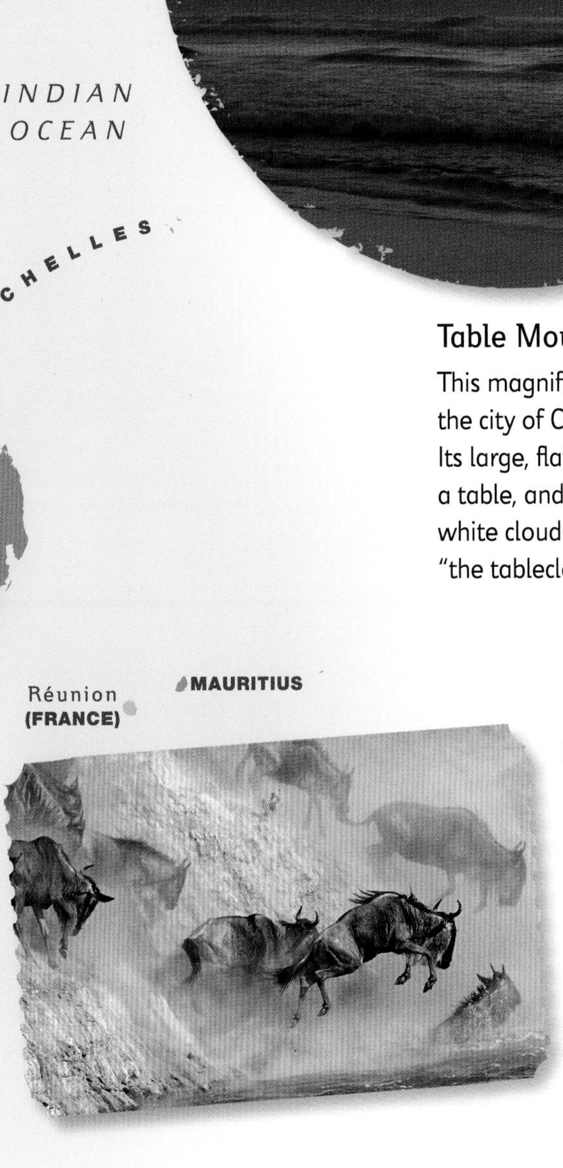

Game reserve

Many African countries have set up game reserves to protect wild animals, such as lions, elephants, and wildebeest, from hunters and poachers.

NORTH AFRICA

Morocco, Algeria, Tunisia, and Libya sit side by side at the northern end of Africa. Towns and cities are dotted along the Mediterranean coast, where lively markets are found alongside ancient ruins. Vast areas of North Africa are sandy desert, with rich oil reserves in some places.

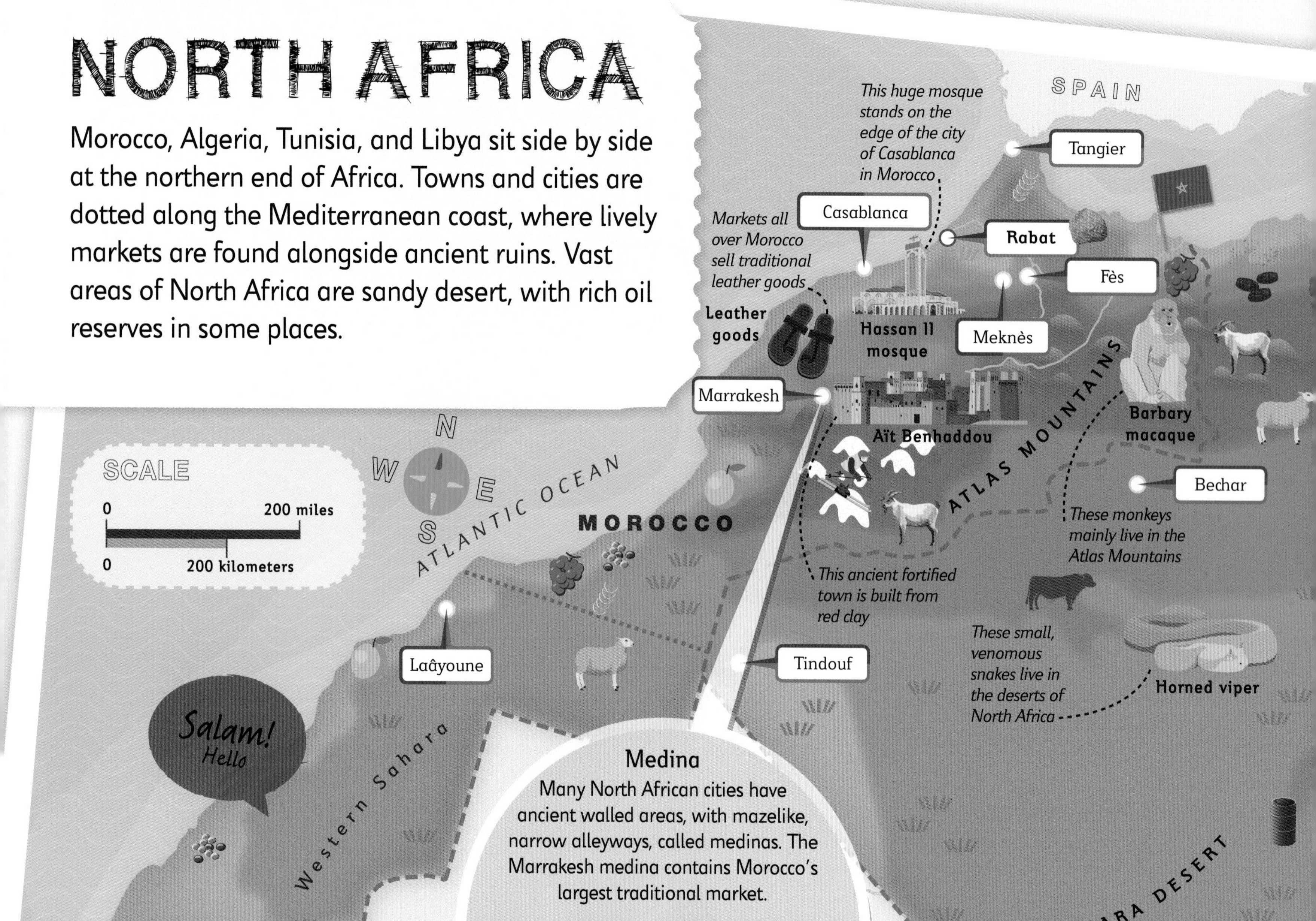

SPAIN
This huge mosque stands on the edge of the city of Casablanca in Morocco
Tangier
Casablanca
Markets all over Morocco sell traditional leather goods
Rabat
Fès
Leather goods
Hassan 11 mosque
Meknès
Marrakesh
Aït Benhaddou
Barbary macaque
ATLAS MOUNTAINS
Bechar
These monkeys mainly live in the Atlas Mountains
SCALE
0
200 miles
0
200 kilometers
N
E
S
W
ATLANTIC OCEAN
MOROCCO
This ancient fortified town is built from red clay
These small, venomous snakes live in the deserts of North Africa
Horned viper
Laâyoune
Tindouf
Salam! Hello
Western Sahara
SAHARA DESERT
The Tuareg are a desert people who traditionally wear blue robes
Tuareg blue robes
MALI
MAURITANIA

Medina

Many North African cities have ancient walled areas, with mazelike, narrow alleyways, called medinas. The Marrakesh medina contains Morocco's largest traditional market.

Moroccan rapper Khtek

Hip-hop music

Hip-hop is popular among young people in North Africa. Female rappers in Morocco often use their lyrics to demand equality for girls and women.

North African cuisine

Tagine, made with meat and fruit, is eaten in many parts of North Africa. Refreshing mint tea is a popular drink.

Tagine
Mint tea
Mint leaves

Striped hyena

These hyenas are found throughout North Africa. They live in caves or dug dens, coming out to search for food at night.

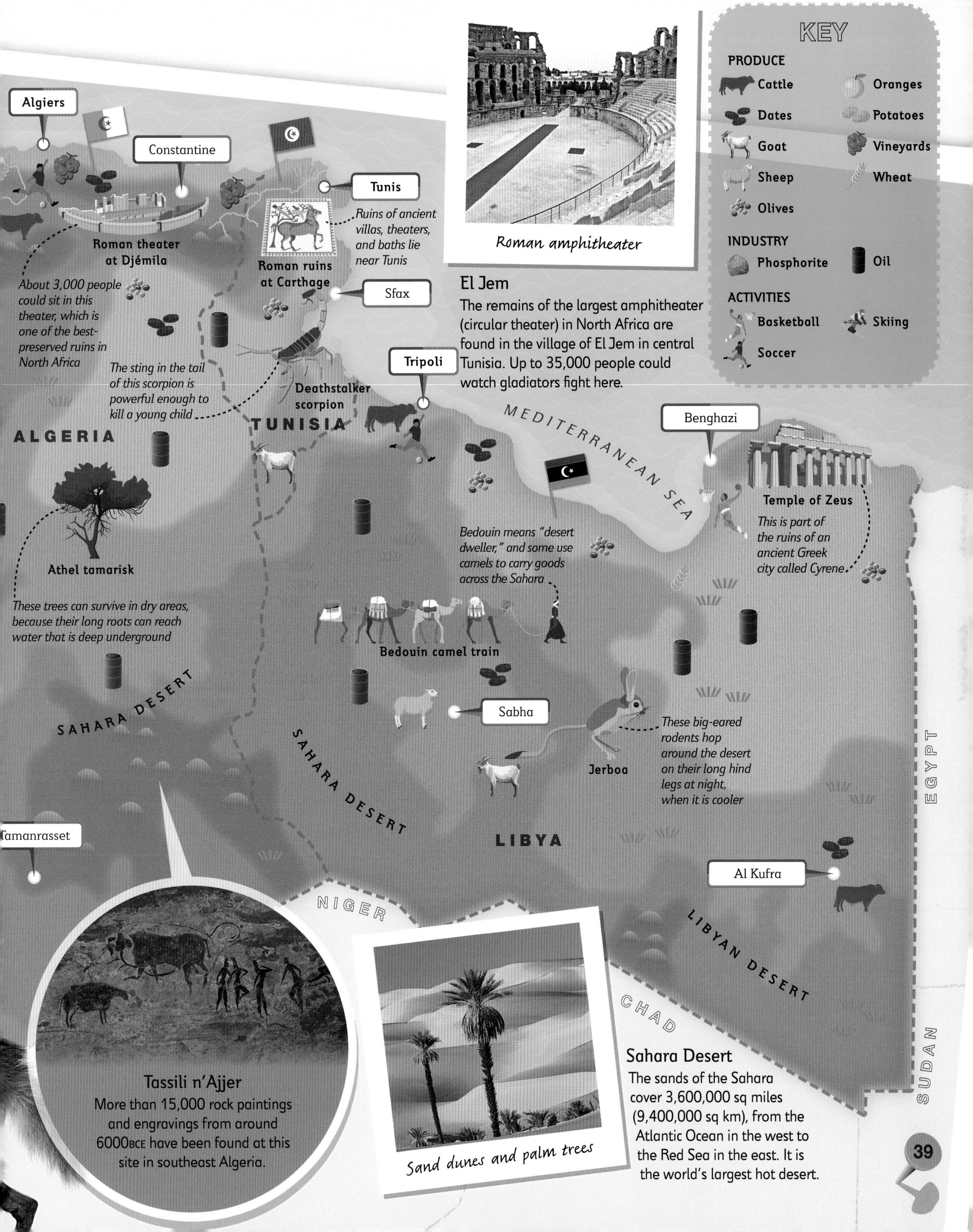

Algiers
Constantine
Tunis
Sfax
Tripoli
Benghazi
Sabha
Al Kufra
Tamanrasset
ALGERIA
TUNISIA
LIBYA
EGYPT
SUDAN
NIGER
CHAD
MEDITERRANEAN SEA
SAHARA DESERT
SAHARA DESERT
LIBYAN DESERT
Roman theater at Djémila
About 3,000 people could sit in this theater, which is one of the best-preserved ruins in North Africa
Roman ruins at Carthage
Ruins of ancient villas, theaters, and baths lie near Tunis
Deathstalker scorpion
The sting in the tail of this scorpion is powerful enough to kill a young child
Athel tamarisk
These trees can survive in dry areas, because their long roots can reach water that is deep underground
Bedouin camel train
Bedouin means "desert dweller," and some use camels to carry goods across the Sahara
Temple of Zeus
This is part of the ruins of an ancient Greek city called Cyrene
Jerboa
These big-eared rodents hop around the desert on their long hind legs at night, when it is cooler

Roman amphitheater

KEY

PRODUCE
- Cattle
- Oranges
- Dates
- Potatoes
- Goat
- Vineyards
- Sheep
- Wheat
- Olives

INDUSTRY
- Phosphorite
- Oil

ACTIVITIES
- Basketball
- Skiing
- Soccer

El Jem

The remains of the largest amphitheater (circular theater) in North Africa are found in the village of El Jem in central Tunisia. Up to 35,000 people could watch gladiators fight here.

Tassili n'Ajjer

More than 15,000 rock paintings and engravings from around 6000BCE have been found at this site in southeast Algeria.

Sand dunes and palm trees

Sahara Desert

The sands of the Sahara cover 3,600,000 sq miles (9,400,000 sq km), from the Atlantic Ocean in the west to the Red Sea in the east. It is the world's largest hot desert.

EGYPT

Much of Egypt is made up of dry, sandy desert, and so most people live along the banks of the Nile River. This very long river is a vital source of water for drinking and farming. Thousands of years ago, pharaohs (kings) built pyramids along the Nile, some of which are still standing.

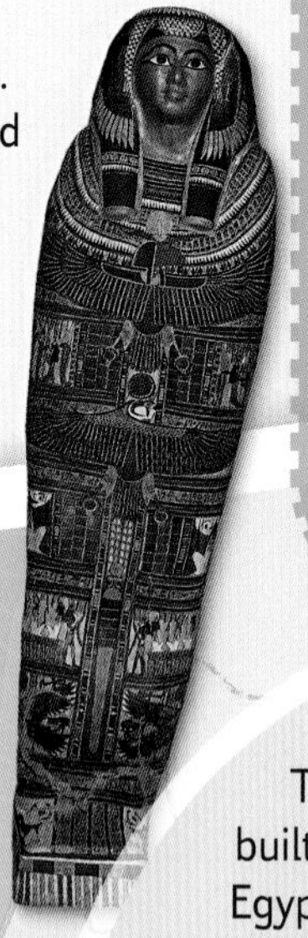

Mummy case
Ancient Egyptians preserved, or mummified, bodies. The specially treated body was wrapped in bandages and the mummy was then placed in a decorated case.

KEY

PRODUCE	INDUSTRY
Rice	Oil
Wheat	Fishing
Oranges	**ACTIVITIES**
Dates	Scuba diving
Cotton	**NATURAL FEATURES**
	Coral reef

Pyramids
These massive structures were built as tombs for the bodies of dead Egyptian kings and queens. The three most famous pyramids are at Giza.

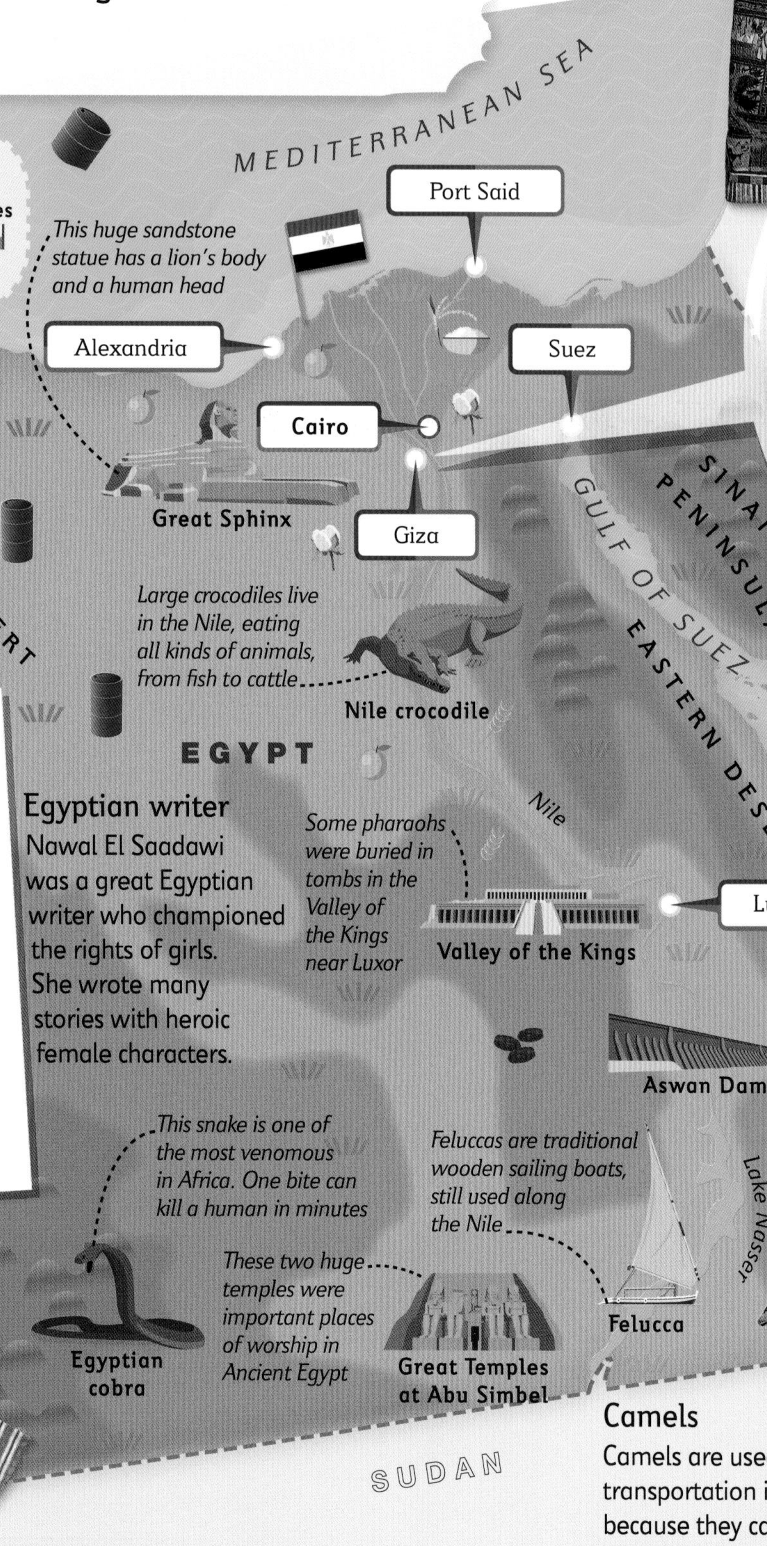

SCALE
0
100 miles
200 miles
0
200 kilometers
N
S
E
W
MEDITERRANEAN SEA
Port Said
Alexandria
Suez
Cairo
Giza
Great Sphinx
This huge sandstone statue has a lion's body and a human head
WESTERN DESERT
LIBYA
SINAI PENINSULA
GULF OF SUEZ
EASTERN DESERT
Large crocodiles live in the Nile, eating all kinds of animals, from fish to cattle
Nile crocodile
EGYPT
Nile
Some pharaohs were buried in tombs in the Valley of the Kings near Luxor
Valley of the Kings
Luxor
RED SEA
SAUDI ARABIA
Salam!
Hello
Aswan Dam
This dam opened in 1970; it generates hydroelectricity and controls flood water
Lake Nasser
This snake is one of the most venomous in Africa. One bite can kill a human in minutes
Egyptian cobra
Feluccas are traditional wooden sailing boats, still used along the Nile
Felucca
These two huge temples were important places of worship in Ancient Egypt
Great Temples at Abu Simbel
SUDAN

Nawal El Saadawi

Egyptian writer
Nawal El Saadawi was a great Egyptian writer who championed the rights of girls. She wrote many stories with heroic female characters.

Cotton tunic

Cotton
Cool and comfortable cotton tunics are a common form of dress in this hot country. Egyptian cotton is known for its high quality.

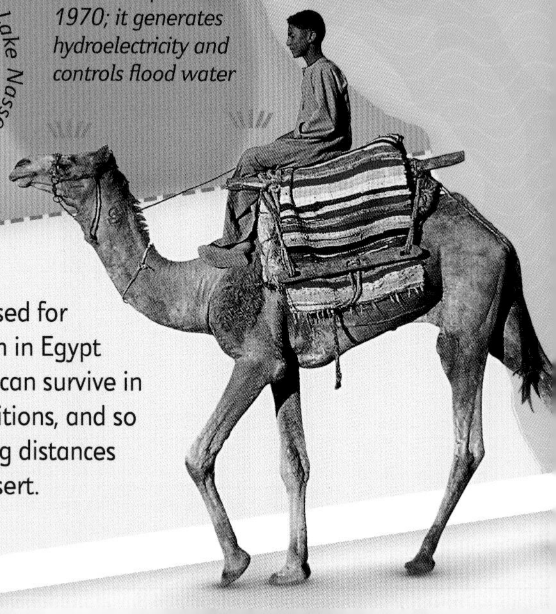

Camels
Camels are used for transportation in Egypt because they can survive in very dry conditions, and so can travel long distances across the desert.

ETHIOPIA AND KENYA

Some of Africa's most spectacular scenery is found in Ethiopia and Kenya. Ethiopia has high mountains where coffee is grown. A wide variety of wildlife live on the plains of Kenya, including lions, elephants, zebras, and giraffes.

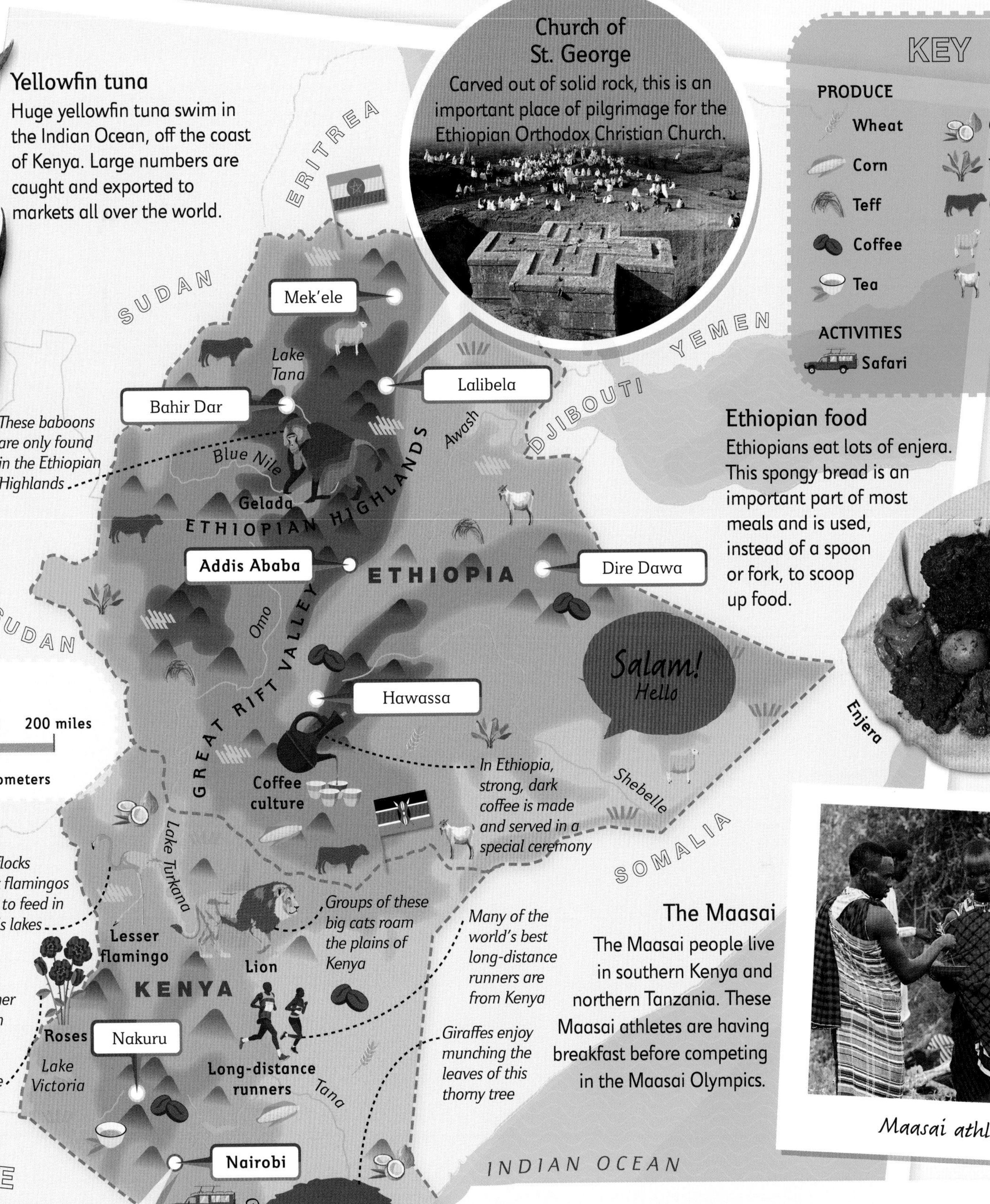

KEY
PRODUCE
Wheat
Coconuts
Corn
Ensete
Teff
Cattle
Coffee
Sheep
Tea
Goats
ACTIVITIES
Safari
ERITREA
SUDAN
SOUTH SUDAN
YEMEN
DJIBOUTI
SOMALIA
UGANDA
TANZANIA
INDIAN OCEAN
Mek'ele
Lake Tana
Lalibela
Bahir Dar
Blue Nile
Awash
Gelada
ETHIOPIAN HIGHLANDS
Addis Ababa
ETHIOPIA
Dire Dawa
Omo
GREAT RIFT VALLEY
Hawassa
Salam! Hello
Coffee culture
Shebelle
Lake Turkana
Lesser flamingo
Lion
KENYA
Roses
Nakuru
Lake Victoria
Long-distance runners
Tana
Nairobi
Galana
Acacia
Mombasa
Jambo! Hello
SCALE
0 100 miles 200 miles
0 200 kilometers
N
W E
S
These baboons are only found in the Ethiopian Highlands
In Ethiopia, strong, dark coffee is made and served in a special ceremony
Huge flocks of pink flamingos gather to feed in Kenya's lakes
Groups of these big cats roam the plains of Kenya
Many of the world's best long-distance runners are from Kenya
Roses and other flowers grown in Kenya are exported for sale in Europe
Giraffes enjoy munching the leaves of this thorny tree

Yellowfin tuna

Yellowfin tuna

Huge yellowfin tuna swim in the Indian Ocean, off the coast of Kenya. Large numbers are caught and exported to markets all over the world.

Church of St. George

Carved out of solid rock, this is an important place of pilgrimage for the Ethiopian Orthodox Christian Church.

Ethiopian food

Ethiopians eat lots of enjera. This spongy bread is an important part of most meals and is used, instead of a spoon or fork, to scoop up food.

Enjera

The Maasai

The Maasai people live in southern Kenya and northern Tanzania. These Maasai athletes are having breakfast before competing in the Maasai Olympics.

Maasai athletes

Giraffe Manor

Giraffes roam the grounds of this hotel, which looks after endangered species. The giraffes often poke their heads through the hotel's indows, hoping to receive a tasty snack.

NIGERIA

About 206 million people live in Nigeria, more than in any other African country. Many different tribal groups live here, each with its own colorful traditions, handicrafts, and music. Nigeria is also Africa's largest producer of oil and has several oil rigs in the Gulf of Guinea.

The Yoruba

The Yoruba are one of Nigeria's largest tribal groups. Their traditional dress includes brightly patterned fabrics and finely carved ivory bracelets.

Ivory bracelet
Yoruba cloth

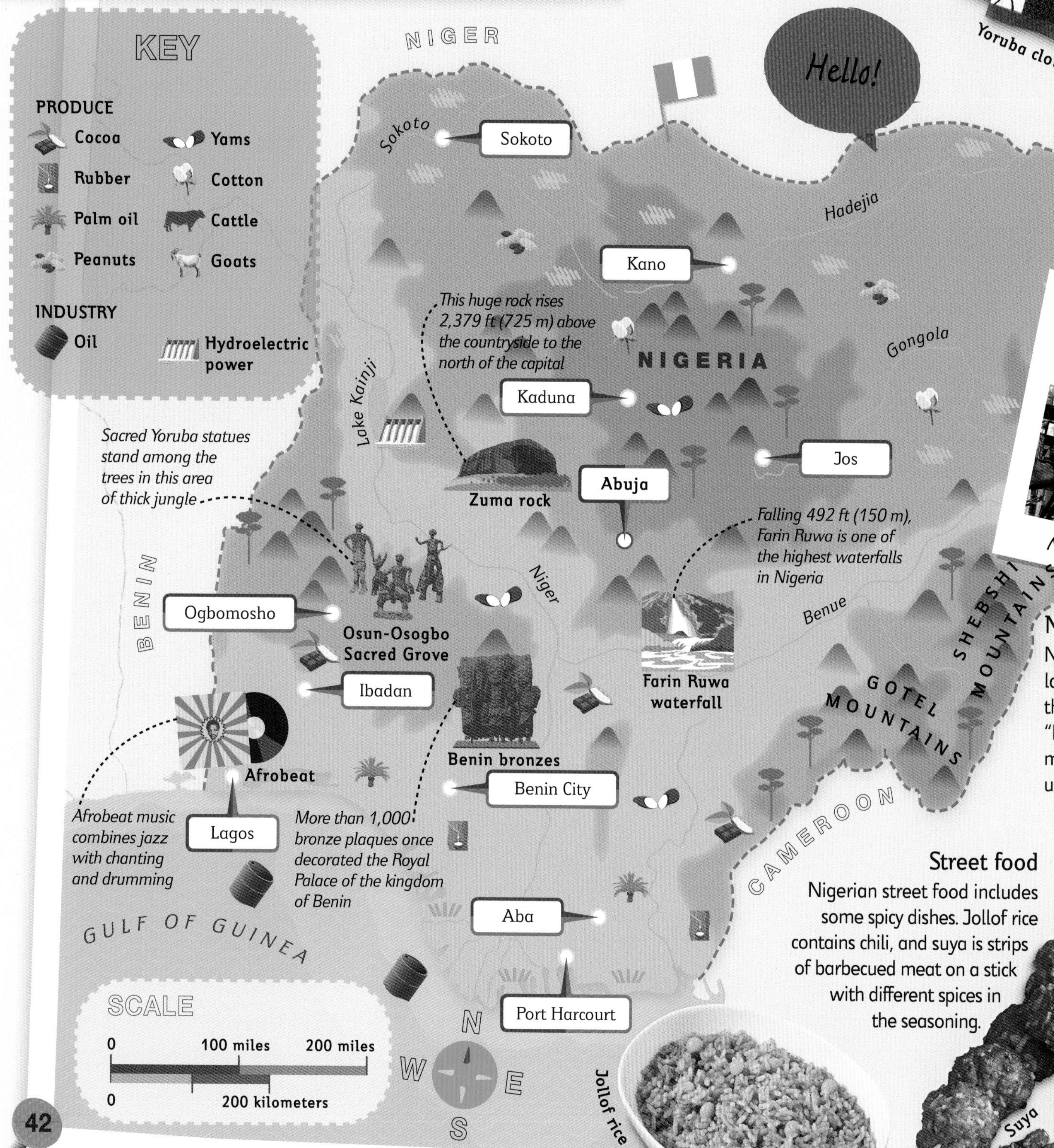

KEY
PRODUCE
Cocoa
Yams
Rubber
Cotton
Palm oil
Cattle
Peanuts
Goats
INDUSTRY
Oil
Hydroelectric power
NIGER
CHAD
Hello!
Sokoto
Sokoto
Hadejia
Maiduguri
Kano
This huge rock rises 2,379 ft (725 m) above the countryside to the north of the capital
Gongola
Lake Kainji
NIGERIA
Kaduna
Sacred Yoruba statues stand among the trees in this area of thick jungle
Jos
Zuma rock
Abuja
Falling 492 ft (150 m), Farin Ruwa is one of the highest waterfalls in Nigeria
BENIN
Niger
Ogbomosho
Osun-Osogbo Sacred Grove
Benue
SHEBSHI MOUNTAINS
Ibadan
Farin Ruwa waterfall
GOTEL MOUNTAINS
Afrobeat
Benin bronzes
Benin City
CAMEROON
Afrobeat music combines jazz with chanting and drumming
Lagos
More than 1,000 bronze plaques once decorated the Royal Palace of the kingdom of Benin
GULF OF GUINEA
Aba
Port Harcourt
SCALE
0
100 miles
200 miles
0
200 kilometers
N
W
E
S

Nigerian film crew

Nollywood

Nigeria has the second largest film industry in the world. Known as "Nollywood," it produces many funny, thrilling, and unique movies.

Street food

Nigerian street food includes some spicy dishes. Jollof rice contains chili, and suya is strips of barbecued meat on a stick with different spices in the seasoning.

Pepper sauce
Jollof rice
Suya

GHANA AND THE IVORY COAST

Ghana was once known as the Gold Coast because of its plentiful gold. The Ivory Coast was famous for its elephant herds, and the elephant is the nation's symbol. Today, both countries grow cocoa beans, which are used to make some of the world's finest chocolate.

Plantain and okra

West Africa has lots of fertile farmland. Crops grown include plantain, a type of cooking banana, and okra, a long, thin vegetable that grows on a plant with large, white flowers.

Plantain

KEY

PRODUCE

- Coffee
- Corn
- Cocoa
- Coconuts
- Bananas
- Yams
- Pineapples
- Cassavas
- Rubber
- Cattle
- Palm oil
- Goats
- Rice

INDUSTRY

- Iron
- Oil
- Gold
- Natural gas
- Bauxite
- Diamonds

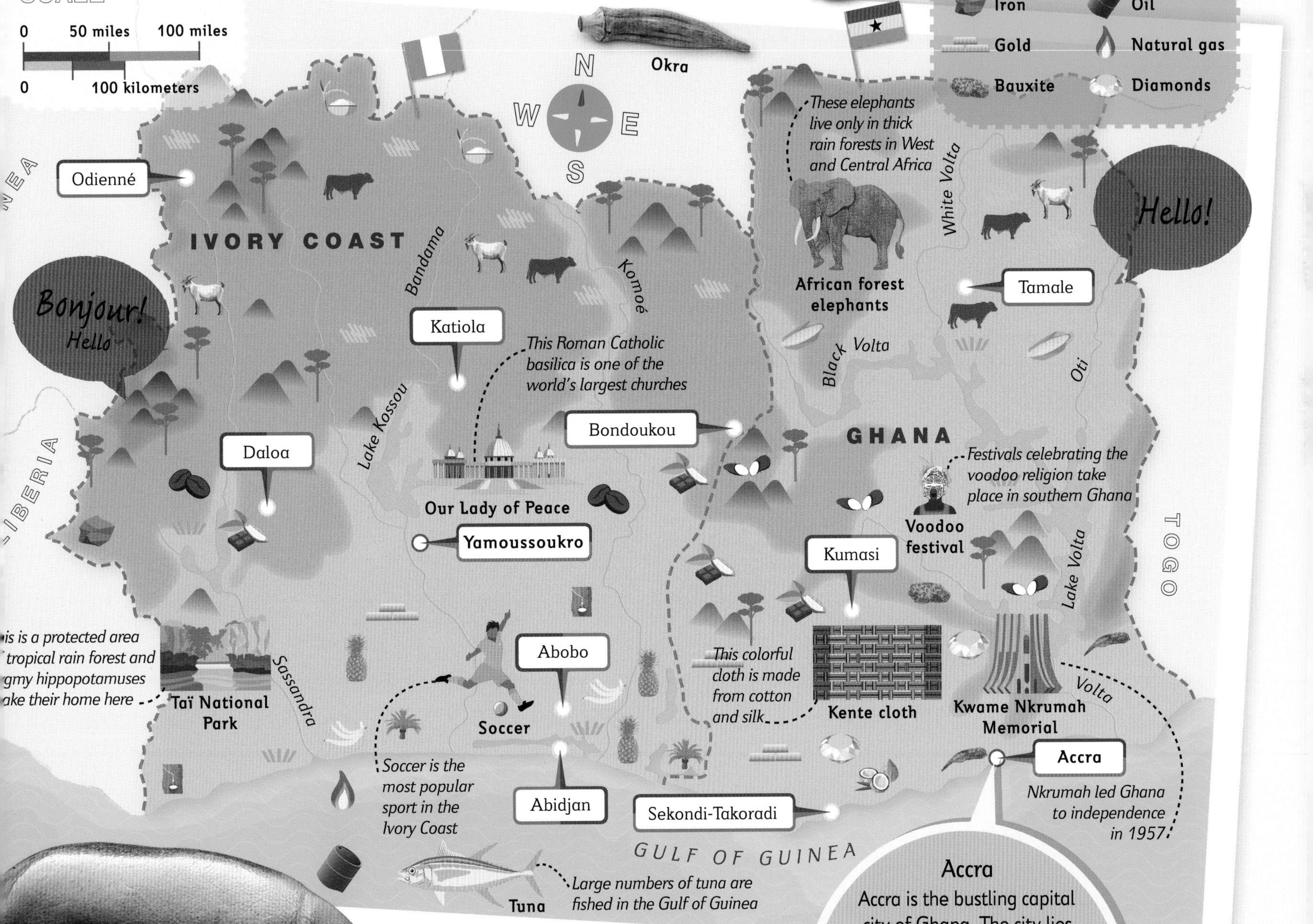

SCALE
0
50 miles
100 miles
0
100 kilometers
N
W
E
S
Okra
IVORY COAST
GHANA
TOGO
LIBERIA
GULF OF GUINEA
Odienné
Bonjour!
Hello
Katiola
Bandama
Komoé
This Roman Catholic basilica is one of the world's largest churches
Lake Kossou
Daloa
Bondoukou
Our Lady of Peace
Yamoussoukro
These elephants live only in thick rain forests in West and Central Africa
African forest elephants
White Volta
Black Volta
Oti
Hello!
Tamale
Festivals celebrating the voodoo religion take place in southern Ghana
Voodoo festival
Kumasi
Lake Volta
Volta
This colorful cloth is made from cotton and silk
Kente cloth
Kwame Nkrumah Memorial
Accra
Nkrumah led Ghana to independence in 1957
Sassandra
Taï National Park
Abobo
Soccer
Soccer is the most popular sport in the Ivory Coast
Abidjan
Sekondi-Takoradi
Large numbers of tuna are fished in the Gulf of Guinea
Tuna

Pygmy hippopotamus

This small hippopotamus lives in the forests and swamps of West Africa. It only ventures out at night, so is rarely seen.

Accra

Accra is the bustling capital city of Ghana. The city lies partly on a cliff.

CONGO (DRC)

The Democratic Republic of the Congo (DRC) is the largest African country south of the Sahara Desert. The world's deepest river, the Congo, runs all across the country, and some of Africa's Great Lakes lie on its eastern border. The Congo rain forest is the second largest in the world.

Mountain gorillas

Virunga National Park

Africa's oldest national park was created in 1925, mainly to provide a safe home for mountain gorillas and other local wildlife. Years of war nearly destroyed the park, but the area is now protected. Thousands of tourists visit the park every year.

KEY
PRODUCE
Oil palms
Cassavas
Corn
Rubber
Coffee
Rice
INDUSTRY
Copper
Cobalt
Tin
Diamonds
ACTIVITIES
Soccer
NATURAL FEATURES
Volcanoes
Bonjour! Hello
CENTRAL AFRICAN REPUBLIC
SOUTH SUDAN
UGANDA
RWANDA
BURUNDI
TANZANIA
ZAMBIA
ANGOLA
REPUBLIC OF THE CONGO
CONGO (DRC)
This small, clever chimpanzee only lives in the Congo rain forest
Bonobo
The Mbuti people live in the forest of the Congo
Mbuti
This shy rain forest animal is related to the giraffe
Okapi
This parrot eats forest fruits, nuts, and flowers
African gray parrot
Congo
Ubangi
Lake Mai-Ndombe
Tshuapa
Kasai
Sankuru
Lulua
Lake Albert
Lake Edward
Lake Tanganyika
Lake Mweru
Kisangani
Bukavu
Kinshasa
Kananga
Mbuji-Mayi
Tshikapa
Likasi
Kolwezi
Lubumbashi
SCALE
0
200 miles
0
200 kilometers
N
W
S

Sapeurs

The sapeurs are a group of people who like to wear finely tailored clothes and who believe in being sophisticated and stylish.

Cobalt mine

Mining

Many valuable minerals are mined in the Congo area, including cobalt. Cobalt has been used since ancient times to give a rich blue colc to paints. It is also used in medicine, batteries, and electronic equipment.

ZAMBIA AND ZIMBABWE

Zambia and Zimbabwe are famous for their spectacular scenery and wildlife. Africa's fourth longest river, the Zambezi, flows down through Zambia, then curves along the border with Zimbabwe on its journey to the Indian Ocean.

Southern yellow-billed hornbill

This bird uses its huge beak to snatch up insects, spiders, and even scorpions from the ground. It sleeps in trees at night to avoid predators.

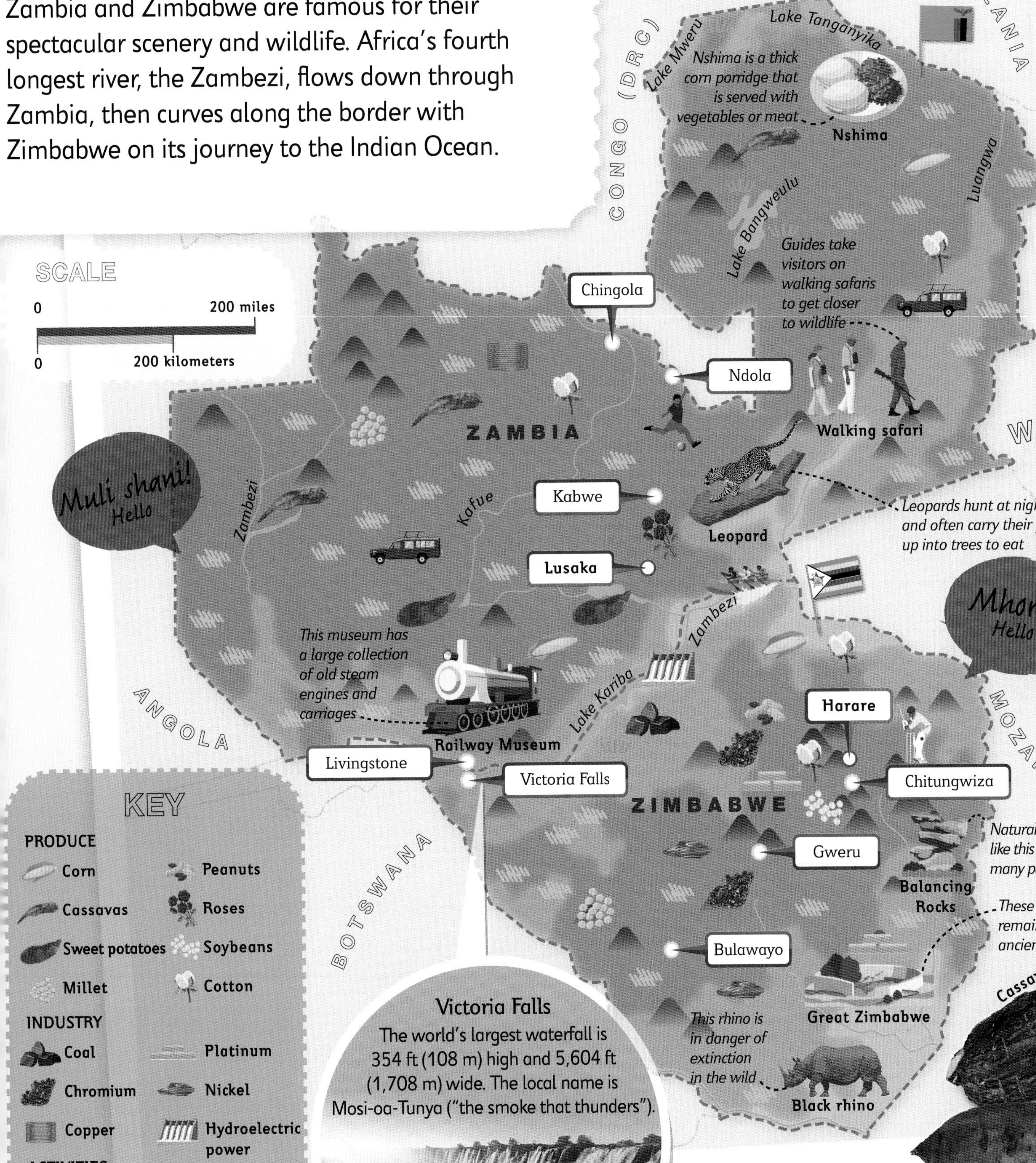

SCALE
0
200 miles
0
200 kilometers
TANZANIA
CONGO (DRC)
MALAWI
ANGOLA
BOTSWANA
MOZAMBIQUE
Lake Mweru
Lake Tanganyika
Nshima is a thick corn porridge that is served with vegetables or meat
Nshima
Luangwa
Lake Bangweulu
Guides take visitors on walking safaris to get closer to wildlife
Walking safari
Chingola
Ndola
ZAMBIA
N
E
S
W
Muli shani! Hello
Zambezi
Kafue
Kabwe
Leopard
Leopards hunt at night and often carry their prey up into trees to eat
Lusaka
Zambezi
Mhoro! Hello
This museum has a large collection of old steam engines and carriages
Railway Museum
Lake Kariba
Harare
Livingstone
Victoria Falls
Chitungwiza
ZIMBABWE
Gweru
Natural rock formations like this are found in many parts of Zimbabwe
Balancing Rocks
These ruins are the remains of an ancient city
Bulawayo
Great Zimbabwe
This rhino is in danger of extinction in the wild
Black rhino
KEY
PRODUCE
Corn
Peanuts
Cassavas
Roses
Sweet potatoes
Soybeans
Millet
Cotton
INDUSTRY
Coal
Platinum
Chromium
Nickel
Copper
Hydroelectric power
ACTIVITIES
Soccer
White-water rafting
Cricket
Safari

Victoria Falls

The world's largest waterfall is 354 ft (108 m) high and 5,604 ft (1,708 m) wide. The local name is Mosi-oa-Tunya ("the smoke that thunders").

Cassava
Sweet potato

Root vegetables

Cassavas and sweet potatoes are a main part of people's diet here. Cassava root can be cooked or made into flour that is used to make bread. Sweet potatoes are often boiled or roasted.

SOUTH AFRICA

South Africa is home to people from many different cultures, which is why it has 11 official languages and 3 capital cities. The landscape is equally varied, ranging from forests to deserts, while the long coastline has many beautiful beaches.

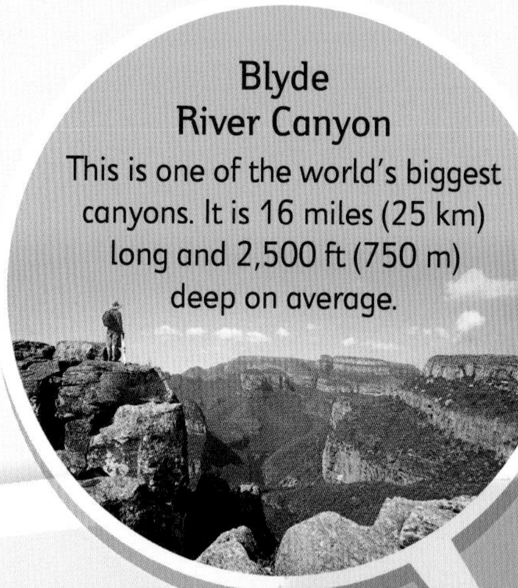

Blyde
River Canyon
This is one of the world's biggest canyons. It is 16 miles (25 km) long and 2,500 ft (750 m) deep on average.

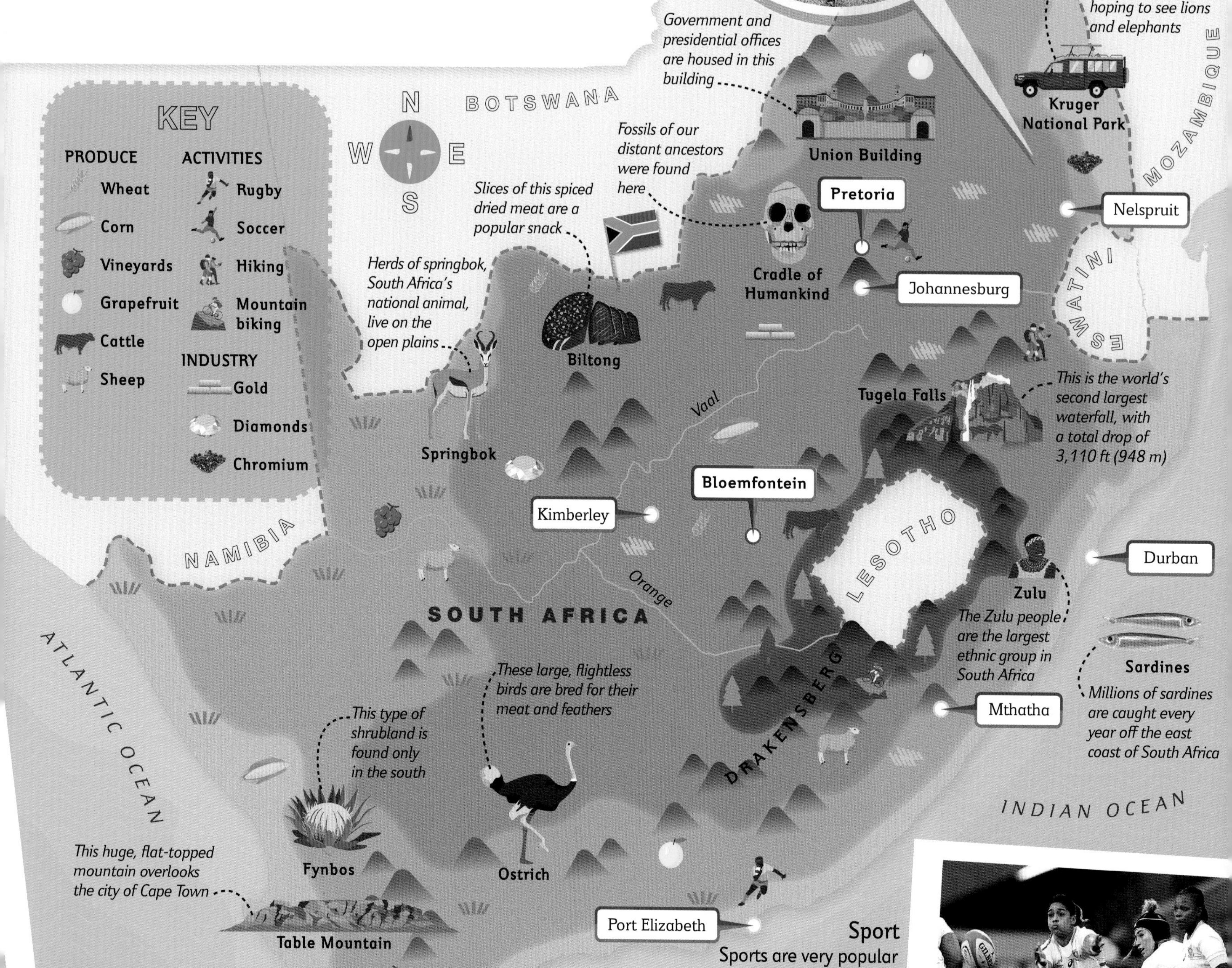

SCALE
0
100 miles
0
100 kilometers
KEY
PRODUCE
Wheat
Corn
Vineyards
Grapefruit
Cattle
Sheep
ACTIVITIES
Rugby
Soccer
Hiking
Mountain biking
INDUSTRY
Gold
Diamonds
Chromium
N
E
S
W
BOTSWANA
NAMIBIA
MOZAMBIQUE
ESWATINI
LESOTHO
SOUTH AFRICA
ATLANTIC OCEAN
INDIAN OCEAN
Government and presidential offices are housed in this building
Union Building
Tourists go on safari by jeep in this large game reserve, hoping to see lions and elephants
Kruger National Park
Fossils of our distant ancestors were found here
Cradle of Humankind
Pretoria
Nelspruit
Johannesburg
Slices of this spiced dried meat are a popular snack
Biltong
Herds of springbok, South Africa's national animal, live on the open plains
Springbok
Tugela Falls
This is the world's second largest waterfall, with a total drop of 3,110 ft (948 m)
Vaal
Orange
Kimberley
Bloemfontein
Durban
Zulu
The Zulu people are the largest ethnic group in South Africa
Sardines
Millions of sardines are caught every year off the east coast of South Africa
Mthatha
DRAKENSBERG
These large, flightless birds are bred for their meat and feathers
Ostrich
This type of shrubland is found only in the south
Fynbos
This huge, flat-topped mountain overlooks the city of Cape Town
Table Mountain
Cape Town
Port Elizabeth

Bunny chow
Bobotie

South African food

Food in South Africa reflects the country's cultural mix. Popular dishes include bunny chow, a hollowed-out loaf filled with curry, and bobotie, minced beef with an egg topping.

Sport

Sports are very popular in South Africa—especialy rugby, cricket, and soccer. The women's national rugby team is known as Springbok Women.

Springbok Women

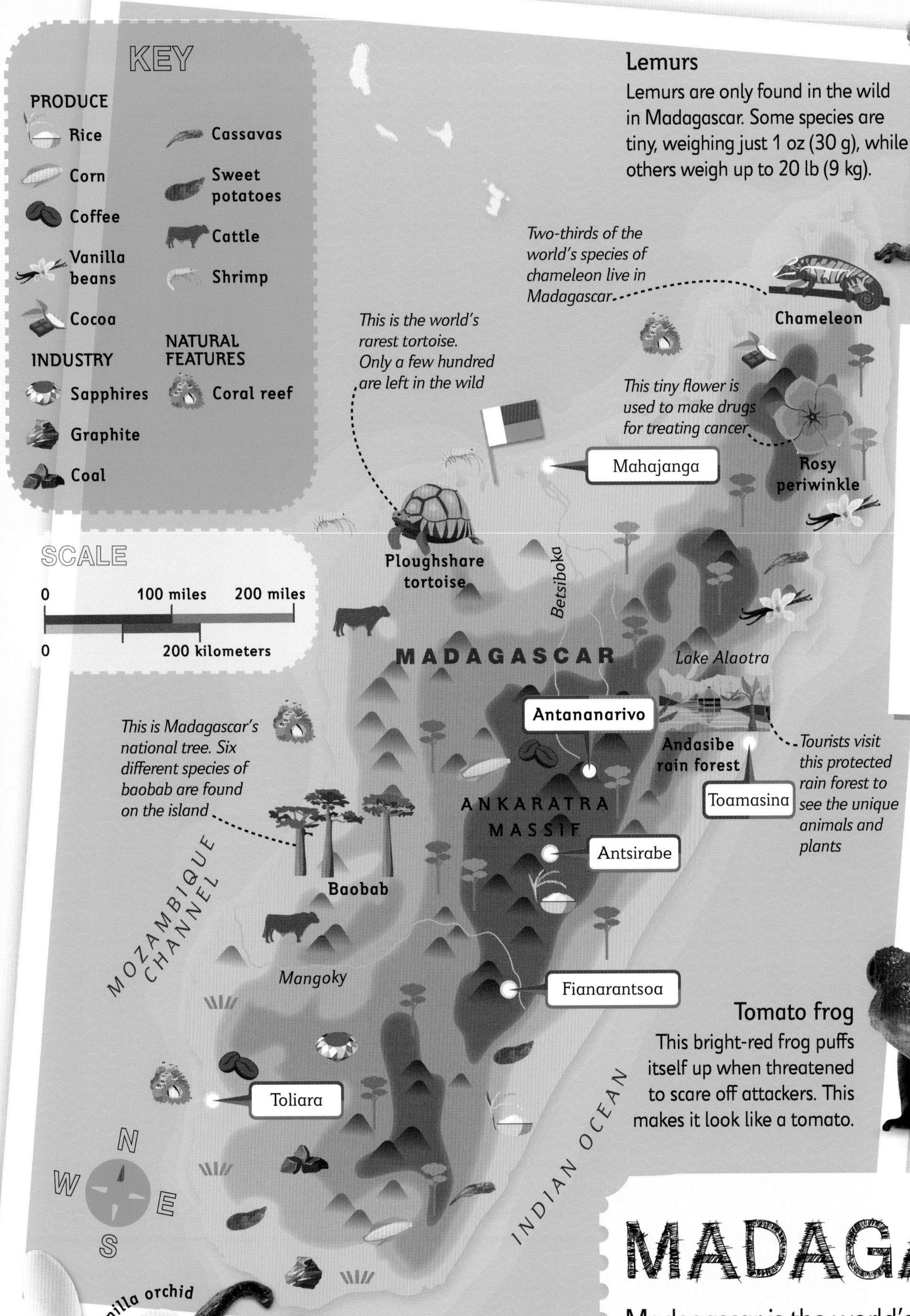
KEY
PRODUCE
Rice
Corn
Coffee
Vanilla beans
Cocoa
Cassavas
Sweet potatoes
Cattle
Shrimp
INDUSTRY
Sapphires
Graphite
Coal
NATURAL FEATURES
Coral reef
SCALE
0
100 miles
200 miles
0
200 kilometers
Two-thirds of the world's species of chameleon live in Madagascar
Chameleon
This is the world's rarest tortoise. Only a few hundred are left in the wild
Ploughshare tortoise
This tiny flower is used to make drugs for treating cancer
Rosy periwinkle
Mahajanga
Betsiboka
MADAGASCAR
Lake Alaotra
Antananarivo
Andasibe rain forest
Toamasina
Tourists visit this protected rain forest to see the unique animals and plants
ANKARATRA MASSIF
Antsirabe
This is Madagascar's national tree. Six different species of baobab are found on the island
Baobab
MOZAMBIQUE CHANNEL
Mangoky
Fianarantsoa
Toliara
INDIAN OCEAN
N
W
E
S

Lemurs

Lemurs are only found in the wild in Madagascar. Some species are tiny, weighing just 1 oz (30 g), while others weigh up to 20 lb (9 kg).

Ring-tailed lemur

Queen's Summer Palace

Ambohimanga

This protected royal compound sits high on a hill northeast of the capital Antananarivo. It contains a number of palaces and tombs of the island's former royal family, as well as sites of religious importance.

Tomato frog

This bright-red frog puffs itself up when threatened to scare off attackers. This makes it look like a tomato.

Vanilla orchid

Vanilla beans

Madagascan vanilla

Vanilla is used to flavor ice cream, cookies, and chocolate, and is used in perfume. It is taken from the beans of a type of orchid. Some of the best vanilla comes from orchids grown in Madagascar.

MADAGASCAR

Madagascar is the world's fourth largest island. Because it is cut off from the rest of Africa, it has many plants and animals that are found nowhere else on Earth. These include lemurs and other forest mammals, many colorful frogs and birds, and around 900 types of orchid, several of which are very rare.

NATURAL WONDERS

The world is full of wonderful natural features that are part of the landscape around us. Across the world, there are lush green rain forests, colorful coral reefs, jagged mountains, smouldering volcanoes, and rushing waterfalls. While under the surface of the Earth there are dark caves, from tiny grottos to huge caverns.

LARGEST RAIN FOREST

The largest rain forest in the world is the Amazon in South America. It covers almost half of the continent.

Seven Natural Wonders

The Seven Natural Wonders of the World are a group of spectacular natural features. They are favorite sites for adventurous people to visit and explore.

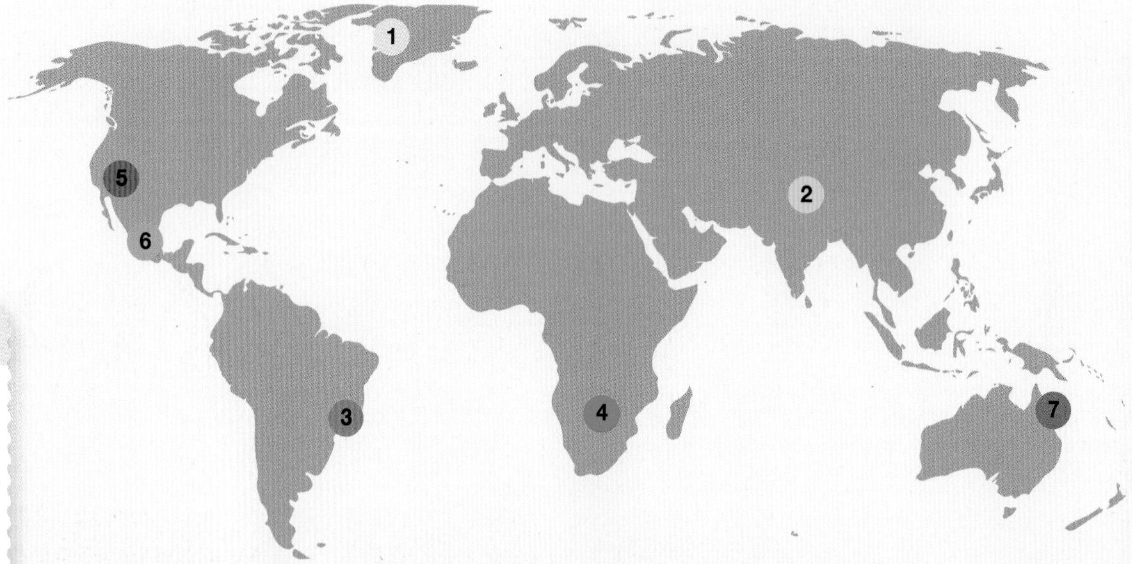

1. NORTHERN LIGHTS

Near the Arctic Circle, amazing light effects known as the Northern Lights, or Aurora Borealis, can be seen in the night sky.

2. MOUNT EVEREST

The world's highest mountain is on the border of Nepal and China.The peak of Mount Everest is a dark pyramid shape.

4. VICTORIA FALLS

Between Zambia and Zimbabwe are the Victoria Falls. The waters of the Zambezi River thunder over these falls.

6. PARÍCUTIN VOLCANO

This volcano rose up and erupted in a farmer's cornfield in Mexico in 1943. Today, people can climb the dormant (inactive) volcano.

3. RIO DE JANEIRO HARBOR

Here, the Brazilian Highlands meet the Atlantic Ocean. Sugar Loaf Mountain marks the entrance of the bay.

5. GRAND CANYON

In Arizona, the Colorado River has formed the massive and majestic Grand Canyon. This is the largest canyon in the world.

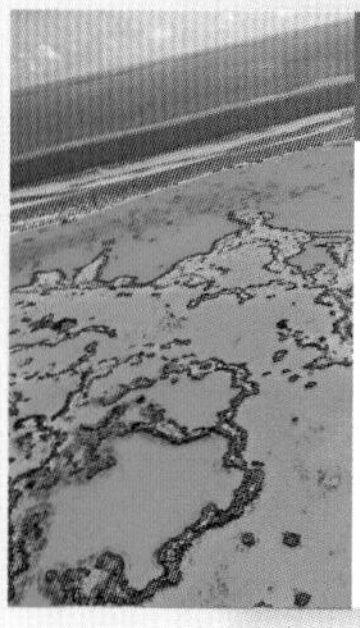

7. GREAT BARRIER REEF

The world's largest coral reef is off the eastern coast of Australia. Thousands of types of fish and coral live here.

Deepest caves

Caves are underground spaces below the surface of the Earth. They form when water wears away some types of rock in the ground. This illustration shows some of the deepest caves in the world.

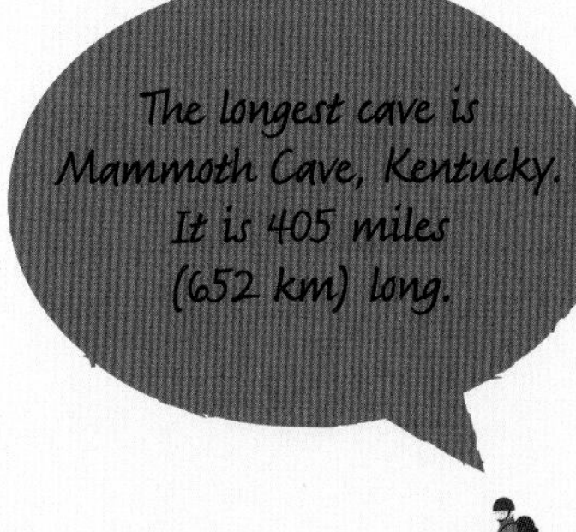
The longest cave is Mammoth Cave, Kentucky. It is 405 miles (652 km) long.

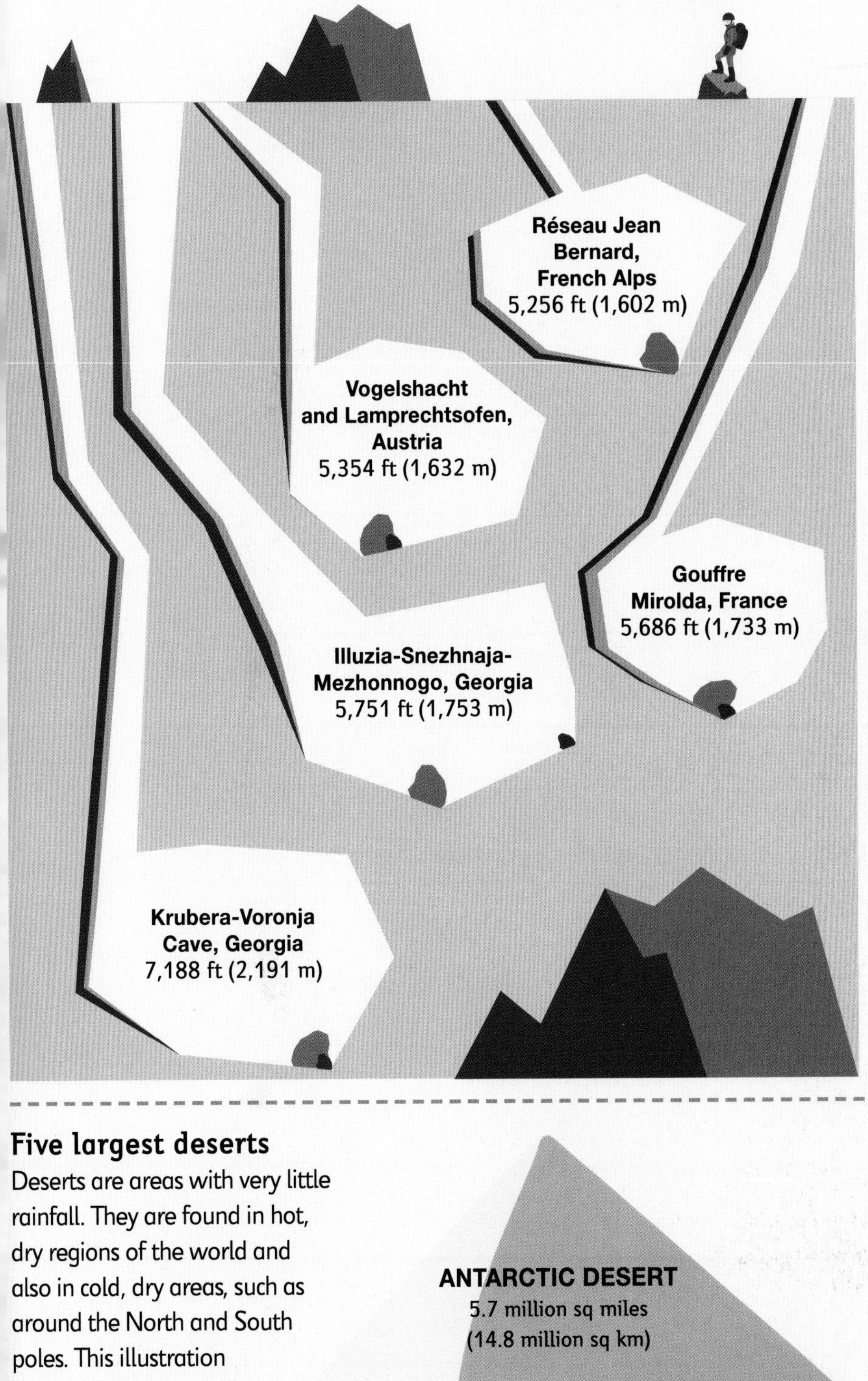
Réseau Jean Bernard, French Alps
5,256 ft (1,602 m)
Vogelshacht and Lamprechtsofen, Austria
5,354 ft (1,632 m)
Gouffre Mirolda, France
5,686 ft (1,733 m)
Illuzia-Snezhnaja-Mezhonnogo, Georgia
5,751 ft (1,753 m)
Krubera-Voronja Cave, Georgia
7,188 ft (2,191 m)

Highest waterfalls

Waterfalls are places where streams of water have a steep drop. They are formed when streams or rivers flow over different types of rock and softer rock is worn away. The five shown below are among the highest waterfalls in the world.

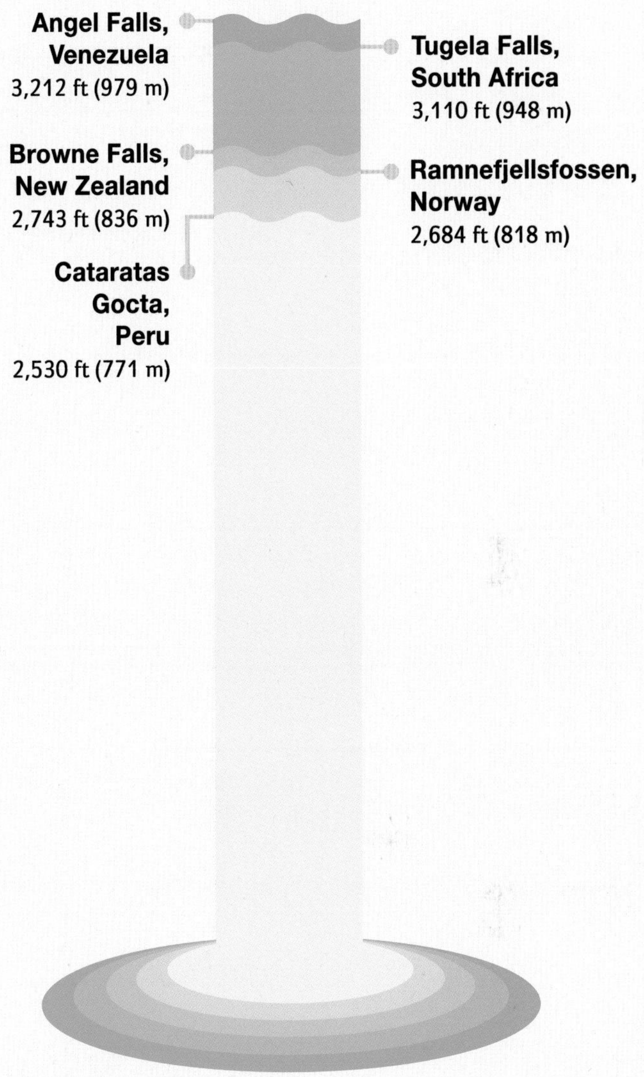
Angel Falls, Venezuela
3,212 ft (979 m)
Tugela Falls, South Africa
3,110 ft (948 m)
Browne Falls, New Zealand
2,743 ft (836 m)
Ramnefjellsfossen, Norway
2,684 ft (818 m)
Cataratas Gocta, Peru
2,530 ft (771 m)

Five largest deserts

Deserts are areas with very little rainfall. They are found in hot, dry regions of the world and also in cold, dry areas, such as around the North and South poles. This illustration shows the largest deserts in the world.

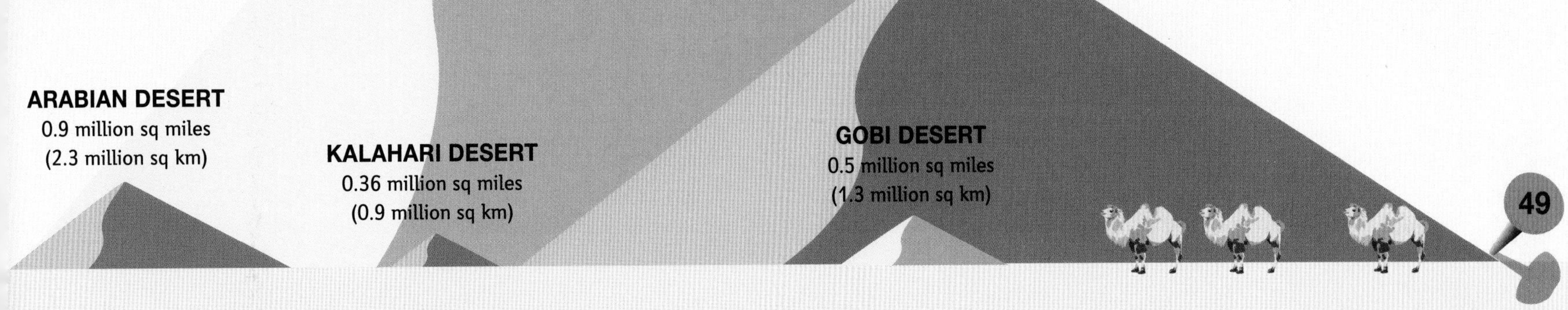
ANTARCTIC DESERT
5.7 million sq miles
(14.8 million sq km)
SAHARA DESERT
3.5 million sq miles
(9 million sq km)
ARABIAN DESERT
0.9 million sq miles
(2.3 million sq km)
KALAHARI DESERT
0.36 million sq miles
(0.9 million sq km)
GOBI DESERT
0.5 million sq miles
(1.3 million sq km)

1. On which island was Napoleon born?
2. What is the name of this colorful building in Moscow?
3. In which country would you find this angelic statue?
4. Which city was the composer Mozart born in?

NORTHERN EUROPE

The northern European countries have fairly small populations, with most people living in towns and cities. There are also large areas of open countryside. Summers are generally warm, but winters are very cold, with limited daylight in the far north.

Eyjafjallajökull

This huge volcano in Iceland is covered by an icecap. It erupted in 2010, producing a vast ash cloud that disrupted air travel across Europe.

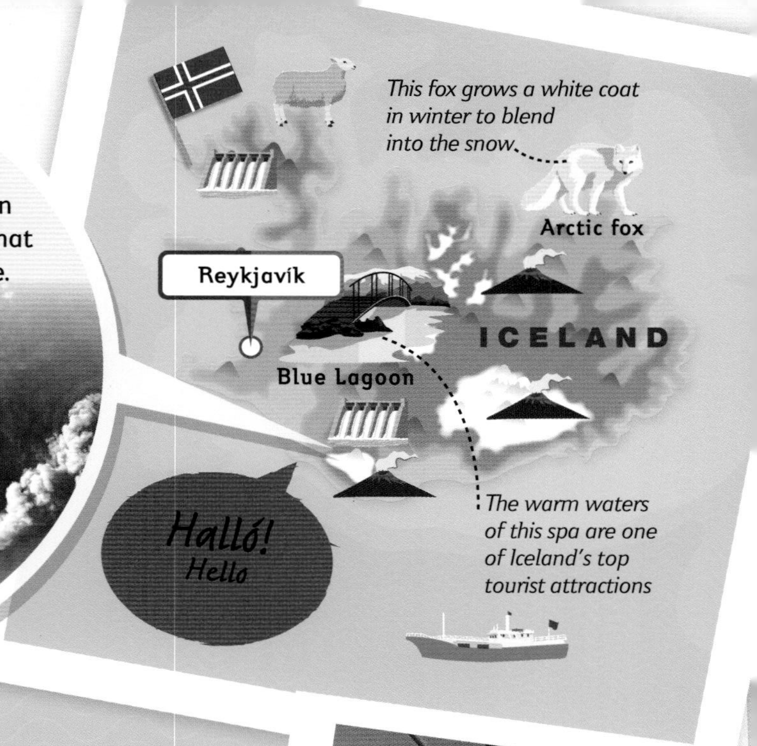

This fox grows a white coat in winter to blend into the snow
Arctic fox
Reykjavík
ICELAND
Blue Lagoon
The warm waters of this spa are one of Iceland's top tourist attractions
Halló!
Hello

Pulpit Rock overlooking Lysefjord

Sami in traditional dress

KEY

PRODUCE
- Sheep
- Cattle
- Potatoes
- Rye
- Wheat
- Sugar beets
- Barley
- Pigs

ACTIVITIES
- Ice hockey
- Soccer
- Cross-country skiing

INDUSTRY
- Lumber
- Shipbuilding
- Hydroelectric power
- Natural gas
- Oil
- Fishing
- Wind power
- Iron ore
- Electronics

NATURAL FEATURES
- Volcanoes

Norway's fjords

Norway's coast is lined with hundreds of narrow inlets, called fjords, with steep cliffs on each side. The cliffs of Pulpit Rock rise a spectacular 1,982 ft (604 m) above the waters of Lysefjord.

N
W
E
S
This strong, ferocious animal can kill prey as big as deer
These cars are very popular in Norway. They are plugged in to be recharged
Tromsø
Wolverine
EV plug-in electric car
Abisko National Park
Kiruna
This park contains Trollsjön lake, the clearest lake in Sweden
The elk is the largest type of deer in the world and lives in northern forests
Elk
NORWEGIAN SEA
This wild cat lives in forests, where it hunts deer and other animals
Lynx
This fast train tilts when it goes around corners
Oulu
Alstom Pendolino
SCALE
0
100 miles
0
100 kilometers

Lapland

This large, snowy region in the far north of Norway, Sweden, and Finland is home to the Sami people. Some keep reindeer and travel by sleigh.

Herring

Herring is known as the "silver of the sea," because of its color and importance to the economy.

SCALE
0
250 miles
500 miles
0
500 kilometers
FINLAND
GULF OF BOTHNIA
BALTIC SEA
ESTONIA
LATVIA
LITHUANIA
RUSSIA
(KALININGRAD)
BELARUS
POLAND
UKRAINE
SLOVAKIA
HUNGARY
MOLDOVA
ROMANIA
SERBIA
BULGARIA
KOSOVO
(Disputed)
NORTH MACEDONIA
ALBANIA
TURKEY
GREECE
AEGEAN SEA
IONIAN SEA
Crete
RUSSIA
(European Russia)
Crimea
(Annexed by Russia)
BLACK SEA
CASPIAN SEA
N
E
S
W

The Alps

This mountain range stretches 750 miles (1,200 km) across the heart of Europe, through France, Monaco, Italy, Germany, Austria, Switzerland, Liechtenstein, and Slovenia. The highest peak is Mont Blanc, at 15,781 ft (4,810 m).

St. Basil's Cathedral

This spectacular building is the focal point of Red Square in Moscow, Russia. It was built in the 16th century and is famous for its unique, brightly colored, onion-shaped domes. It has been a museum since 1928.

EUROPE

The landscape of Europe is very varied. It includes dense forests, high mountain ranges, broad plains, remote islands, and sun-soaked beaches. The continent is home to many fine historic buildings. Countries range in size from the tiny state of Liechtenstein to Russia, the biggest country in the world.

Northern European forest
The pine forests of Nordic countries such as Norway, Sweden, and Finland are an important source of lumber.

Paris
Paris, the capital of France, is an elegant city that mixes old and new styles of architecture effortlessly. At its center is the Eiffel Tower, one of the most famous structures on Earth.

Mediterranean Sea
The countries that surround the warm waters of the Mediterranean Sea enjoy hot, dry summers and mild winters. Thousands of visitors are drawn to their sunny beaches every year.

ICELAND
ATLANTIC OCEAN
NORWEGIAN SEA
Faroe Islands
Shetland Islands
NORWAY
NORTH SEA
DENMARK
IRELAND
Isle of Man
UNITED KINGDOM
NETHERLANDS
BELGIUM
GERMANY
Channel Islands
LUXEMBOURG
FRANCE
BAY OF BISCAY
Azores
SWITZERLAND
SAN MARINO
ANDORRA
MONACO
PORTUGAL
SPAIN
ITALY
Corsica
Sardinia
VATICAN CITY
Majorca
Minorca
Ibiza
Balearic Islands
Gibraltar
MEDITERRANEAN SEA
TYRRHENIA SEA
Sicily
Madeira

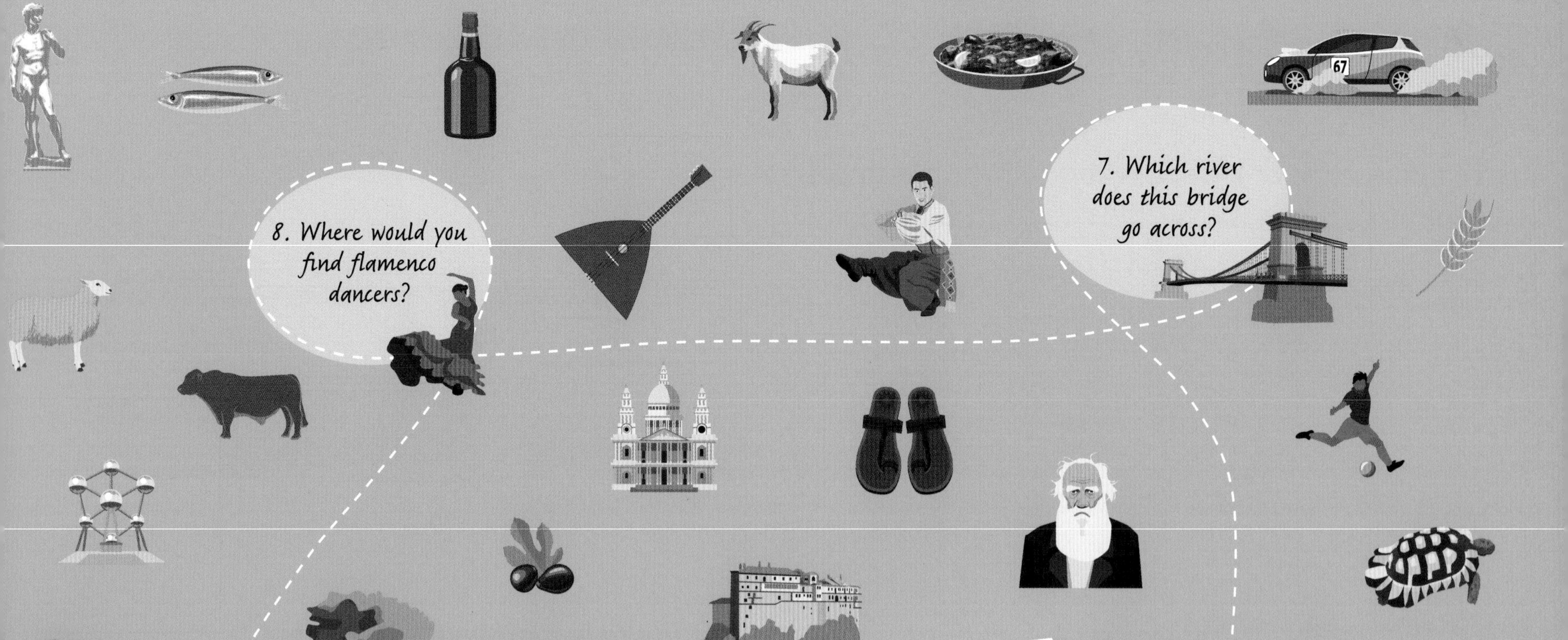
8. Where would you find flamenco dancers?
7. Which river does this bridge go across?
67

EUROPE

With many unique cultures and languages, Europe is a varied and busy continent. It has rich traditions of classical music, literature, art, sports, and cooking. The continent has medieval castles and cathedrals, as well as beautiful historic towns and cities.

5. Which country is the car maker Skoda based in?
6. Which country produces more than 400 kinds of cheese?
You can find all the answers and more quizzes on pages 120–121.

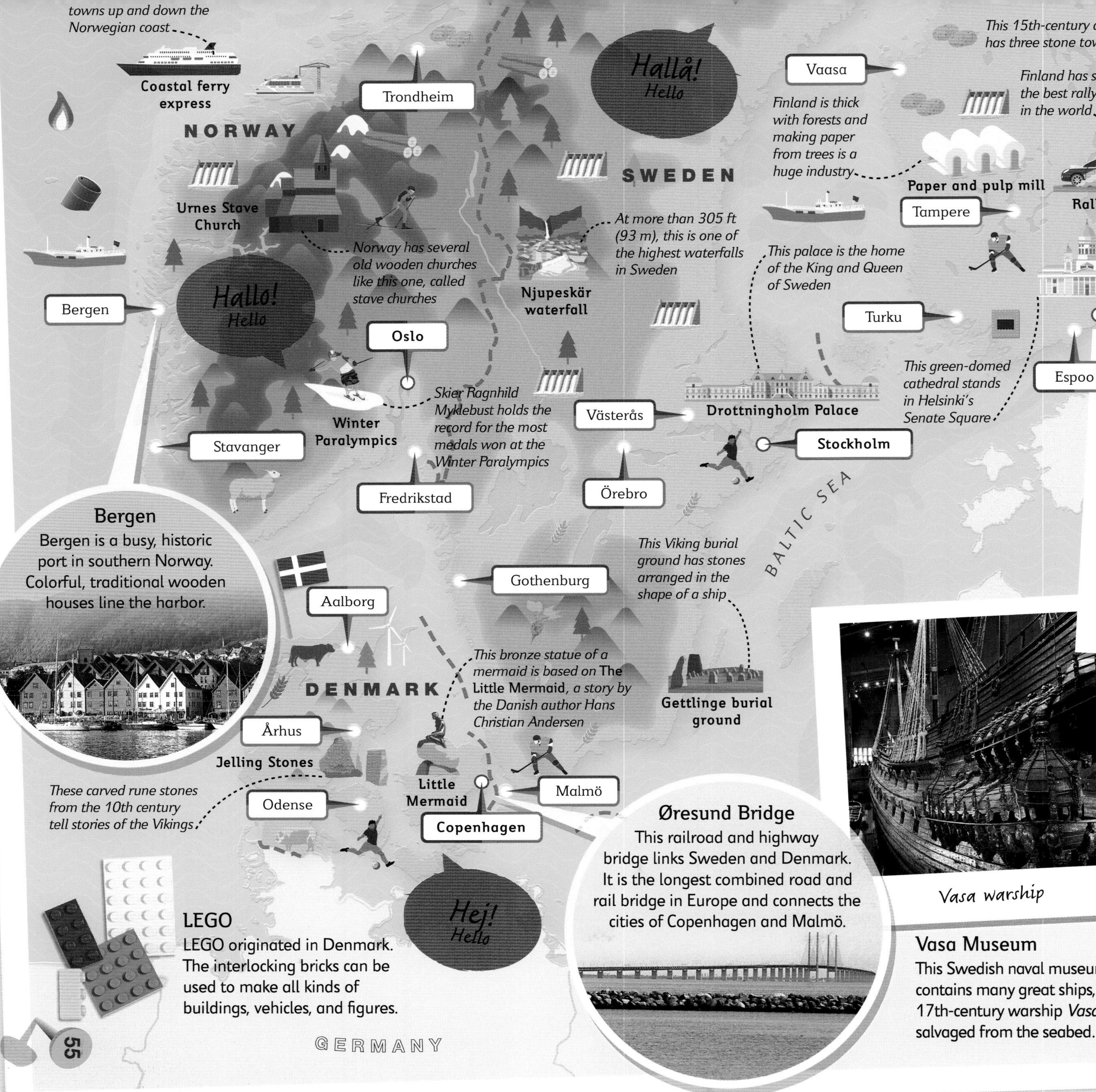
towns up and down the Norwegian coast
Coastal ferry express
NORWAY
Trondheim
Urnes Stave Church
Norway has several old wooden churches like this one, called stave churches
Hallo!
Hello
Bergen
Oslo
Winter Paralympics
Skier Ragnhild Myklebust holds the record for the most medals won at the Winter Paralympics
Stavanger
Fredrikstad
Hallå!
Hello
SWEDEN
At more than 305 ft (93 m), this is one of the highest waterfalls in Sweden
Njupeskär waterfall
Västerås
Örebro
Drottningholm Palace
This palace is the home of the King and Queen of Sweden
Stockholm
Gothenburg
This Viking burial ground has stones arranged in the shape of a ship
Gettlinge burial ground
BALTIC SEA
Aalborg
DENMARK
Århus
Jelling Stones
These carved rune stones from the 10th century tell stories of the Vikings
Odense
This bronze statue of a mermaid is based on The Little Mermaid, a story by the Danish author Hans Christian Andersen
Little Mermaid
Copenhagen
Malmö
Hej!
Hello
GERMANY
Vaasa
Finland is thick with forests and making paper from trees is a huge industry
Paper and pulp mill
Tampere
Turku
This green-domed cathedral stands in Helsinki's Senate Square
Espoo
Helsinki
Helsinki Cathedral
Rally driving
Finland has some of the best rally drivers in the world
Olavinlinna Castle
This 15th-century castle has three stone towers
Hei!
Hello
RUSSIA

Bergen

Bergen is a busy, historic port in southern Norway. Colorful, traditional wooden houses line the harbor.

LEGO

LEGO originated in Denmark. The interlocking bricks can be used to make all kinds of buildings, vehicles, and figures.

Øresund Bridge

This railroad and highway bridge links Sweden and Denmark. It is the longest combined road and rail bridge in Europe and connects the cities of Copenhagen and Malmö.

Traditional Finnish sauna

Saunas

Small wooden saunas are very popular in Finland and nearly every house has one. Water is thrown over hot stones to produce steam, which cleanses and relaxes the body.

Vasa warship

Vasa Museum

This Swedish naval museum in Stockholm contains many great ships, including the 17th-century warship *Vasa*, which was salvaged from the seabed.

BRITISH ISLES

The British Isles is a group of islands off the northwest coast of Europe. They consist of the United Kingdom, or UK (England, Scotland, Wales, and Northern Ireland), and Ireland. These islands share a varied history. The weather is influenced by the sea and it often rains. Ireland is known as the "Emerald Isle," because the rain makes it so green.

Traditional Scottish dress

Scottish traditions

For special occasions, some Scots wear woollen kilts, woven from different colored threads to form a pattern called tartan. Different clans (groups) have their own design of tartan. Some Scots also play the bagpipes, a type of wind instrument.

Fish and chips
Tea

Food and drink

Fried fish and chips are a popular meal, especially by the coast. Tea is widely drunk, usually with milk and sometimes sugar.

William Shakespeare

English playwright

William Shakespeare was one of the world's greatest writers. Born in Stratford-upon-Avon, England, in 1564, he wrote many poems and plays that are still performed today.

KEY

PRODUCE
- Wheat
- Fruit
- Potatoes
- Sheep
- Shellfish
- Cattle
- Vineyards
- Cheese

INDUSTRY
- Cars
- Fishing

RESOURCES
- Oil
- Gas
- Steel

ACTIVITIES
- Soccer
- Rock climbing
- Hiking
- Surfing
- Cricket

SCALE

0 — 50 miles — 100 miles

0 — 100 kilometers

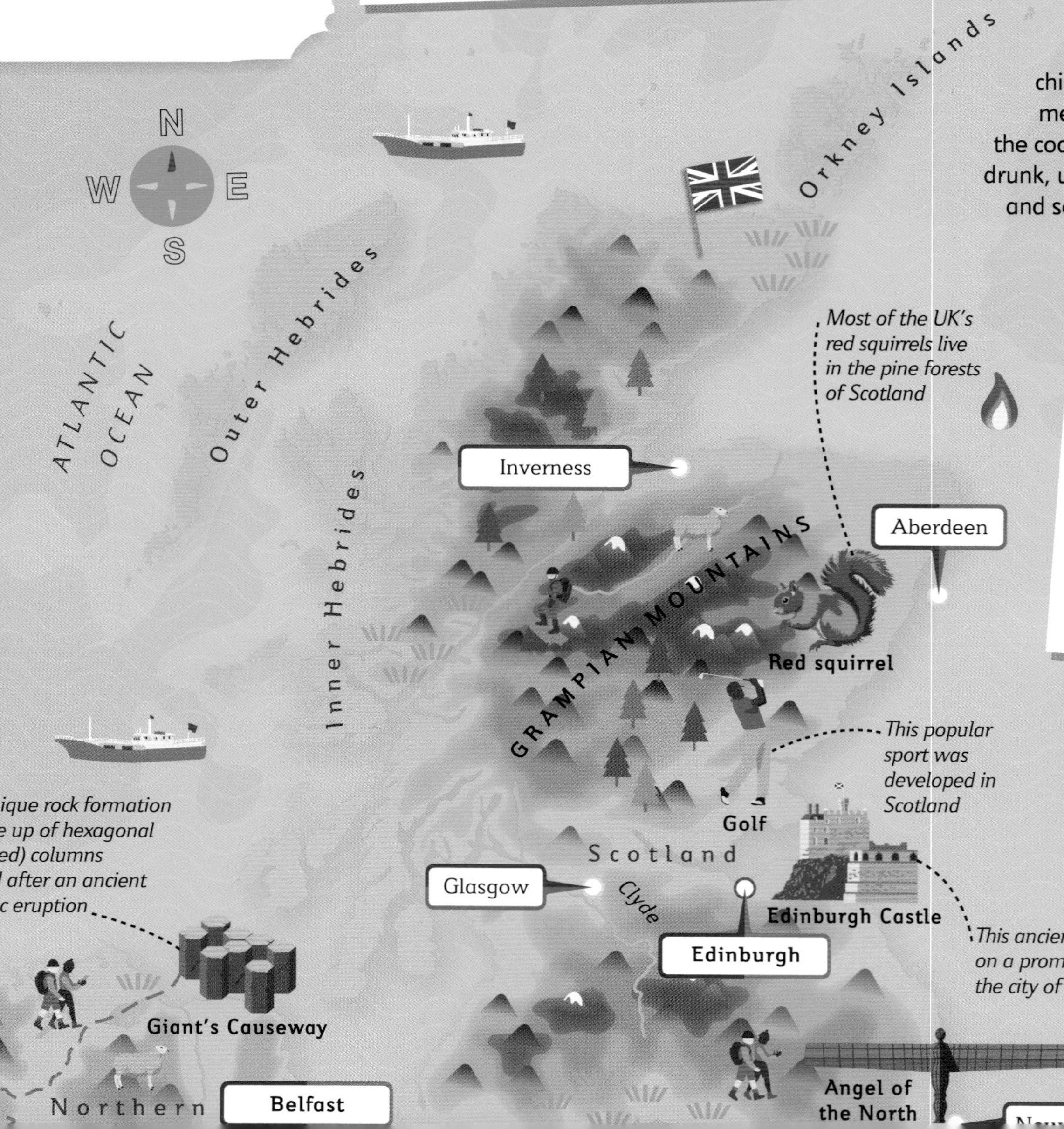

N
W
E
S
ATLANTIC OCEAN
Outer Hebrides
Inner Hebrides
Orkney Islands
Shetland Islands
Inverness
Aberdeen
GRAMPIAN MOUNTAINS
Most of the UK's red squirrels live in the pine forests of Scotland
Red squirrel
This popular sport was developed in Scotland
Golf
Scotland
Glasgow
Clyde
Edinburgh Castle
Edinburgh
This ancient fortress is built on a prominent rock above the city of Edinburgh
This unique rock formation is made up of hexagonal (six-sided) columns formed after an ancient volcanic eruption
Giant's Causeway
Northern
Belfast
Angel of the North
The wings of this huge steel statue are 177 ft (54 m) across

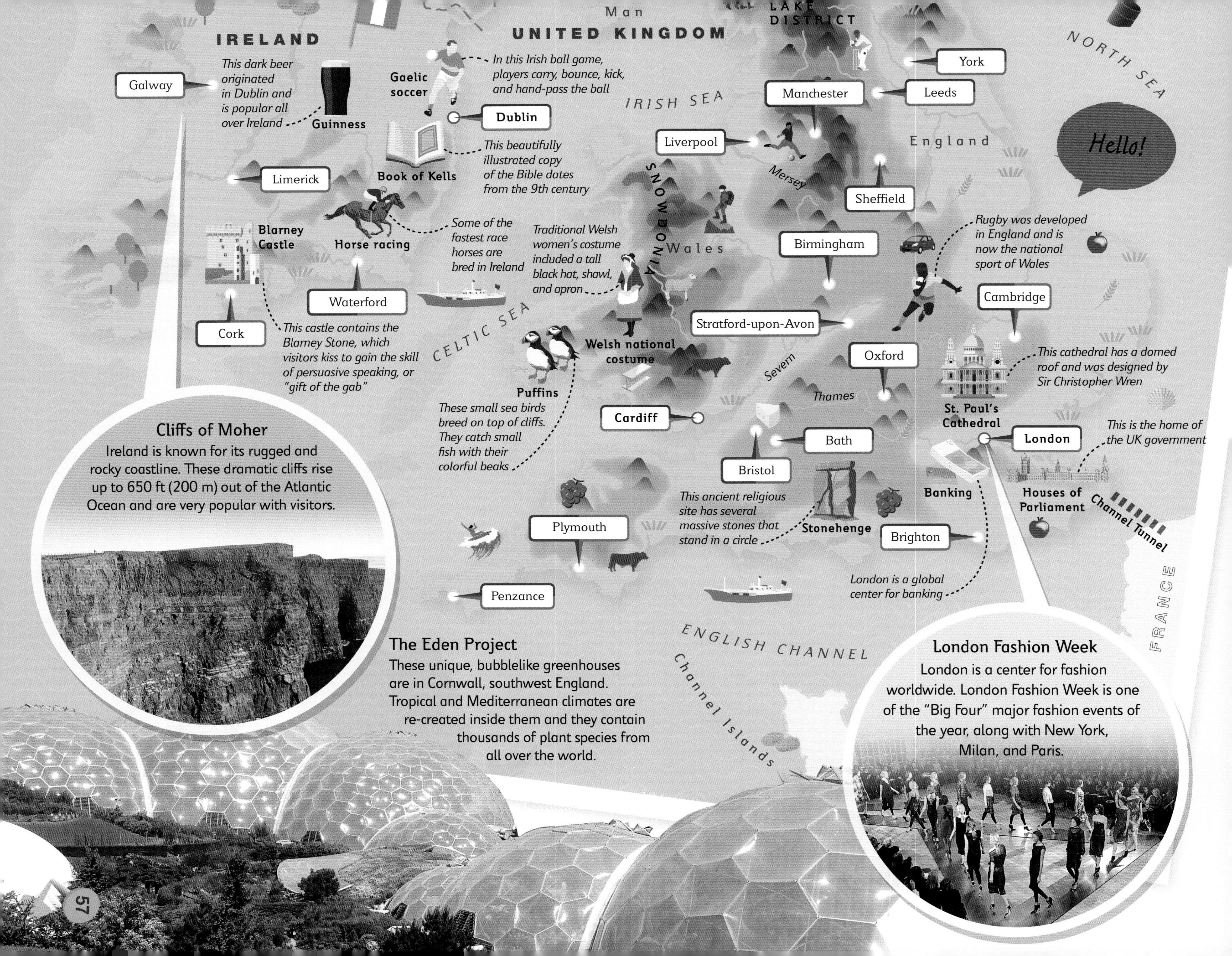
IRELAND
UNITED KINGDOM
Man
LAKE DISTRICT
NORTH SEA
IRISH SEA
CELTIC SEA
ENGLISH CHANNEL
Channel Islands
FRANCE
England
Wales
SNOWDONIA
Mersey
Severn
Thames
Hello!
Galway
Limerick
Cork
Waterford
Dublin
Liverpool
Manchester
Leeds
York
Sheffield
Birmingham
Stratford-upon-Avon
Oxford
Cambridge
London
Cardiff
Bristol
Bath
Brighton
Plymouth
Penzance
This dark beer originated in Dublin and is popular all over Ireland
Guinness
Gaelic soccer
In this Irish ball game, players carry, bounce, kick, and hand-pass the ball
Book of Kells
This beautifully illustrated copy of the Bible dates from the 9th century
Horse racing
Some of the fastest race horses are bred in Ireland
Blarney Castle
This castle contains the Blarney Stone, which visitors kiss to gain the skill of persuasive speaking, or "gift of the gab"
Traditional Welsh women's costume included a tall black hat, shawl, and apron
Welsh national costume
Puffins
These small sea birds breed on top of cliffs. They catch small fish with their colorful beaks
Rugby was developed in England and is now the national sport of Wales
This cathedral has a domed roof and was designed by Sir Christopher Wren
St. Paul's Cathedral
This is the home of the UK government
Houses of Parliament
Channel Tunnel
Banking
London is a global center for banking
Stonehenge
This ancient religious site has several massive stones that stand in a circle

Cliffs of Moher

Ireland is known for its rugged and rocky coastline. These dramatic cliffs rise up to 650 ft (200 m) out of the Atlantic Ocean and are very popular with visitors.

The Eden Project

These unique, bubblelike greenhouses are in Cornwall, southwest England. Tropical and Mediterranean climates are re-created inside them and they contain thousands of plant species from all over the world.

London Fashion Week

London is a center for fashion worldwide. London Fashion Week is one of the "Big Four" major fashion events of the year, along with New York, Milan, and Paris.

FRANCE

France is known worldwide for its food, wine, and beautiful countryside. Today, most French people live in towns and cities. France is highly industrialized and has one of the fastest train networks, the TGV. The arts, such as painting, and sports, particularly cycling, are very popular.

Water Lilies, by Monet

Art

Millions of people visit France's museums every year to see paintings and sculptures by artists such as Claude Monet and Auguste Rodin.

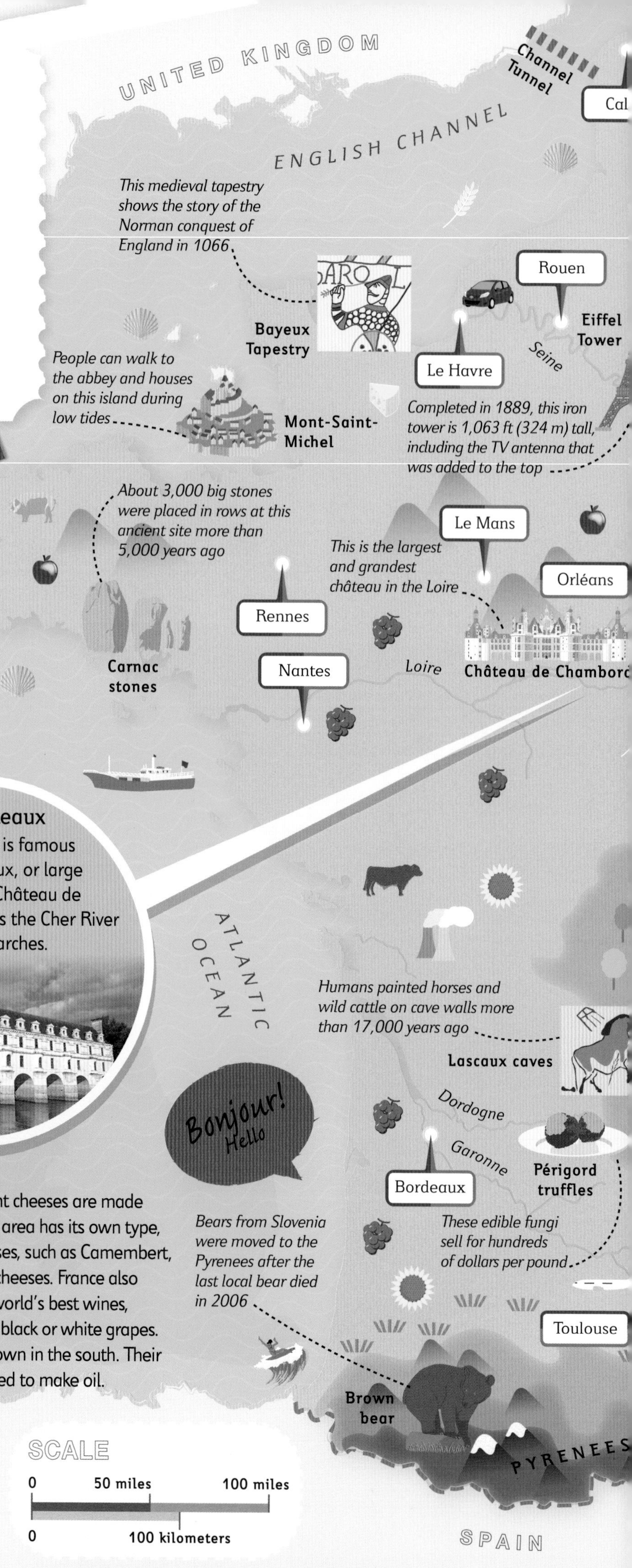

UNITED KINGDOM
Channel Tunnel
Cal
ENGLISH CHANNEL
This medieval tapestry shows the story of the Norman conquest of England in 1066
Bayeux Tapestry
Rouen
Eiffel Tower
Seine
Le Havre
People can walk to the abbey and houses on this island during low tides
Mont-Saint-Michel
Completed in 1889, this iron tower is 1,063 ft (324 m) tall, including the TV antenna that was added to the top
About 3,000 big stones were placed in rows at this ancient site more than 5,000 years ago
Le Mans
This is the largest and grandest château in the Loire
Orléans
Rennes
Carnac stones
Nantes
Loire
Château de Chambord
ATLANTIC OCEAN
Humans painted horses and wild cattle on cave walls more than 17,000 years ago
Lascaux caves
Dordogne
Garonne
Bonjour! Hello
Bordeaux
Périgord truffles
These edible fungi sell for hundreds of dollars per pound
Bears from Slovenia were moved to the Pyrenees after the last local bear died in 2006
Toulouse
Brown bear
PYRENEES
SCALE
0 50 miles 100 miles
0 100 kilometers
SPAIN

Loire châteaux

The Loire Valley is famous for its 42 châteaux, or large country houses. Château de Chenonceau sits across the Cher River on a row of arches.

Sunflower
Camembert cheese
Grapes

Cheese and wine

More than 400 different cheeses are made in France. Almost every area has its own type, ranging from soft cheeses, such as Camembert, to hard and even blue cheeses. France also produces some of the world's best wines, made from the juice of black or white grapes. Sunflowers are grown in the south. Their seeds are pressed to make oil.

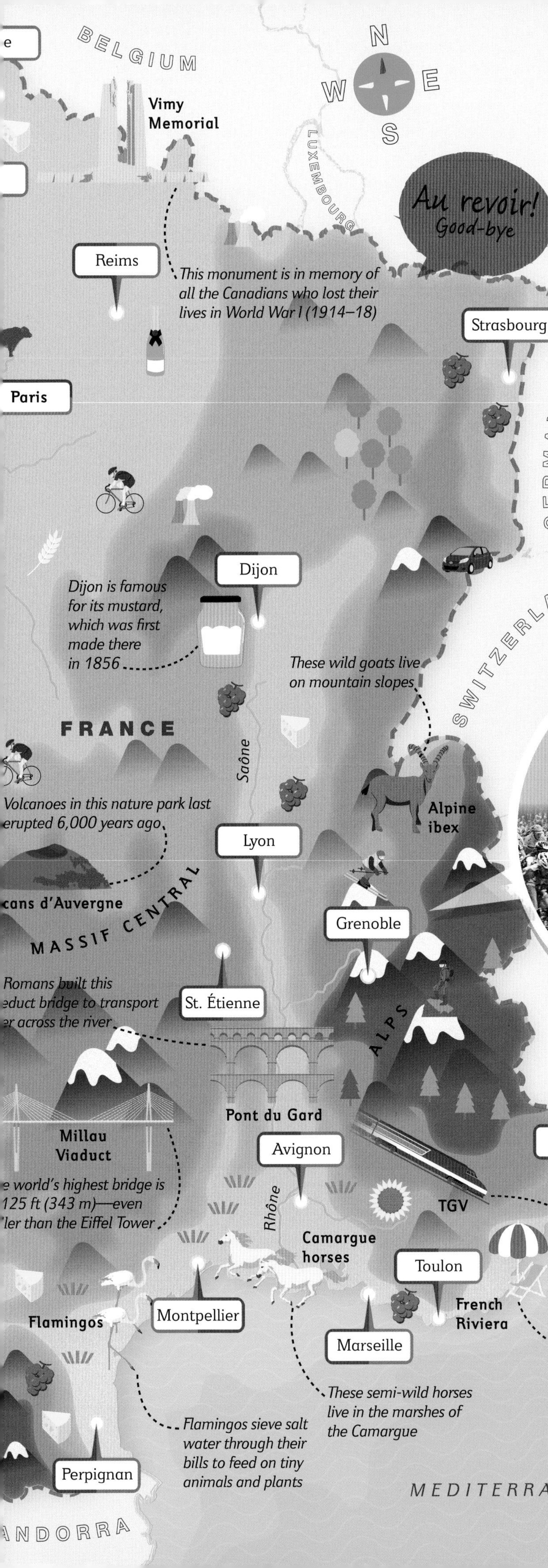
BELGIUM
N
W
E
S
Vimy Memorial
LUXEMBOURG
Au revoir!
Good-bye
Reims
This monument is in memory of all the Canadians who lost their lives in World War I (1914–18)
Strasbourg
Paris
GERMANY
Dijon
Dijon is famous for its mustard, which was first made there in 1856
These wild goats live on mountain slopes
SWITZERLAND
FRANCE
Saône
Volcanoes in this nature park last erupted 6,000 years ago
Alpine ibex
Lyon
cans d'Auvergne
MASSIF CENTRAL
Grenoble
Romans built this
educt bridge to transport
er across the river
St. Étienne
ALPS
ITALY
Pont du Gard
Millau Viaduct
e world's highest bridge is
125 ft (343 m)—even
ller than the Eiffel Tower
Avignon
Nice
MONACO
Monaco is a small city-state that is independent from France
Rhône
TGV
Camargue horses
Toulon
High-speed trains connect France's major cities
Flamingos
Montpellier
French Riviera
Marseille
The southeast coast is famous for its seaside resorts and the Cannes Film Festival
These semi-wild horses live in the marshes of the Camargue
Napoleon Bonaparte was born in Corsica in 1769. He became emperor of France in 1804 and died in 1821
Flamingos sieve salt water through their bills to feed on tiny animals and plants
Corsica
Perpignan
MEDITERRANEAN SEA
ANDORRA

French street market

Outdoor markets

Every French village and town has an outdoor market that opens at least one day a week. People can buy fresh fruits and vegetables grown at nearby farms and local produce, such as cheese.

Café culture

French people enjoy meeting up with their friends in cafés. They often have a croissant (a flaky pastry) and coffee for breakfast. In the evenings, popular drinks include beer, wine, or champagne (a sparkling wine).

Coffee
Croissants

Tour de France

The world's most famous bicycle race lasts for three weeks and passes through the Alps and Pyrenees before finishing in Paris.

KEY

PRODUCE
- Vineyards
- Sunflowers
- Cattle
- Wheat
- Apples
- Cheese
- Champagne
- Shellfish
- Pigs

INDUSTRY
- Nuclear power
- Aircraft manufacture
- Fishing
- Cars

ACTIVITIES
- Mountain climbing
- Skiing
- Cycling
- Surfing

NETHERLANDS, BELGIUM, AND LUXEMBOURG

These three densely populated countries are known as the Low Countries, because most of the land is flat, and some of it is below sea level. This flat land makes cycling popular.

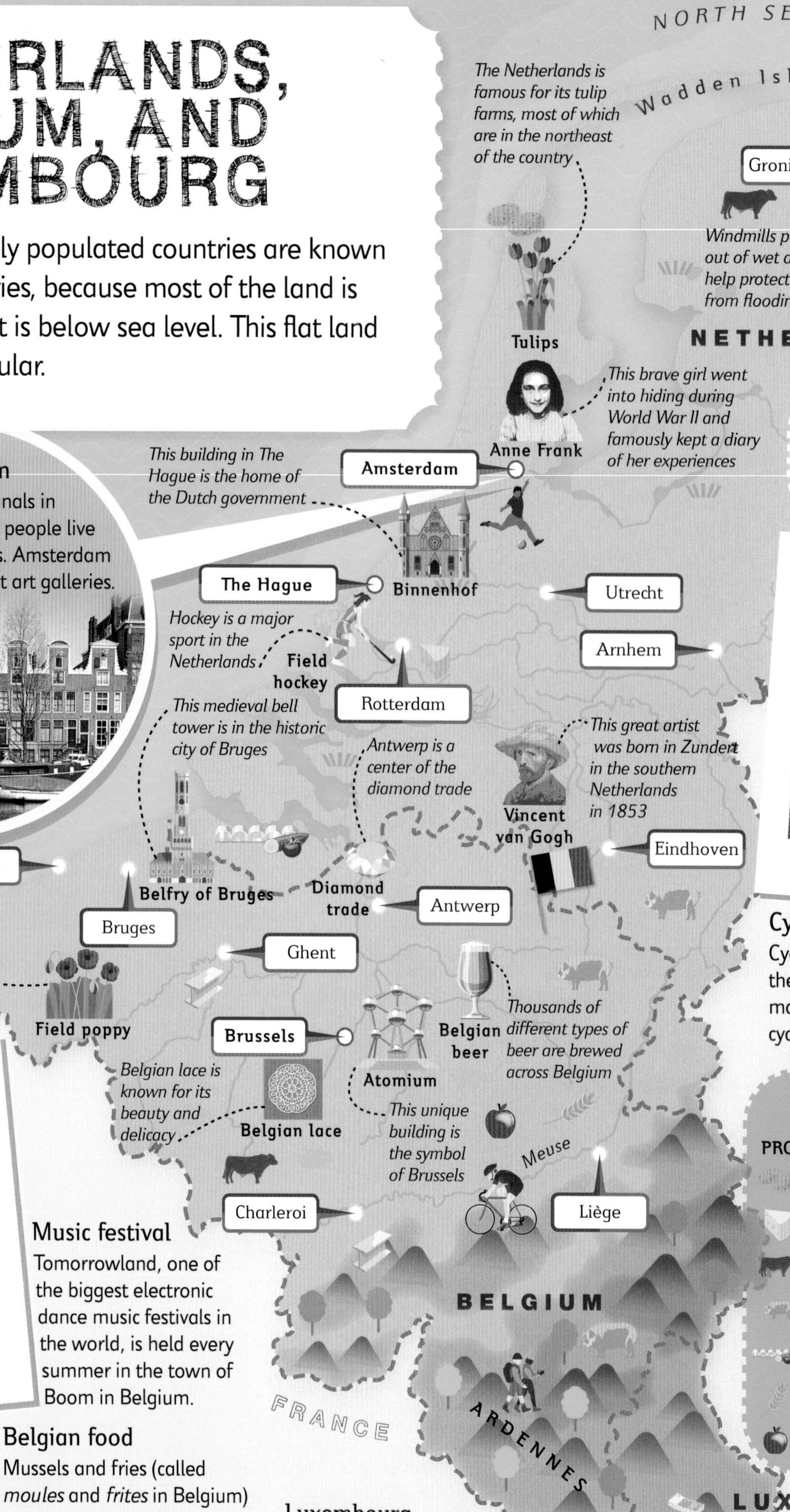

NORTH SEA
Wadden Islands
N
W
E
S
The Netherlands is famous for its tulip farms, most of which are in the northeast of the country
Groningen
Windmills pump water out of wet areas and help protect land from flooding
Windmill
Tulips
NETHERLANDS
This brave girl went into hiding during World War II and famously kept a diary of her experiences
Anne Frank
SCALE
0
50 miles
0
50 kilometers
This building in The Hague is the home of the Dutch government
Amsterdam
The Hague
Binnenhof
Utrecht
Hockey is a major sport in the Netherlands
Field hockey
Arnhem
Rotterdam
This medieval bell tower is in the historic city of Bruges
Antwerp is a center of the diamond trade
This great artist was born in Zundert in the southern Netherlands in 1853
Vincent van Gogh
Eindhoven
Ostend
Belfry of Bruges
Diamond trade
Antwerp
Red poppies grow in the fields of Belgium
Bruges
Ghent
Field poppy
Brussels
Belgian beer
Thousands of different types of beer are brewed across Belgium
Atomium
Belgian lace is known for its beauty and delicacy
Belgian lace
This unique building is the symbol of Brussels
Meuse
Charleroi
Liège
BELGIUM
FRANCE
ARDENNES
LUXEMBOURG
Luxembourg City
KEY
PRODUCE
Potatoes
Cheese
Cattle
Pigs
Greenhouses
Wheat
Fruit
INDUSTRY
Steel
Gas
Banking
ACTIVITIES
Soccer
Hiking
Cycling

Amsterdam

There are many canals in Amsterdam and lots of people live in waterfront apartments. Amsterdam also has several important art galleries.

Cycle lanes

Cycling

Cycle lanes are found throughout the Netherlands and Belgium, making it safe and quick for cyclists on the move.

Tomorrowland

Music festival

Tomorrowland, one of the biggest electronic dance music festivals in the world, is held every summer in the town of Boom in Belgium.

Belgian food

Mussels and fries (called *moules* and *frites* in Belgium) is a favorite Belgian dish. Another specialty is rich and creamy Belgian chocolate.

Moules and frites

Luxembourg

There are many ancient castles to be found in Luxembourg. This small country is also a major financial center.

Vianden Castle in Luxembourg is a popular tourist destination

SWITZERLAND AND AUSTRIA

Switzerland and Austria are mountainous countries in the middle of Europe. The Alps run through both countries, providing snow-covered slopes that are used for winter sports and beautiful alpine valleys, where hiking is popular in the summer.

Lipizzaner and rider

Spanish Riding School

The Spanish Riding School in Vienna teaches traditional horse-riding techniques and is home to the Lipizzaner, a breed of white horse.

Le Corbusier

This Swiss-French architect designed stylish modern buildings, often featuring straight lines and bright blocks of colors.

Sachertorte

This rich chocolate cake is served in coffee houses, where Austrians love to meet up. Coffee houses are an important part of Austrian social life, especially in Vienna.

This cathedral has a multicolored roof
CZECH REPUBLIC
SLOVAKIA
Vienna
Stephansdom
Linz
Danube
Neusiedler See
HUNGARY
The great composer Wolfgang Amadeus Mozart was born in Salzburg in 1756
Salzburg
Mozart
Graz
N
E
S
W
AUSTRIA
SLOVENIA
GERMANY
Liechtenstein is one of the smallest countries in the world and specializes in banking
Innsbruck
ALPS
This Swiss author wrote Heidi, a novel about a young girl who lives in the Alps
Zürich
Basel
Chamois
These wild goats are hunted for their meat
Gentiana
Johanna Spyri
LIECHTENSTEIN
Bern
Watches
This flower grows in the mountains and is used to flavor drinks
SWITZERLAND
SCALE
0
50 miles
0
50 kilometers
ITALY
Lausanne
Alpine horns are used in the mountains to play music or send signals
Hornblower
Red Cross
Geneva is home to the Red Cross, which provides care to people in need around the world
KEY
PRODUCE
Cheese
Cattle
Vineyards
Apricots
INDUSTRY
Lumber
Banking
Hydroelectric power
ACTIVITIES
Skiing
Hiking
Mountain climbing

Matterhorn

On the Swiss-Italian border is the dramatic Matterhorn. It has a pyramid-shaped peak and is one of the highest mountains in Europe.

Skiing in the Alps

The snowy Alps are great for winter sports, such as skiing and snowboarding. Competitions, such as downhill racing, are held for both children and adults.

Downhill racer

Alpine marmot

Marmots live high up in the Alps, eating grass and shrubs. They are sociable little animals that whistle to each other. In winter, they hibernate in burrows.

GERMANY

Germany is one of the largest and most important countries in Europe. The Rhine River cuts through mountainous landscape and passes pretty villages in southern Germany, while farther north there are large industrial cities. Germany is a major exporter of many quality goods, including cars.

Modern design

The Bauhaus was an art school in Germany. It promoted a clean, bold, modern look in art, architecture, and craft and had a huge influence throughout the world.

BAUHAUS

The Bauhaus

KEY

INDUSTRY
- Iron
- Coal
- Lumber
- Cars
- Shipbuilding
- Wind power
- Finance and banking

PRODUCE
- Wheat
- Sugar beets
- Cattle
- Vineyards
- Apples

ACTIVITIES
- Hiking
- Skiing

Angela Merkel

Chancellor

The political leader of Germany is called the chancellor. Angela Merkel was born in Hamburg and was one of Germany's longest-serving chancellors, from 2005 to 2021.

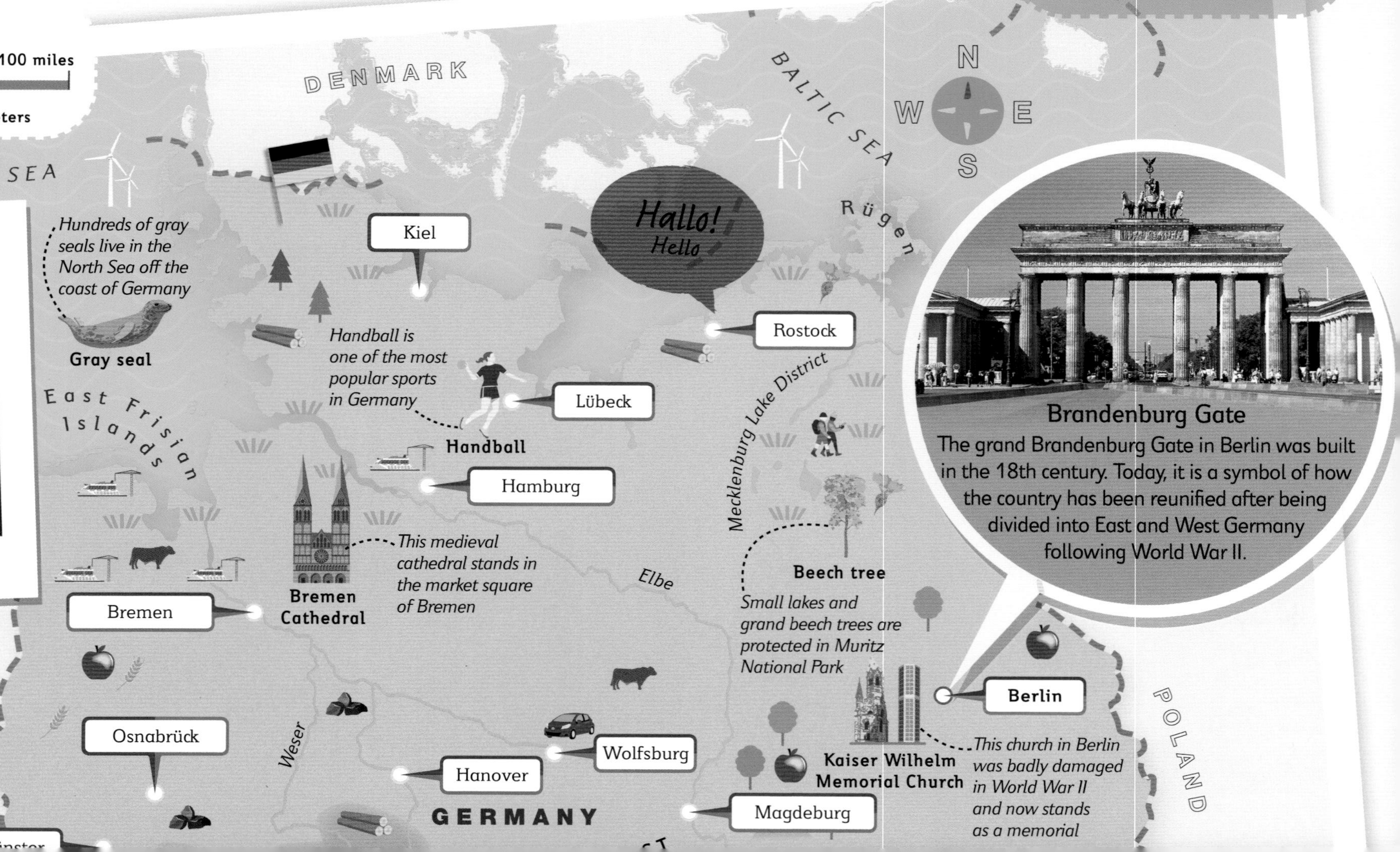
SCALE
0
50 miles
100 miles
0
50 kilometers
100 kilometers
NORTH SEA
DENMARK
BALTIC SEA
N
W
E
S
Rügen
Hallo!
Hello
Hundreds of gray seals live in the North Sea off the coast of Germany
Gray seal
East Frisian Islands
Kiel
Handball is one of the most popular sports in Germany
Handball
Lübeck
Rostock
Hamburg
Mecklenburg Lake District
This medieval cathedral stands in the market square of Bremen
Bremen Cathedral
Bremen
Elbe
Beech tree
Small lakes and grand beech trees are protected in Muritz National Park
Berlin
POLAND
This church in Berlin was badly damaged in World War II and now stands as a memorial
Kaiser Wilhelm Memorial Church
Osnabrück
Weser
Hanover
Wolfsburg
GERMANY
Magdeburg
Münster

Brandenburg Gate

The grand Brandenburg Gate in Berlin was built in the 18th century. Today, it is a symbol of how the country has been reunified after being divided into East and West Germany following World War II.

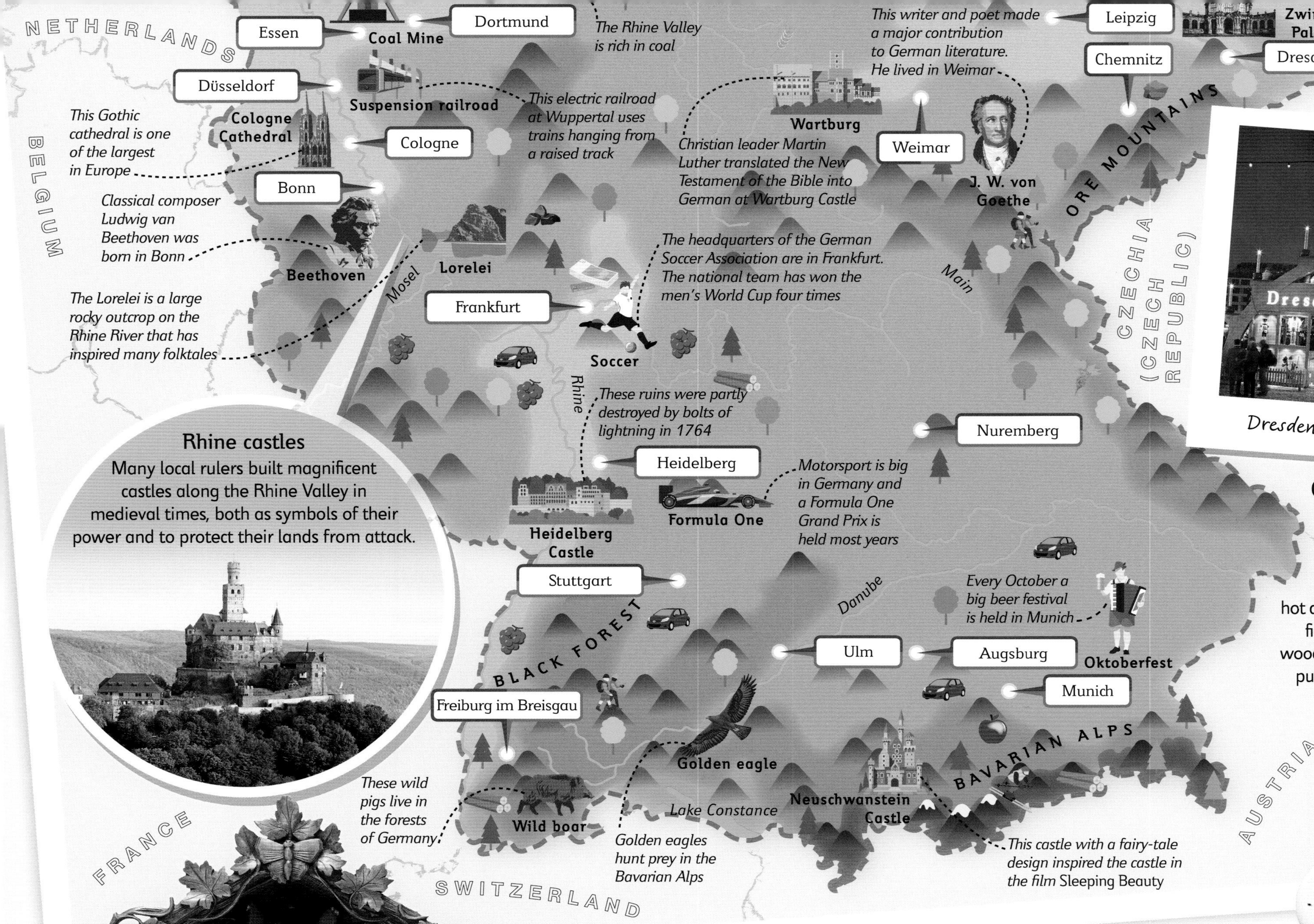
NETHERLANDS
BELGIUM
FRANCE
SWITZERLAND
AUSTRIA
CZECHIA (CZECH REPUBLIC)
Essen
Coal Mine
Dortmund
The Rhine Valley is rich in coal
Düsseldorf
Suspension railroad
This electric railroad at Wuppertal uses trains hanging from a raised track
Cologne Cathedral
This Gothic cathedral is one of the largest in Europe
Cologne
Bonn
Classical composer Ludwig van Beethoven was born in Bonn
Beethoven
Lorelei
The Lorelei is a large rocky outcrop on the Rhine River that has inspired many folktales
Mosel
Frankfurt
Soccer
The headquarters of the German Soccer Association are in Frankfurt. The national team has won the men's World Cup four times
Rhine
These ruins were partly destroyed by bolts of lightning in 1764
Heidelberg
Heidelberg Castle
Formula One
Motorsport is big in Germany and a Formula One Grand Prix is held most years
Stuttgart
BLACK FOREST
Freiburg im Breisgau
These wild pigs live in the forests of Germany
Wild boar
Golden eagle
Golden eagles hunt prey in the Bavarian Alps
Lake Constance
Neuschwanstein Castle
This castle with a fairy-tale design inspired the castle in the film Sleeping Beauty
BAVARIAN ALPS
Danube
Ulm
Augsburg
Munich
Oktoberfest
Every October a big beer festival is held in Munich
Nuremberg
Main
Wartburg
Christian leader Martin Luther translated the New Testament of the Bible into German at Wartburg Castle
Weimar
J. W. von Goethe
This writer and poet made a major contribution to German literature. He lived in Weimar
ORE MOUNTAINS
Leipzig
Chemnitz
Zwinger Palace
Dresden
This beautiful Baroque palace was built for the ruler of Saxony in 1709

Rhine castles

Many local rulers built magnificent castles along the Rhine Valley in medieval times, both as symbols of their power and to protect their lands from attack.

Dresdner Striezelmarkt
575.

Dresden Christmas market

Christmas markets

At Christmastime, markets are held all over Germany, selling seasonal foods, such as hot chestnuts and marzipan figures. Markets also sell wooden toys and candles to put on the Christmas tree.

Cuckoo clock

The cuckoo clock became popular in the Black Forest and surrounding area in the 19th century. When the hour is struck, the clock makes a sound like a cuckoo and a model cuckoo pops out.

Whole-wheat bread

German baking

Baking bread, cakes, and pastries is a German specialty. Crusty whole-wheat, dark rye, and multigrain breads are popular. Pretzels are sweet or salty bread made in the shape of a knot. Black Forest cake is a cream and chocolate cake topped with cherries.

Black Forest cake

Pretzels

SPAIN AND PORTUGAL

Spain and Portugal are part of sunny southern Europe. Both countries have long coastlines and spectacular scenery, making them popular with vacationers. The sea is a major source of food, and fishing is an important industry in both countries.

Portuguese tiles

Decorative tiles are found on homes and churches and are sometimes used as street signs. They often show scenes including cities, flowers, and fishing boats.

Decorative tiles

Many people walk to this cathedral on a Christian pilgrimage
Santiago de Compostela Cathedral
Santiago de Compostela
León
Esla
These gray wolves live in the forests and grassy planes of northern Portugal and Spain
Iberian wolf
This house is decorated with more than 300 scallop shells
Braga
Port is a special type of strong, sweet wine that is made in the Douro Valley
Guimarães
House of Shells
Porto
Douro
Salamanca
Port
Moliceiro boat
Aveiro
Luis de Camoes
This great Portuguese poet lived in the 16th century
Coimbra
Fado
Tagus
Nazaré
PORTUGAL
Bark is cut from cork trees and used to make wine corks
Cork
Guadiana
This temple in Evora was once an important place of worship
Badajoz
Belém Tower
Lisbon
Roman temple
Evora
Setúbal
Guadiana
Olá! Hello
Seville
Pastel de nata
Faro
Sherry is a strong type of wine made from white grapes grown in Jerez
Sherry
Jerez de la Frontera
SCALE
0
100 miles
0
100 kilometers
Cádiz

These traditional boats from Aveiro have a half-moon shape and are painted in bright colors
ATLANTIC OCEAN
Fado is traditional Portuguese music that is often accompanied by guitar
This 16th-century fort sits at the entrance to Lisbon's harbor
Many people visit the Azores to see dolphins
Dolphin watching
Azores
Ponta Delgada
Madeira
Levadas
The levadas are a system of channels built to carry water along the mountains
Madeira and the Azores
These islands in the middle of the Atlantic Ocean belong to Portugal. They are a popular destination for cruise ships to visit.
Funchal
Canary Islands
These Spanish islands are found off North Africa's west coast.
Santa Cruz de Tenerife
Canary Islands
Las Palmas de Gran Canaria

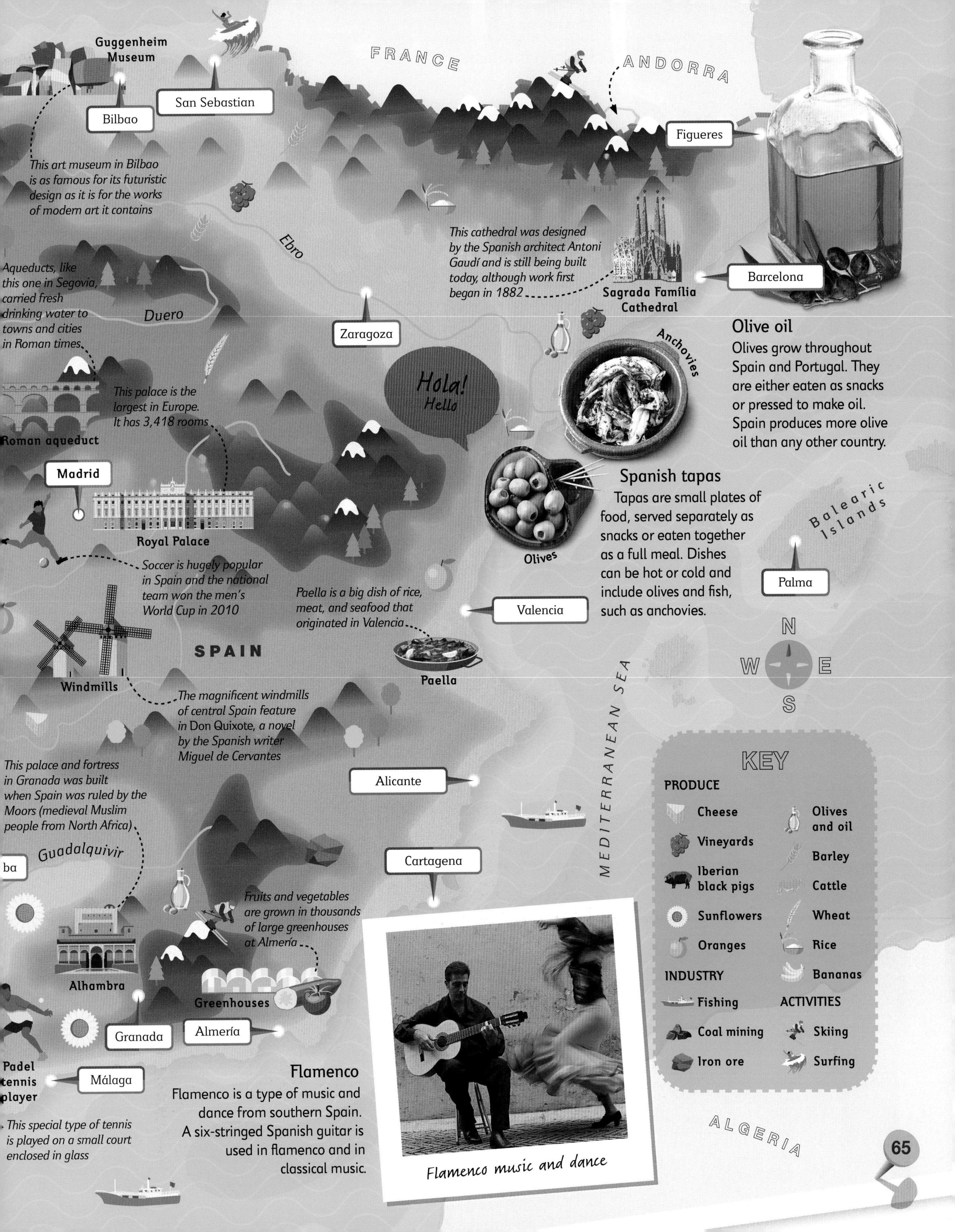
Guggenheim Museum
San Sebastian
Bilbao
FRANCE
ANDORRA
Figueres
This art museum in Bilbao is as famous for its futuristic design as it is for the works of modern art it contains
Ebro
This cathedral was designed by the Spanish architect Antoni Gaudí and is still being built today, although work first began in 1882
Sagrada Família Cathedral
Barcelona
Aqueducts, like this one in Segovia, carried fresh drinking water to towns and cities in Roman times
Duero
Zaragoza
Anchovies
Hola!
Hello
Roman aqueduct
This palace is the largest in Europe. It has 3,418 rooms
Madrid
Royal Palace
Olives
Soccer is hugely popular in Spain and the national team won the men's World Cup in 2010
Paella is a big dish of rice, meat, and seafood that originated in Valencia
Valencia
Balearic Islands
Palma
SPAIN
Windmills
Paella
N
W
E
S
MEDITERRANEAN SEA
The magnificent windmills of central Spain feature in Don Quixote, a novel by the Spanish writer Miguel de Cervantes
This palace and fortress in Granada was built when Spain was ruled by the Moors (medieval Muslim people from North Africa)
Alicante
Guadalquivir
ba
Cartagena
Fruits and vegetables are grown in thousands of large greenhouses at Almería
Alhambra
Greenhouses
Granada
Almería
Padel tennis player
Málaga
This special type of tennis is played on a small court enclosed in glass
KEY
PRODUCE
Cheese
Olives and oil
Vineyards
Barley
Iberian black pigs
Cattle
Sunflowers
Wheat
Oranges
Rice
INDUSTRY
Bananas
Fishing
ACTIVITIES
Coal mining
Skiing
Iron ore
Surfing
ALGERIA

Olive oil

Olives grow throughout Spain and Portugal. They are either eaten as snacks or pressed to make oil. Spain produces more olive oil than any other country.

Spanish tapas

Tapas are small plates of food, served separately as snacks or eaten together as a full meal. Dishes can be hot or cold and include olives and fish, such as anchovies.

Flamenco

Flamenco is a type of music and dance from southern Spain. A six-stringed Spanish guitar is used in flamenco and in classical music.

Flamenco music and dance

ITALY

Italy stretches down from the Alps in the north to the Mediterrean island of Sicily in the south. The country is shaped like a boot, with its toe almost touching Sicily. In ancient times, the Romans built a great empire that was ruled from Rome. Italy is also famous for its art and architecture.

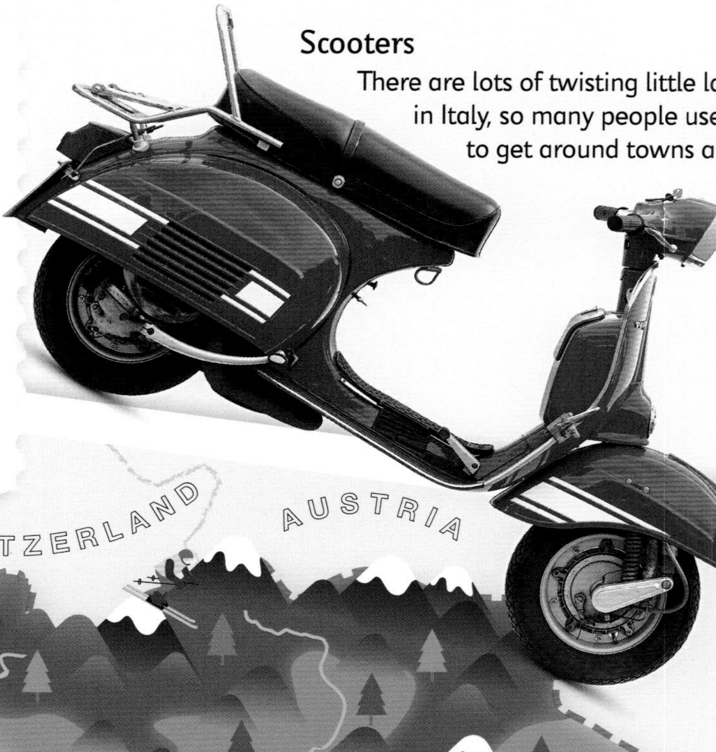

Scooters

There are lots of twisting little lanes and streets in Italy, so many people use small scooters to get around towns and cities.

The Last Supper

Leonardo da Vinci

Leonardo da Vinci was one of the world's greatest artists and inventors. In the late 15th century he painted *The Last Supper*, an oil painting showing Jesus Christ's last meal with his disciples (followers).

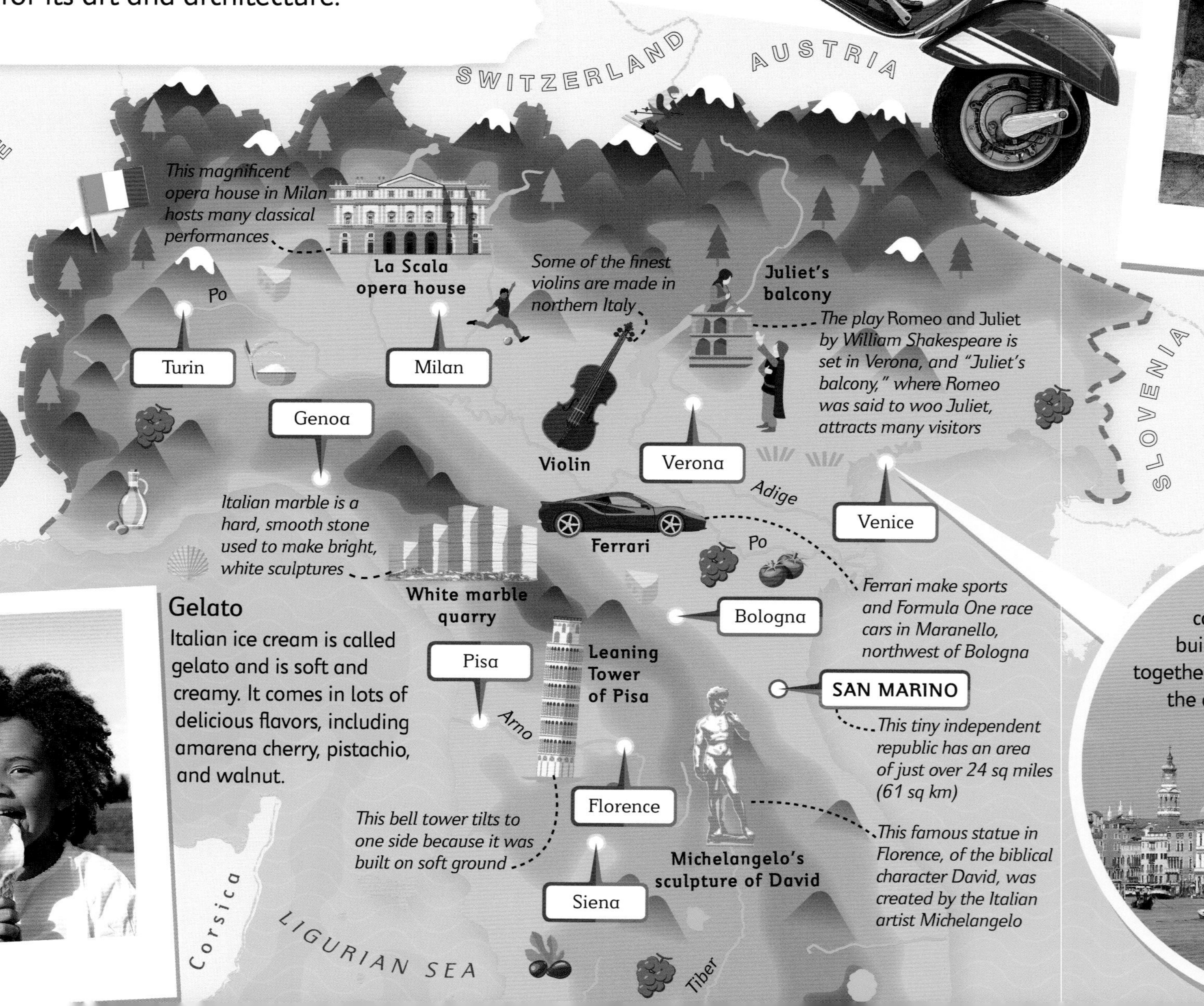
SWITZERLAND
AUSTRIA
FRANCE
SLOVENIA
CROATIA
Ciao! Hello
This magnificent opera house in Milan hosts many classical performances
La Scala opera house
Po
Turin
Milan
Genoa
Some of the finest violins are made in northern Italy
Violin
Juliet's balcony
The play Romeo and Juliet by William Shakespeare is set in Verona, and "Juliet's balcony," where Romeo was said to woo Juliet, attracts many visitors
Verona
Adige
Venice
Italian marble is a hard, smooth stone used to make bright, white sculptures
White marble quarry
Ferrari
Po
Ferrari make sports and Formula One race cars in Maranello, northwest of Bologna
Bologna
Pisa
Arno
Leaning Tower of Pisa
SAN MARINO
This tiny independent republic has an area of just over 24 sq miles (61 sq km)
Florence
This bell tower tilts to one side because it was built on soft ground
Michelangelo's sculpture of David
This famous statue in Florence, of the biblical character David, was created by the Italian artist Michelangelo
Siena
Corsica
LIGURIAN SEA
Tiber

Gelato

Italian ice cream is called gelato and is soft and creamy. It comes in lots of delicious flavors, including amarena cherry, pistachio, and walnut.

Gelato

Venice

Venice is a city of canals instead of streets. It is built on 118 small islands linked together by bridges. People travel around the city on boats called gondolas.

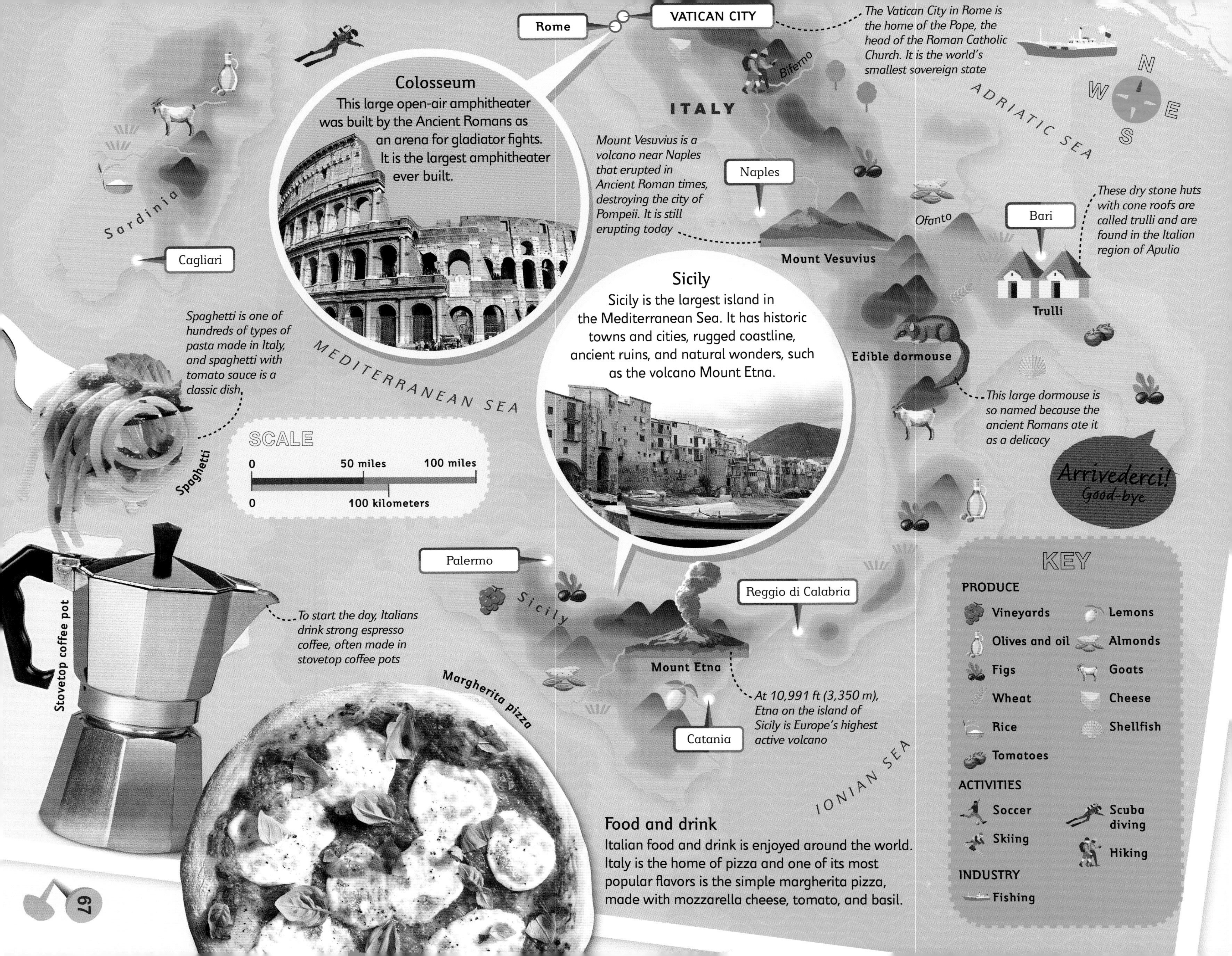

Rome
VATICAN CITY
ITALY
Biferno
ADRIATIC SEA
N
W
E
S
Naples
Mount Vesuvius
Ofanto
Bari
Trulli
Edible dormouse
Sardinia
Cagliari
MEDITERRANEAN SEA
Spaghetti
SCALE
0
50 miles
100 miles
0
100 kilometers
Arrivederci!
Good-bye
Palermo
Sicily
Reggio di Calabria
Mount Etna
Catania
IONIAN SEA
Stovetop coffee pot
Margherita pizza
KEY
PRODUCE
Vineyards
Lemons
Olives and oil
Almonds
Figs
Goats
Wheat
Cheese
Rice
Shellfish
Tomatoes
ACTIVITIES
Soccer
Scuba diving
Skiing
Hiking
INDUSTRY
Fishing

The Vatican City in Rome is the home of the Pope, the head of the Roman Catholic Church. It is the world's smallest sovereign state

Colosseum

This large open-air amphitheater was built by the Ancient Romans as an arena for gladiator fights. It is the largest amphitheater ever built.

Mount Vesuvius is a volcano near Naples that erupted in Ancient Roman times, destroying the city of Pompeii. It is still erupting today

These dry stone huts with cone roofs are called trulli and are found in the Italian region of Apulia

Sicily

Sicily is the largest island in the Mediterranean Sea. It has historic towns and cities, rugged coastline, ancient ruins, and natural wonders, such as the volcano Mount Etna.

Spaghetti is one of hundreds of types of pasta made in Italy, and spaghetti with tomato sauce is a classic dish

This large dormouse is so named because the ancient Romans ate it as a delicacy

To start the day, Italians drink strong espresso coffee, often made in stovetop coffee pots

At 10,991 ft (3,350 m), Etna on the island of Sicily is Europe's highest active volcano

Food and drink

Italian food and drink is enjoyed around the world. Italy is the home of pizza and one of its most popular flavors is the simple margherita pizza, made with mozzarella cheese, tomato, and basil.

CENTRAL EUROPE

Central Europe is a region of historic cities and ancient castles. Farming is important in Poland, as are industries such as coal mining and steel. To the south, people enjoy hiking and skiing in the rugged mountains of Czechia and Slovakia.

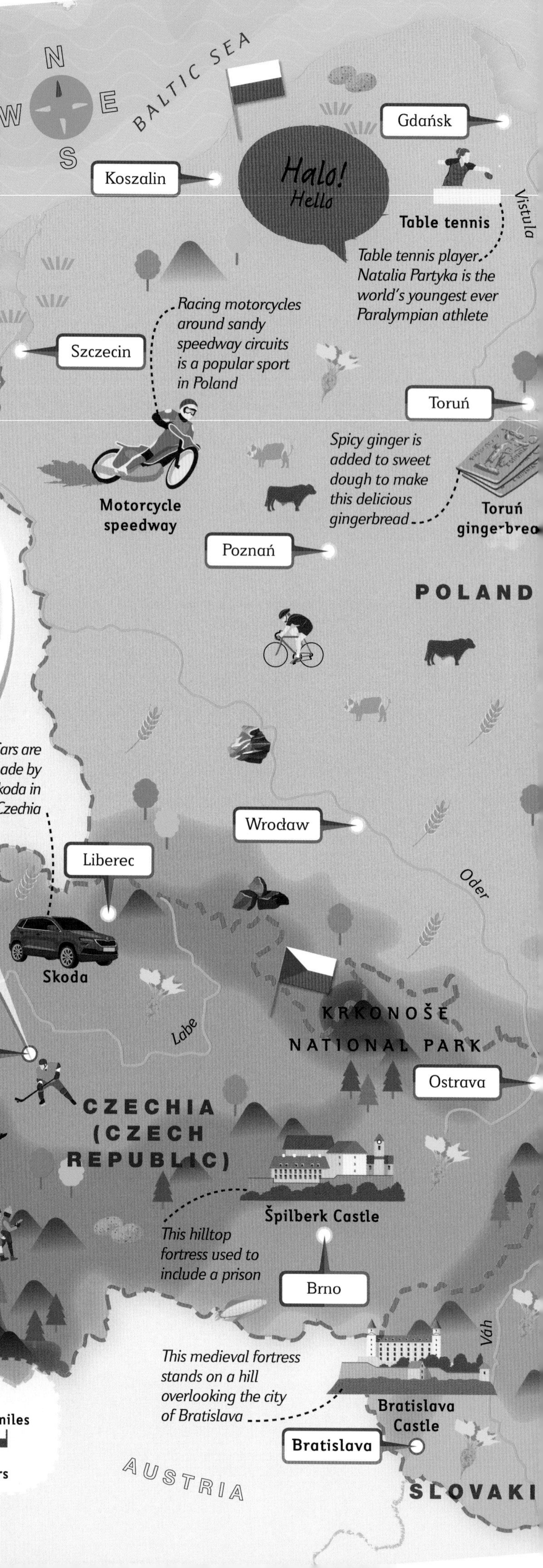

N
W
E
S
BALTIC SEA
Gdańsk
Koszalin
Halo!
Hello
Table tennis
Vistula
Table tennis player Natalia Partyka is the world's youngest ever Paralympian athlete
Racing motorcycles around sandy speedway circuits is a popular sport in Poland
Szczecin
Toruń
Spicy ginger is added to sweet dough to make this delicious gingerbread
Toruń gingerbrea
Motorcycle speedway
Poznań
POLAND
GERMANY
Cars are made by Skoda in Czechia
Wrocław
Liberec
Oder
Hops are used to brew beer, a Czech specialty
Skoda
Hops
Labe
KRKONOŠE NATIONAL PARK
Prague
Ostrava
CZECHIA (CZECH REPUBLIC)
Ahoj!
Hello
Špilberk Castle
This hilltop fortress used to include a prison
Brno
Váh
This medieval fortress stands on a hill overlooking the city of Bratislava
Bratislava Castle
Bratislava
AUSTRIA
SLOVAKI
SCALE
0
50 miles
0
50 kilometers

Charles Bridge

This medieval stone bridge is lined with statues. It crosses the Vltava River in Prague.

Astronomical clock

Astronomical Clock

This 600-year-old clock is in the Old Town Square of Prague. Every hour, mechanical statues move and perform.

Bohemian glass

Glassmaking is a traditional craft in Bohemia, the eastern half of the Czechia. Hand-cut, colored, and gold-plated glasses are made in studios across Bohemia.

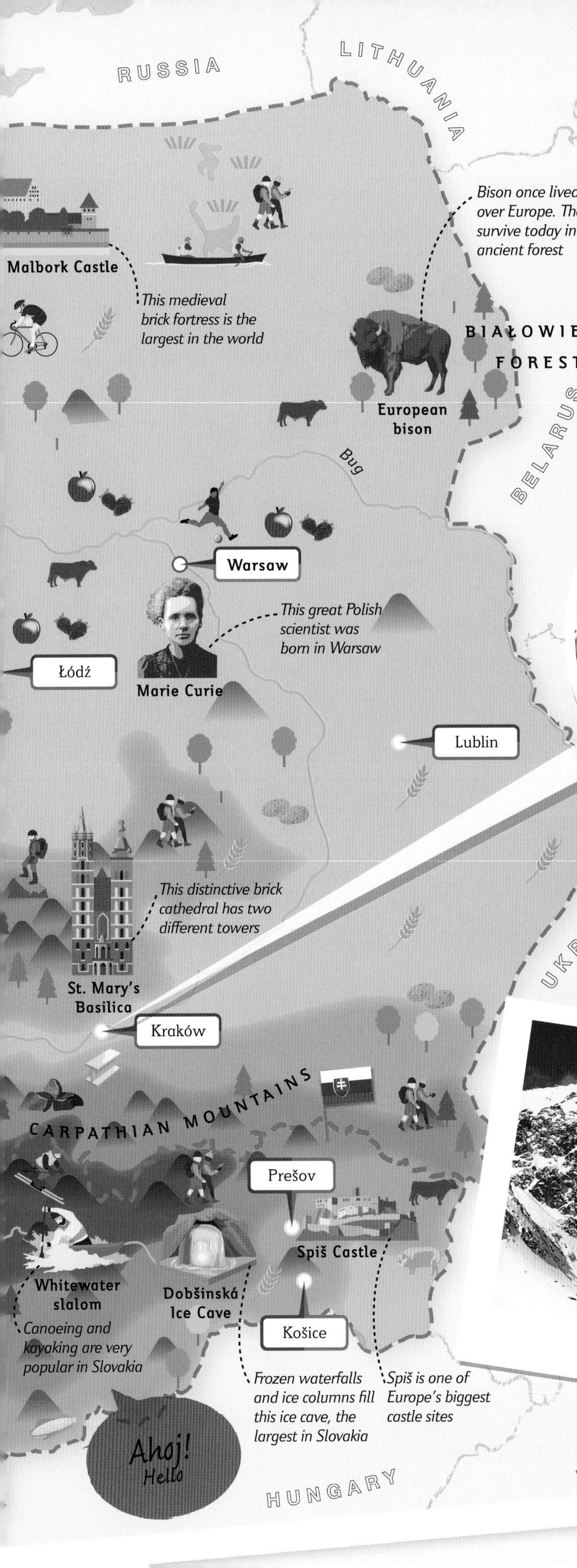
RUSSIA
LITHUANIA
Malbork Castle
This medieval brick fortress is the largest in the world
Bison once lived all over Europe. They survive today in this ancient forest
BIAŁOWIEŻA FOREST
European bison
BELARUS
Bug
Warsaw
This great Polish scientist was born in Warsaw
Marie Curie
Łódź
Lublin
This distinctive brick cathedral has two different towers
St. Mary's Basilica
Kraków
UKRAINE
CARPATHIAN MOUNTAINS
Prešov
Spiš Castle
Whitewater slalom
Canoeing and kayaking are very popular in Slovakia
Dobšinská Ice Cave
Frozen waterfalls and ice columns fill this ice cave, the largest in Slovakia
Košice
Spiš is one of Europe's biggest castle sites
Ahoj! Hello
HUNGARY
ROMANIA

Local produce

Many different berries grow in the fields and forests of central Europe. Milk from Polish cows is used in creamy cheeses, Slovakian pork makes Pressburg saláma sausage, and Chlebičky open sandwiches are a Czech delicacy.

Gooseberries
Raspberries
Black currants
Slovakian Pressburg saláma
Polish cheese
Czech Chlebičky

Market square

Kraków medieval market square is the largest in Europe. The beautiful buildings and many bars and cafés attract lots of visitors.

Cable car

KEY

PRODUCE

- Cattle
- Potatoes
- Pigs
- Wheat
- Sugar beets
- Corn
- Strawberries
- Apples

INDUSTRY

- Coal
- Silver
- Steel

ACTIVITIES

- Hiking
- Soccer
- Ice hockey
- Skiing
- Rock climbing
- Cycling
- Canoeing

High Tatras

The High Tatra Mountains lie between Poland and Slovakia. Cable cars carry passengers to the top of Lomnický Peak, one of the highest mountains in Slovakia.

HUNGARY, CROATIA, AND SLOVENIA

Hungary's historic capital, Budapest, lies on the banks of the Danube River, which flows through the country. Many crops are grown on the fertile plains. Croatia's coastline is dotted with hundreds of small islands that are fun to sail around. Slovenia has serene lakes and high mountains that are great for skiing.

Széchenyi Baths

The waters of these baths in Hungary are heated by two thermal springs. The ornate interior makes it feel as if you are swimming inside a cathedral.

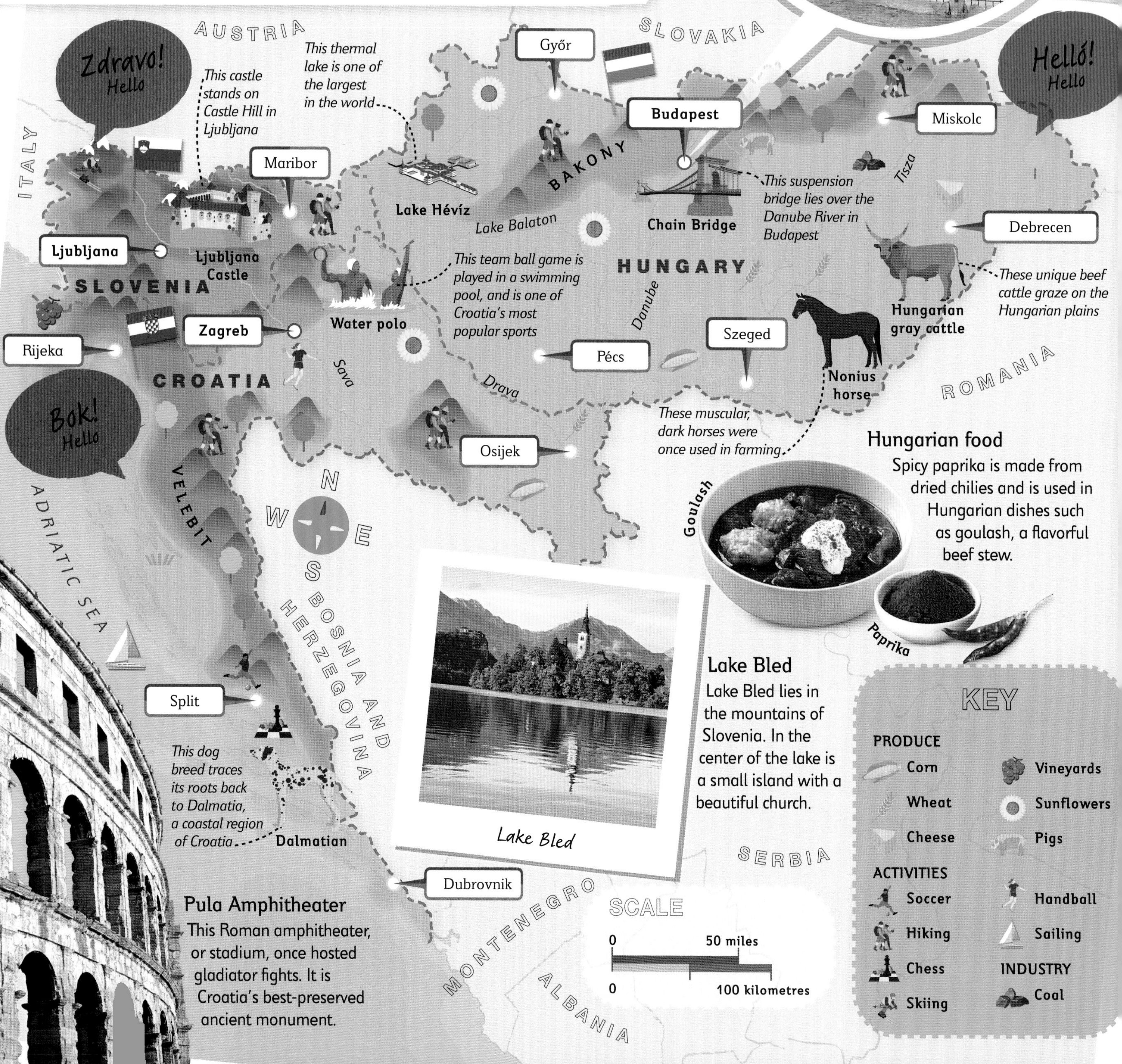

AUSTRIA
SLOVAKIA
ITALY
ROMANIA
SERBIA
MONTENEGRO
ALBANIA
BOSNIA AND HERZEGOVINA
ADRIATIC SEA
Zdravo! Hello
Helló! Hello
Bok! Hello
This castle stands on Castle Hill in Ljubljana
This thermal lake is one of the largest in the world
Győr
Budapest
Miskolc
Maribor
BAKONY
Tisza
Lake Hévíz
Lake Balaton
Chain Bridge
This suspension bridge lies over the Danube River in Budapest
Debrecen
Ljubljana
Ljubljana Castle
SLOVENIA
This team ball game is played in a swimming pool, and is one of Croatia's most popular sports
HUNGARY
These unique beef cattle graze on the Hungarian plains
Danube
Hungarian gray cattle
Zagreb
Water polo
Szeged
Rijeka
Pécs
Sava
CROATIA
Drava
Nonius horse
These muscular, dark horses were once used in farming
Osijek
VELEBIT
N
W
E
S
Split
This dog breed traces its roots back to Dalmatia, a coastal region of Croatia
Dalmatian
Dubrovnik
KEY
PRODUCE
Corn
Vineyards
Wheat
Sunflowers
Cheese
Pigs
ACTIVITIES
Soccer
Handball
Hiking
Sailing
Chess
INDUSTRY
Skiing
Coal
SCALE
0
50 miles
0
100 kilometres
Goulash
Paprika
Lake Bled

Hungarian food

Spicy paprika is made from dried chilies and is used in Hungarian dishes such as goulash, a flavorful beef stew.

Lake Bled

Lake Bled lies in the mountains of Slovenia. In the center of the lake is a small island with a beautiful church.

Pula Amphitheater

This Roman amphitheater, or stadium, once hosted gladiator fights. It is Croatia's best-preserved ancient monument.

UKRAINE

Ukraine is the second largest country in Europe. The country's flag is blue and yellow, representing the sky and the golden wheat and bright sunflowers that cover large areas of the landscape. Industry is important, with Ukraine being a major producer of hydroelectric power, steel, and coal.

Children's Parade

Children's Day

Children's Day is a special day that honors all children around the world. It is celebrated by a parade on June 1 every year in Kyiv, the capital of Ukraine.

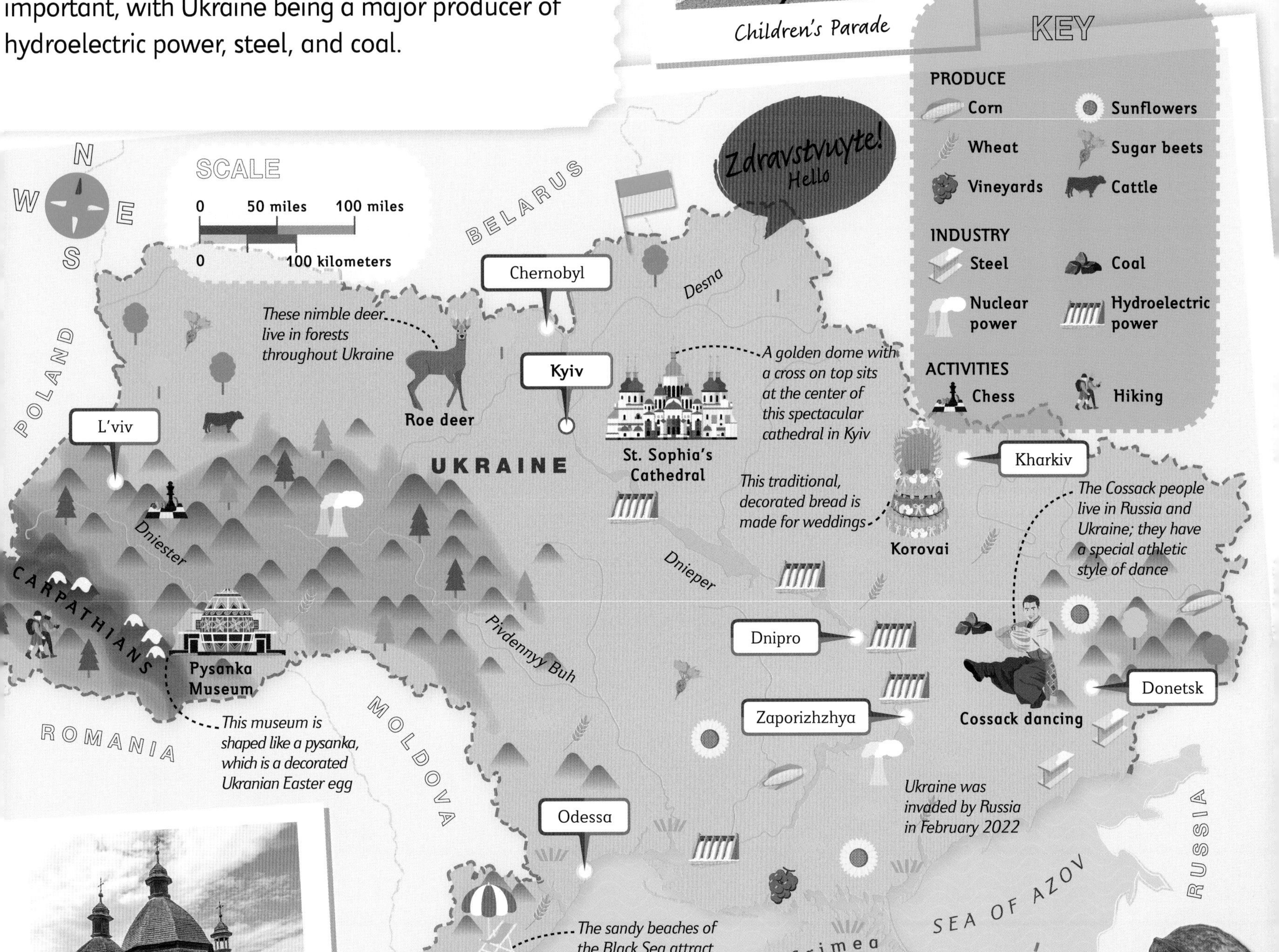

KEY
PRODUCE
Corn
Sunflowers
Wheat
Sugar beets
Vineyards
Cattle
INDUSTRY
Steel
Coal
Nuclear power
Hydroelectric power
ACTIVITIES
Chess
Hiking
SCALE
0
50 miles
100 miles
0
100 kilometers
N
W
E
S
Zdravstvuyte!
Hello
BELARUS
POLAND
ROMANIA
MOLDOVA
RUSSIA
Chernobyl
Kyiv
L'viv
Kharkiv
Dnipro
Zaporizhzhya
Donetsk
Odessa
UKRAINE
Desna
Dniester
Dnieper
Pivdennyy Buh
CARPATHIANS
These nimble deer live in forests throughout Ukraine
Roe deer
A golden dome with a cross on top sits at the center of this spectacular cathedral in Kyiv
St. Sophia's Cathedral
This traditional, decorated bread is made for weddings
Korovai
The Cossack people live in Russia and Ukraine; they have a special athletic style of dance
Cossack dancing
Pysanka Museum
This museum is shaped like a pysanka, which is a decorated Ukranian Easter egg
Ukraine was invaded by Russia in February 2022
Black Sea resorts
The sandy beaches of the Black Sea attract lots of visitors in the summer months
Crimea
Since 2014, Crimea has been annexed by Russia
SEA OF AZOV
BLACK SEA

Trinity Church, Zhovkva

Wooden churches

Ukraine is known for its traditional wooden churches. There is a range of styles, with churches in different parts of the country having their own unique shape and look.

Honey
Walnuts

Honey and walnuts

Bees are kept throughout Ukraine for their sweet, sticky honey. Crunchy walnuts are an important crop.

ROMANIA AND BULGARIA

Among the mountains and forests of Romania are dramatic castles and ancient stone churches. Bulgaria is also mountainous and on the sides of the valleys are vineyards that produce grapes for wine. In the summer months many tourists visit the Black Sea.

Carpathians

Rocky peaks and breathtaking scenery are features of the Carpathians, a chain of mountains that curves through the heart of Romania. In the valleys below the mountain tops are groves of pine forest.

Horezu Monastery fresco

Horseshoe bat

Caves in the Carpathian Mountains are home to hundreds of horseshoe bats. They come out at night to feed on flying insects.

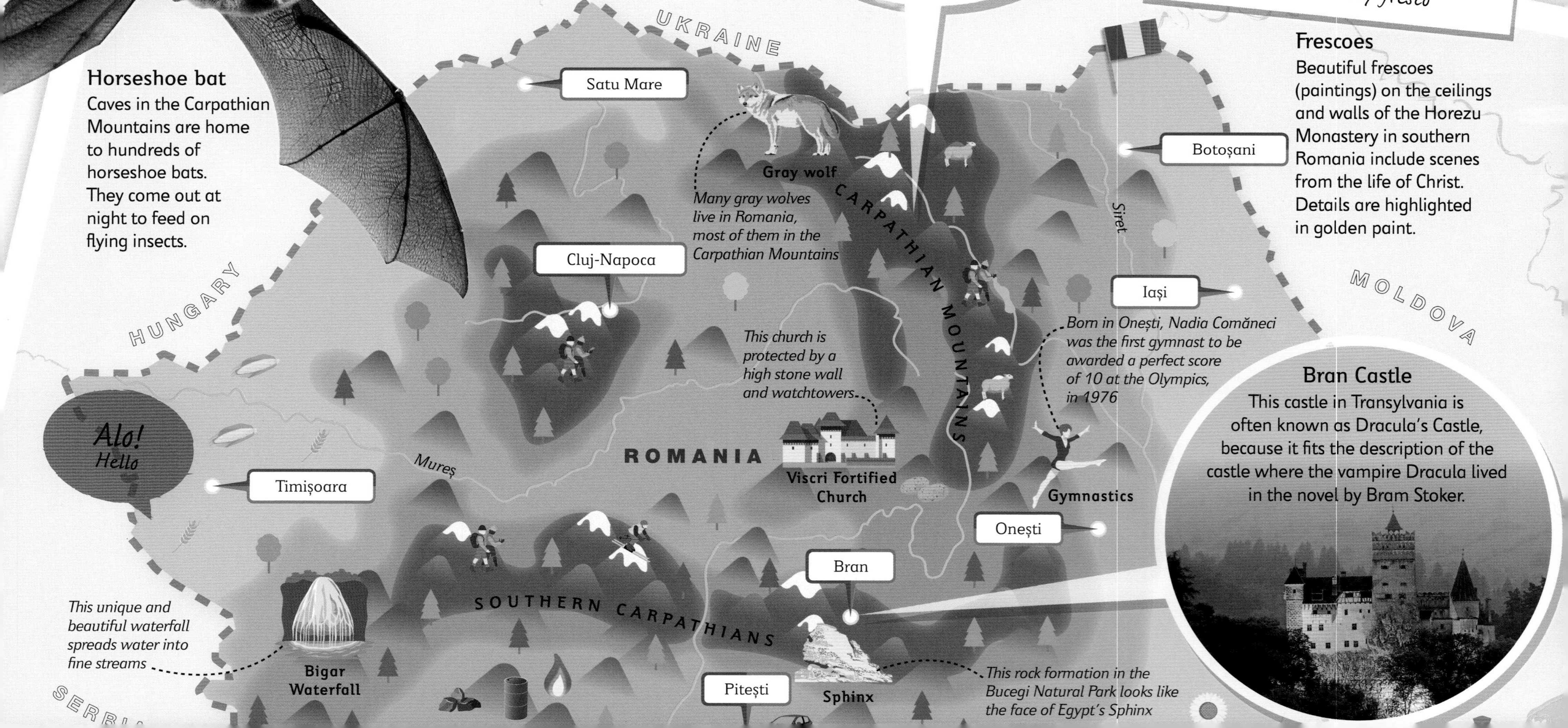

UKRAINE
HUNGARY
MOLDOVA
SERBIA
Satu Mare
Cluj-Napoca
Botoșani
Iași
Timișoara
Onești
Bran
Pitești
Siret
Mureș
ROMANIA
CARPATHIAN MOUNTAINS
SOUTHERN CARPATHIANS
Gray wolf
Many gray wolves live in Romania, most of them in the Carpathian Mountains
This church is protected by a high stone wall and watchtowers
Viscri Fortified Church
Born in Onești, Nadia Comăneci was the first gymnast to be awarded a perfect score of 10 at the Olympics, in 1976
Gymnastics
Alo! Hello
This unique and beautiful waterfall spreads water into fine streams
Bigar Waterfall
Sphinx
This rock formation in the Bucegi Natural Park looks like the face of Egypt's Sphinx

Frescoes

Beautiful frescoes (paintings) on the ceilings and walls of the Horezu Monastery in southern Romania include scenes from the life of Christ. Details are highlighted in golden paint.

Bran Castle

This castle in Transylvania is often known as Dracula's Castle, because it fits the description of the castle where the vampire Dracula lived in the novel by Bram Stoker.

Alexander Nevsky Cathedral

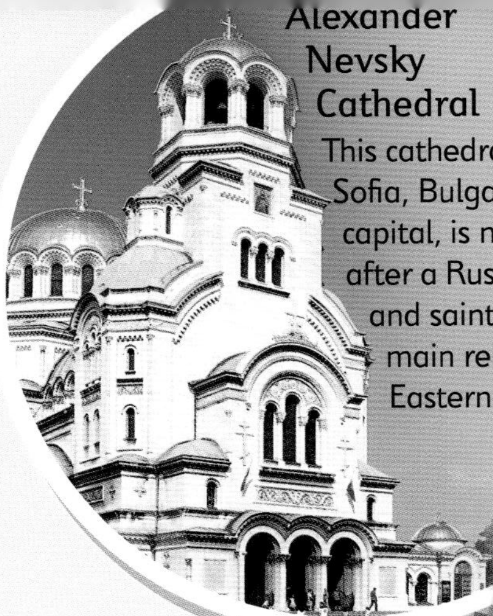

This cathedral in Sofia, Bulgaria's capital, is named after a Russian prince and saint. Bulgaria's main religion is Eastern Orthodox.

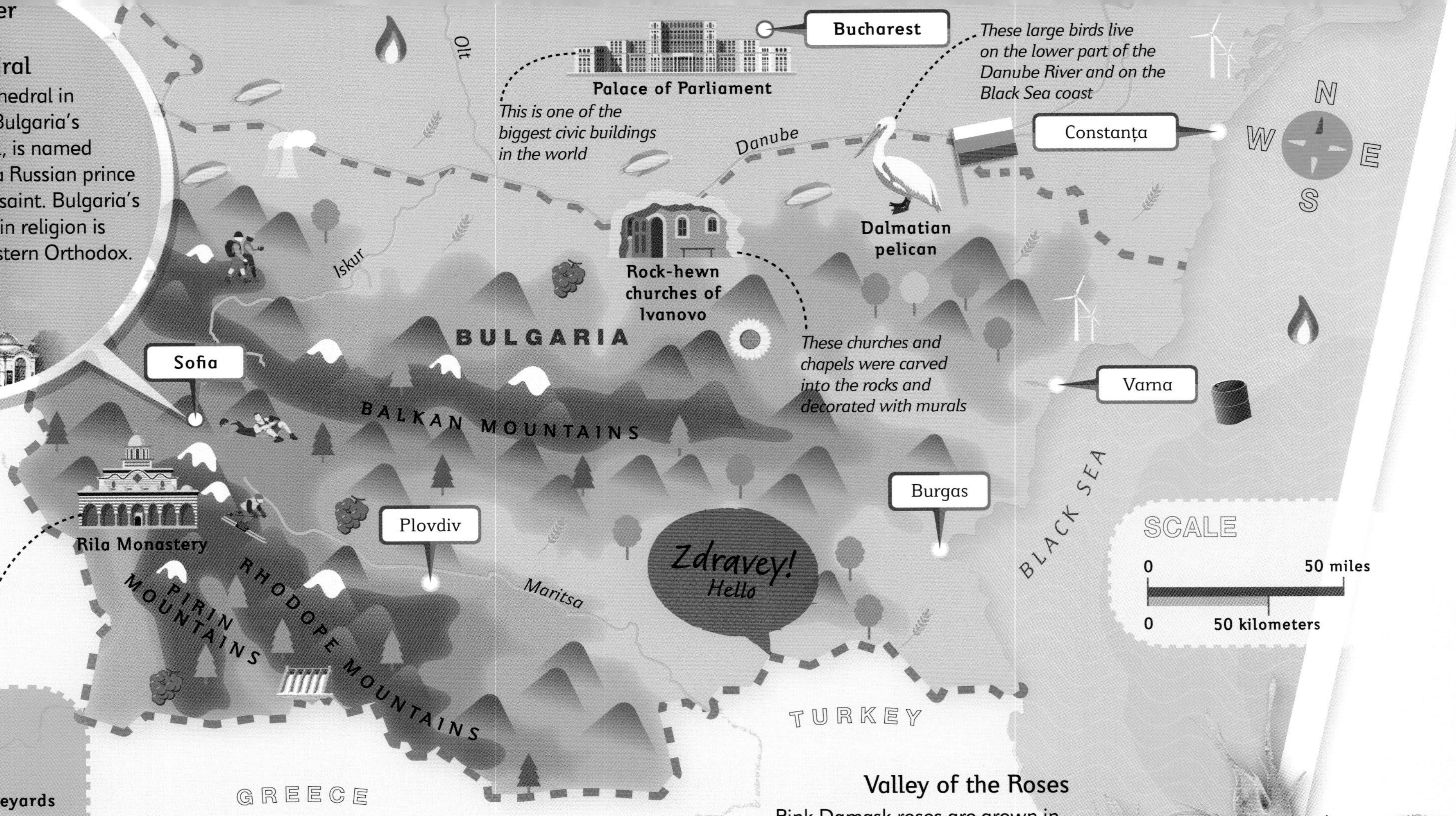

Olt
Bucharest
Palace of Parliament
This is one of the biggest civic buildings in the world
These large birds live on the lower part of the Danube River and on the Black Sea coast
Danube
Constanța
N
W
E
S
Dalmatian pelican
Iskur
Rock-hewn churches of Ivanovo
BULGARIA
These churches and chapels were carved into the rocks and decorated with murals
Sofia
Varna
BALKAN MOUNTAINS
NORTH MACEDONIA
Rila Monastery
This monastery is an important holy site in the Eastern Orthodox Church
Plovdiv
Burgas
BLACK SEA
Zdravey!
Hello
Maritsa
PIRIN MOUNTAINS
RHODOPE MOUNTAINS
TURKEY
GREECE
SCALE
0
50 miles
0
50 kilometers

KEY

PRODUCE
- Wheat
- Vineyards
- Sunflowers
- Sheep
- Corn
- Potatoes

INDUSTRY
- Wind power
- Natural gas
- Coal
- Cars
- Oil
- Hydroelectric power
- Nuclear power

ACTIVITIES
- Hiking
- Wrestling
- Skiing

Valley of the Roses

Pink Damask roses are grown in the center of Bulgaria. The petals are used to make rose oil, which is used in perfumes, and rosewater, which is a food flavoring.

Pirin Mountains, Bulgaria

Hiking

Mountainous landscapes, such as the Carpathians of Romania and the Pirin Mountains in southwest Bulgaria, are popular places for hiking and exploring. The Pirin Mountains are known for their many beautiful, crystal-clear lakes.

Damask rose

Rose oil

GREECE

Greece is the home of one of the world's first great civilizations and has a long and fascinating history. There are ancient remains, magnificent mountains, hundreds of islands with glorious beaches to explore, and delicious traditional food to enjoy. Greece's many attractions have made it popular with tourists.

Monasteries

Medieval monks built more than 20 monasteries at Metéora, each perched at the top of one of the tall rock pillars found at this spectacular site. Today, only six of them remain.

KEY

PRODUCE
- Olives and oil
- Vineyards
- Wheat
- Cotton
- Figs
- Goats
- Sheep
- Cheese
- Marble
- Bauxite
- Leather
- Shellfish

NATURAL FEATURES
- Dolphin
- Coral reef

ACTIVITIES
- Hiking
- Soccer
- Tourism

Dancing

Traditional dancing plays an important role in many Greek celebrations. These are happy, sociable occasions with lots of lively music.

Traditional Greek dancers

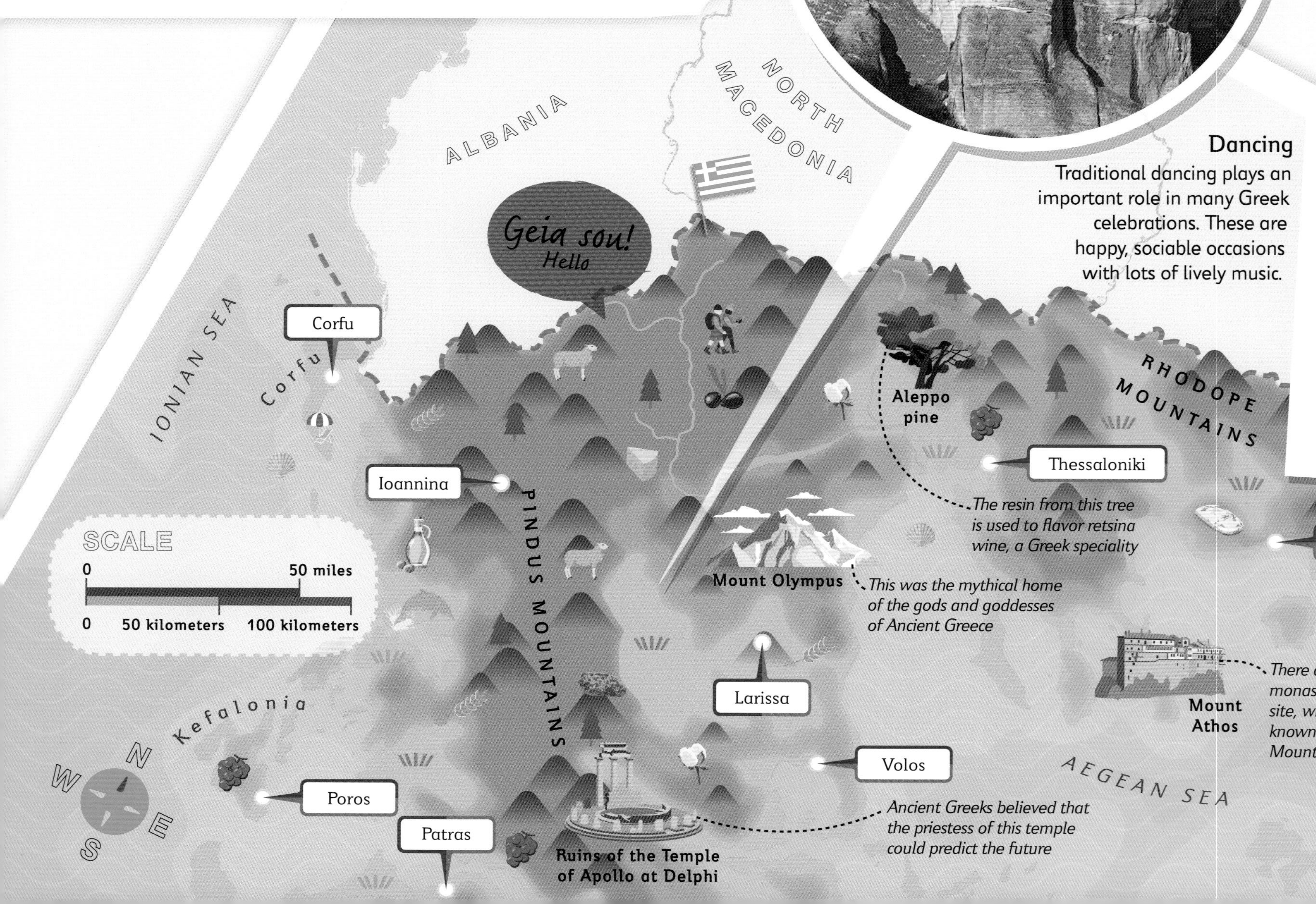

ALBANIA
NORTH MACEDONIA
BULGARIA
IONIAN SEA
AEGEAN SEA
Geia sou!
Hello
Corfu
Corfu
Ioannina
Kefalonia
Poros
Patras
PINDUS MOUNTAINS
Ruins of the Temple of Apollo at Delphi
Ancient Greeks believed that the priestess of this temple could predict the future
Larissa
Volos
Mount Olympus
This was the mythical home of the gods and goddesses of Ancient Greece
Aleppo pine
The resin from this tree is used to flavor retsina wine, a Greek speciality
Thessaloniki
RHODOPE MOUNTAINS
Kavala
Mount Athos
There are 20 monasteries at this site, which is also known as the Holy Mountain
SCALE
0
50 miles
0
50 kilometers
100 kilometers
N
E
S
W

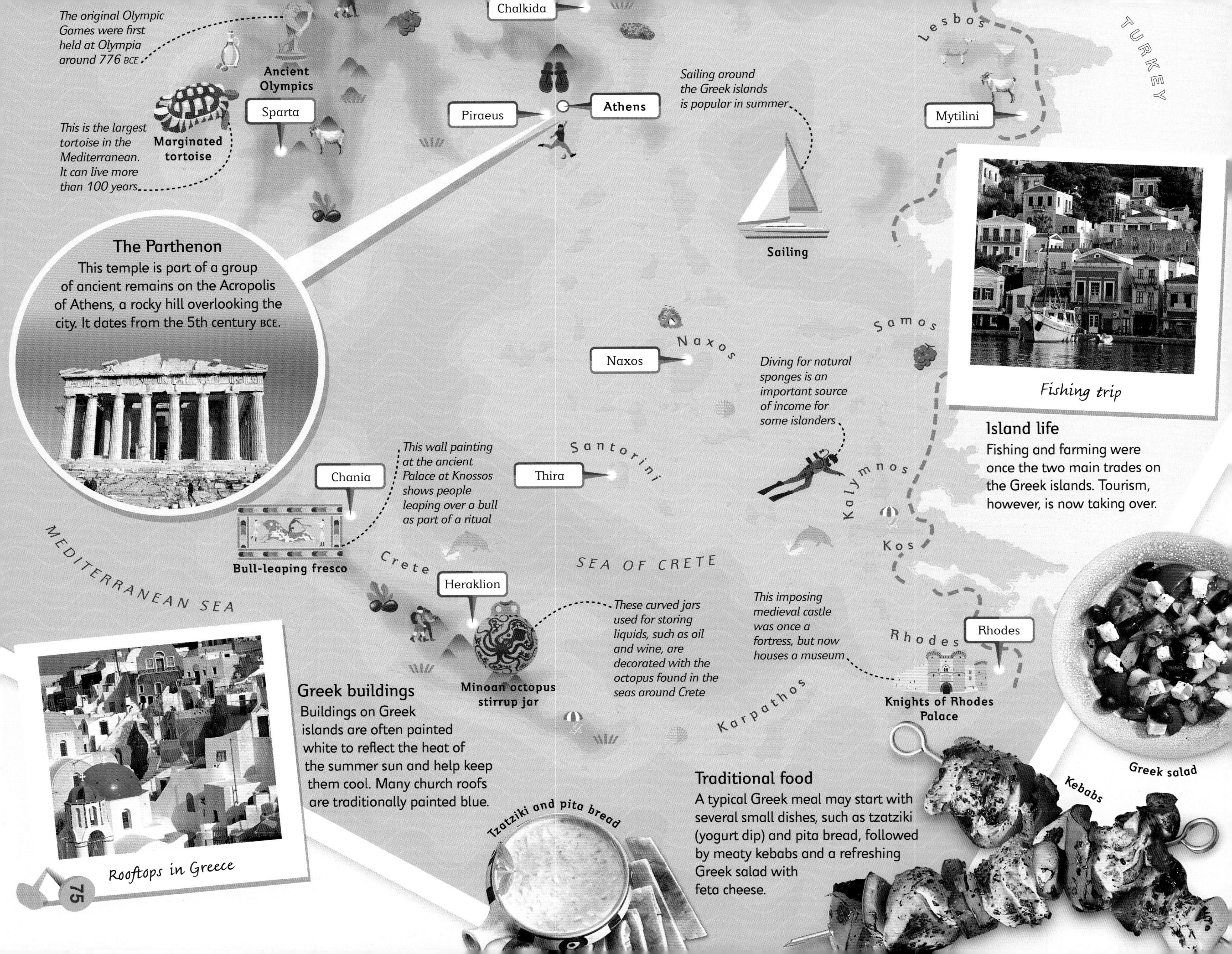

The original Olympic Games were first held at Olympia around 776 BCE
Ancient Olympics
Sparta
This is the largest tortoise in the Mediterranean. It can live more than 100 years
Marginated tortoise
Chalkida
Piraeus
Athens
Sailing around the Greek islands is popular in summer
Sailing
Lesbos
Mytilini
TURKEY
Samos
Naxos
Diving for natural sponges is an important source of income for some islanders
Santorini
Thira
Kalymnos
Kos
This wall painting at the ancient Palace at Knossos shows people leaping over a bull as part of a ritual
Chania
Bull-leaping fresco
MEDITERRANEAN SEA
Crete
Heraklion
SEA OF CRETE
These curved jars used for storing liquids, such as oil and wine, are decorated with the octopus found in the seas around Crete
Minoan octopus stirrup jar
This imposing medieval castle was once a fortress, but now houses a museum
Rhodes
Knights of Rhodes Palace
Karpathos
Tzatziki and pita bread
Kebabs
Greek salad

The Parthenon

This temple is part of a group of ancient remains on the Acropolis of Athens, a rocky hill overlooking the city. It dates from the 5th century BCE.

Fishing trip

Island life

Fishing and farming were once the two main trades on the Greek islands. Tourism, however, is now taking over.

Greek buildings

Buildings on Greek islands are often painted white to reflect the heat of the summer sun and help keep them cool. Many church roofs are traditionally painted blue.

Traditional food

A typical Greek meal may start with several small dishes, such as tzatziki (yogurt dip) and pita bread, followed by meaty kebabs and a refreshing Greek salad with feta cheese.

Rooftops in Greece

EUROPEAN RUSSIA AND THE BALTICS

Russia is the largest country in the world and stretches across two continents: Europe and Asia. European Russia lies to the west of the Ural Mountains. The small Baltic countries of Estonia, Latvia, and Lithuania are on the east coast of the Baltic Sea.

Matryoshka doll

Wooden painted Matryoshka dolls are nested dolls that fit one inside the other. The largest doll is a mother figure and the smallest is a baby. The dolls are popular as ornaments worldwide.

Raekoja plats

In Tallinn's old town stands Raekoja Plats (Town Hall Square.) This lovely square has many attractive medieval buildings and in the summer is filled with outdoor cafés.

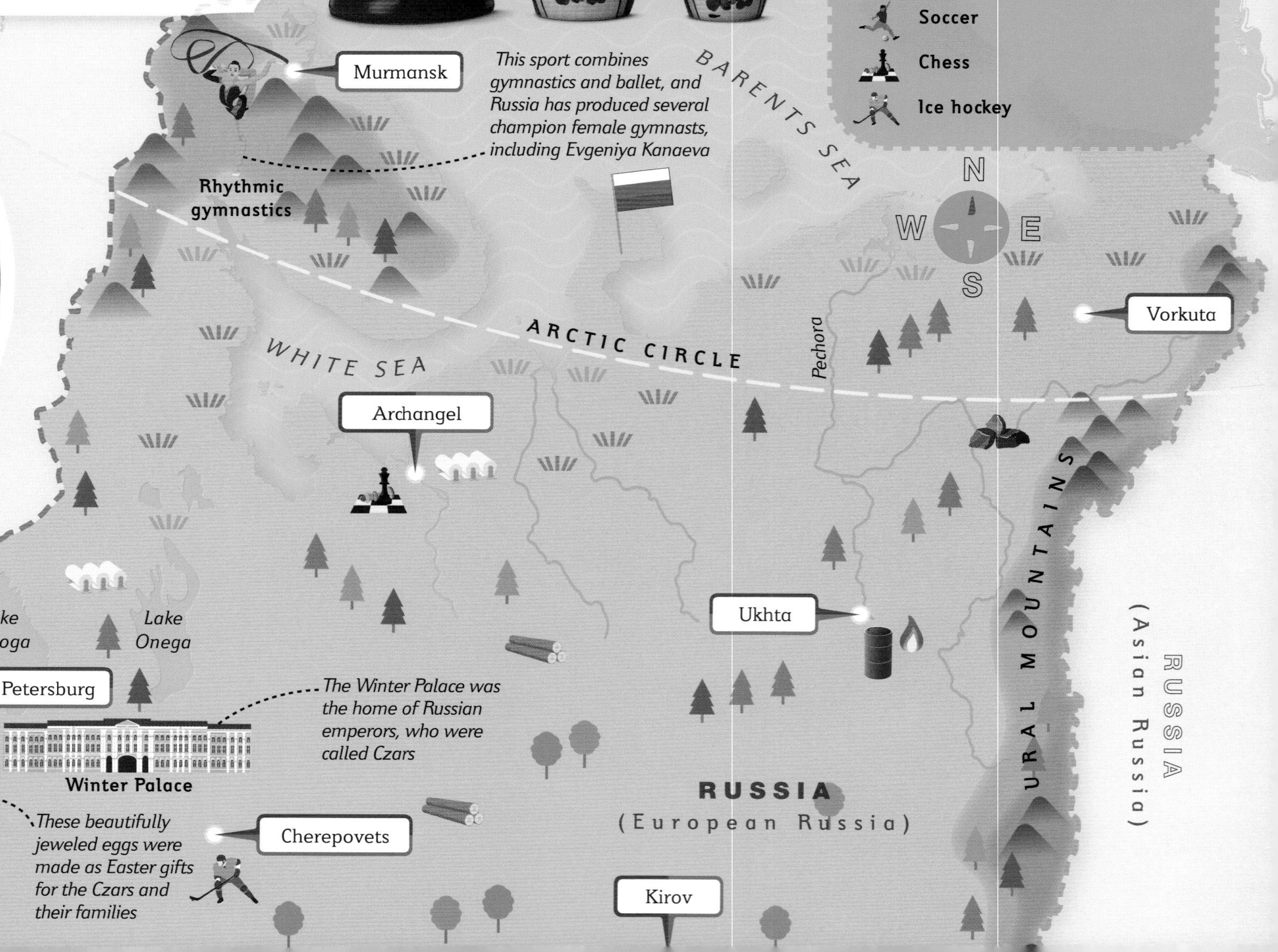
KEY
PRODUCE
Vineyards
Watermelons
Strawberries
Raspberries
Potatoes
Sunflowers
Lumber
INDUSTRY
Oil
Gas
Aircraft
Coal
Cars
Shipbuilding
Pulp and paper
SPORT
Soccer
Chess
Ice hockey
N
W
E
S
BARENTS SEA
WHITE SEA
ARCTIC CIRCLE
BALTIC SEA
FINLAND
Murmansk
Rhythmic gymnastics
This sport combines gymnastics and ballet, and Russia has produced several champion female gymnasts, including Evgeniya Kanaeva
Archangel
Pechora
Vorkuta
Ukhta
Kirov
Cherepovets
URAL MOUNTAINS
RUSSIA
(Asian Russia)
RUSSIA
(European Russia)
Lake Ladoga
Lake Onega
St. Petersburg
The Winter Palace was the home of Russian emperors, who were called Czars
Winter Palace
Fabergé egg
These beautifully jeweled eggs were made as Easter gifts for the Czars and their families
Tallinn
ESTONIA
Estonian National Museum
This museum has a modern, wedge-shaped design
Riga
Riga Cathedral
This cathedral is known for its large pipe organ and concerts are held regularly
LATVIA
Thousands of crosses stand on this hill, which is a symbol of the Christian faith for Lithuanians
Hill of Crosses
LITHUANIA

Shchi
Raspberries

Tasty food

Shchi is a Russian cabbage soup. It also includes other vegetables, such as tomatoes, carrots, and even nettles. Meat can be added, too. Raspberries are another favorite delicacy, grown in southwestern Russia.

Bolshoi ballet dancers

The Bolshoi

The Bolshoi is the world's oldest ballet company. Its classically trained dancers perform at the Bolshoi Theater in Moscow and at theaters in other parts of the world.

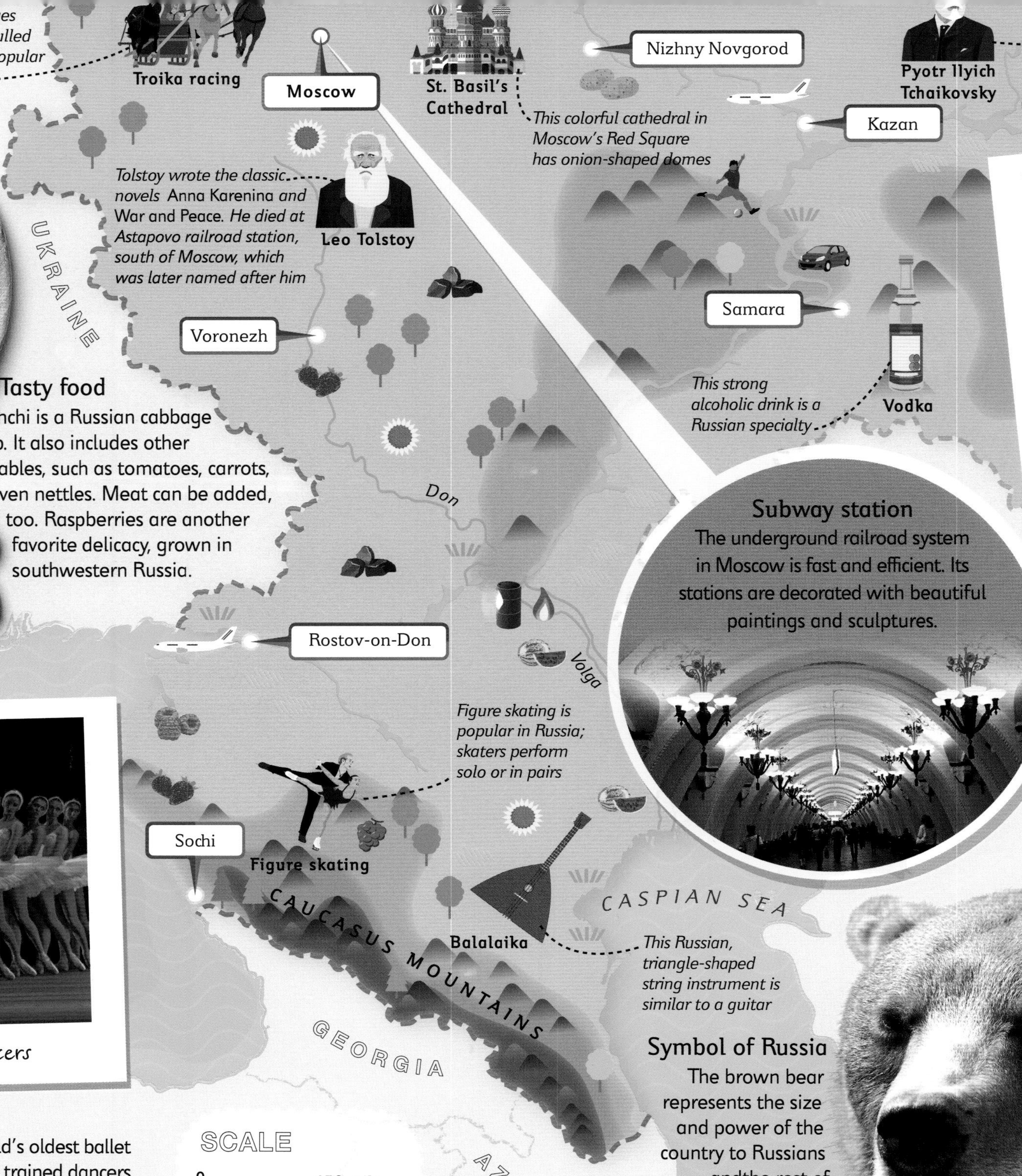
Racing troikas—carriages mounted on skis and pulled by three horses—is a popular sport in winter
Troika racing
Moscow
St. Basil's Cathedral
This colorful cathedral in Moscow's Red Square has onion-shaped domes
Nizhny Novgorod
Pyotr Ilyich Tchaikovsky
Tchaikovksy was one of the first Russian composers to become popular worldwide. His ballets include The Nutcracker
Kazan
UKRAINE
Tolstoy wrote the classic novels Anna Karenina and War and Peace. He died at Astapovo railroad station, south of Moscow, which was later named after him
Leo Tolstoy
Voronezh
Samara
This strong alcoholic drink is a Russian specialty
Vodka
Don
Rostov-on-Don
Volga
Figure skating is popular in Russia; skaters perform solo or in pairs
Sochi
Figure skating
CAUCASUS MOUNTAINS
Balalaika
This Russian, triangle-shaped string instrument is similar to a guitar
CASPIAN SEA
KAZAKHSTAN
GEORGIA
AZERBAIJAN
SCALE
0
150 miles
0
150 kilometres

Subway station

The underground railroad system in Moscow is fast and efficient. Its stations are decorated with beautiful paintings and sculptures.

Dacha and garden

Dachas

Some people who live in big Russian cities have a second home in the country, known as a dacha. Here, they go to relax and grow fruit and vegetables in the garden.

Symbol of Russia

The brown bear represents the size and power of the country to Russians andthe rest of the world.

RIVERS, LAKES, AND MOUNTAINS

Earth's surface is crisscrossed with streams and rivers, lakes, and high mountains. Many rivers begin as streams high up in the mountains, flow downhill through valleys to low-lying areas, and then pour out into seas. Lakes are large pools of water surrounded by land. Mountains are formed over millions of years, as huge areas of land push into each other, forcing the ground upward.

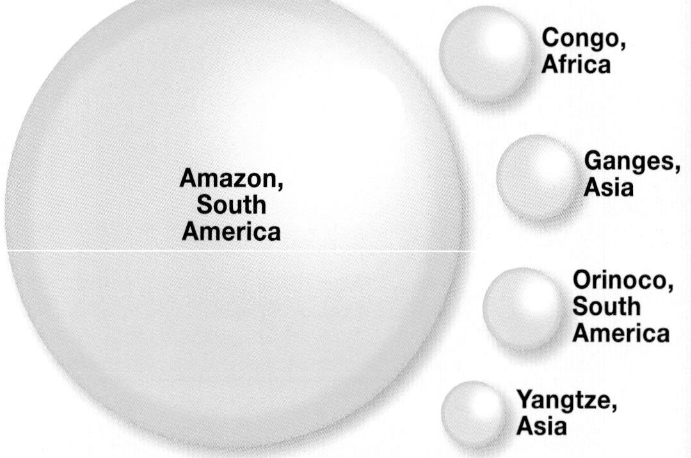

Amazon, South America
Congo, Africa
Ganges, Asia
Orinoco, South America
Yangtze, Asia

Five rivers with the most water

The Amazon has the most water by far. Its closest rivals each hold less than one-fifth of the water that flows along the Amazon. Rivers with the most water are formed in places with heavy rainfall, such as rain forests. They also have wide surface areas to catch the rain.

Five longest rivers

The longest rivers in the world flow across large continents. They begin in the mountains and flow all the way to the open sea.

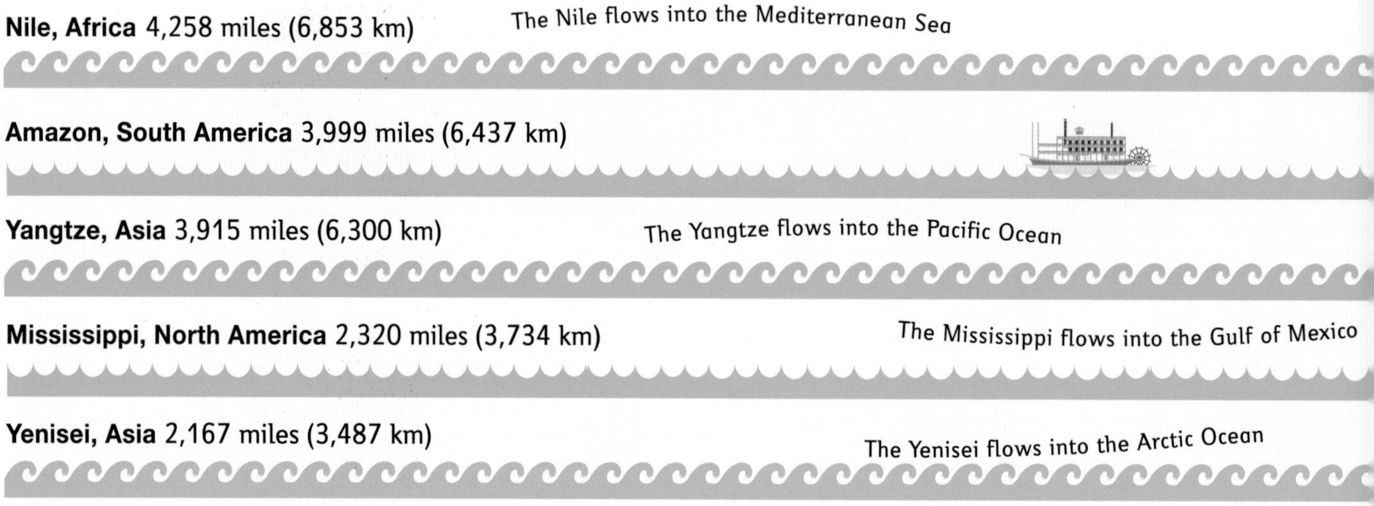

Nile, Africa 4,258 miles (6,853 km)
The Nile flows into the Mediterranean Sea
Amazon, South America 3,999 miles (6,437 km)
Yangtze, Asia 3,915 miles (6,300 km)
The Yangtze flows into the Pacific Ocean
Mississippi, North America 2,320 miles (3,734 km)
The Mississippi flows into the Gulf of Mexico
Yenisei, Asia 2,167 miles (3,487 km)
The Yenisei flows into the Arctic Ocean

Five highest mountains

The highest mountains in the world are all in Asia. They are found in the borderlands between China, India, Nepal, and Pakistan. There is little difference in height between them, but there is no doubt that Mount Everest has the highest peak.

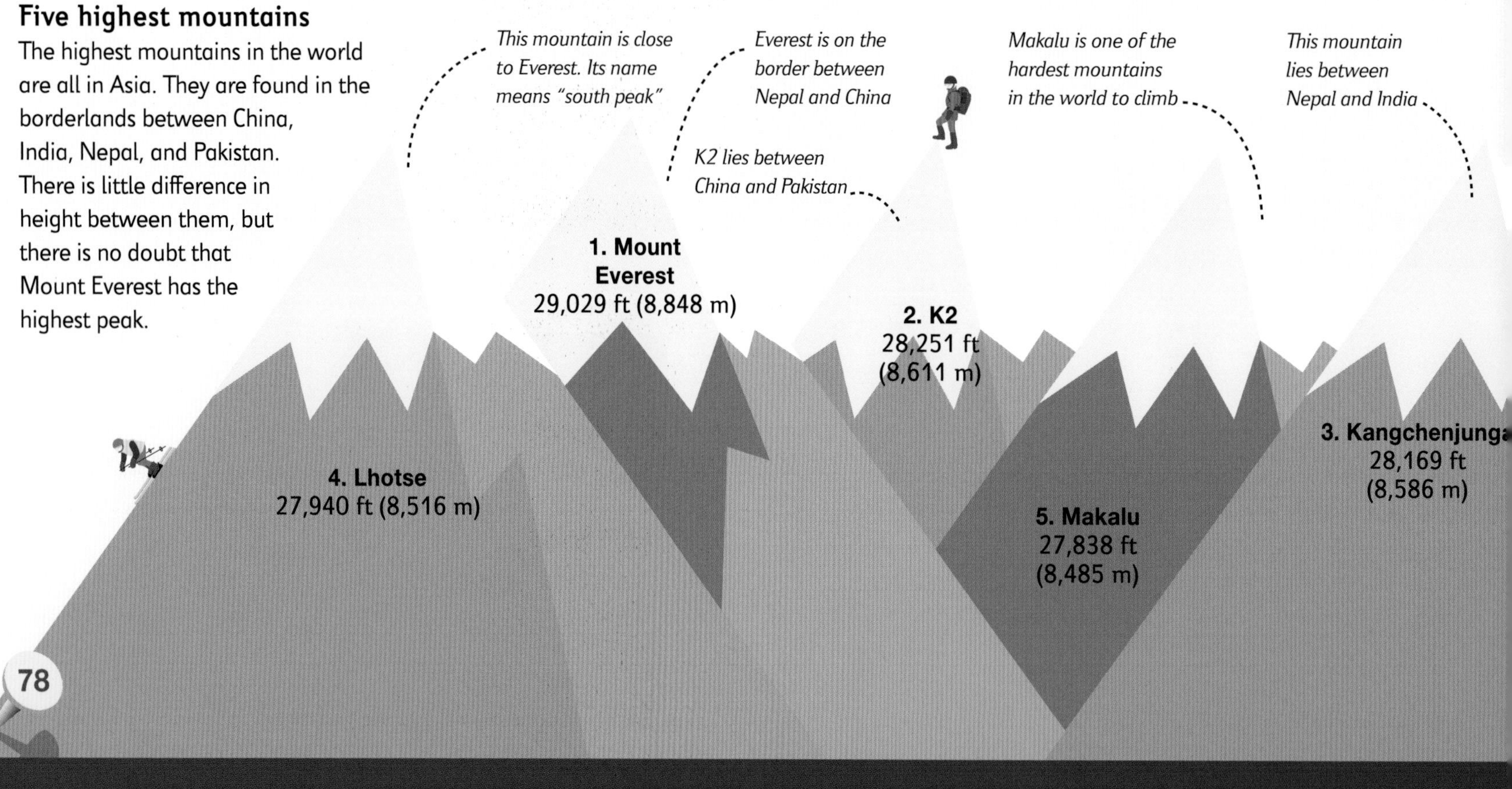

This mountain is close to Everest. Its name means "south peak"
Everest is on the border between Nepal and China
K2 lies between China and Pakistan
Makalu is one of the hardest mountains in the world to climb
This mountain lies between Nepal and India
1. Mount Everest 29,029 ft (8,848 m)
2. K2 28,251 ft (8,611 m)
3. Kangchenjunga 28,169 ft (8,586 m)
4. Lhotse 27,940 ft (8,516 m)
5. Makalu 27,838 ft (8,485 m)

Three largest lakes

The three biggest lakes are spread across four different continents. The largest is the Caspian Sea, which borders Asia and Europe. It has salty water and is both a sea and a lake. Lake Superior is the world's largest freshwater lake.

Victoria is the largest tropical lake and is the source of the Nile River.

1. Caspian Sea, Asia and Europe
143,000 sq miles
(371,000 sq km)

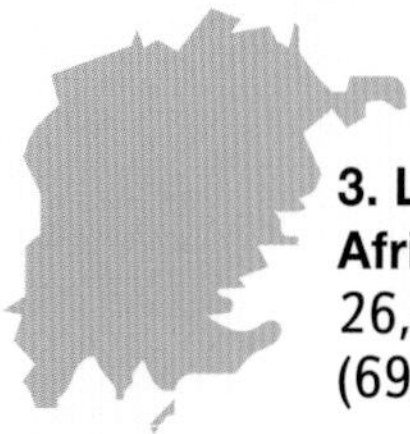

3. Lake Victoria, Africa
26,828 sq miles
(69,485 sq km)

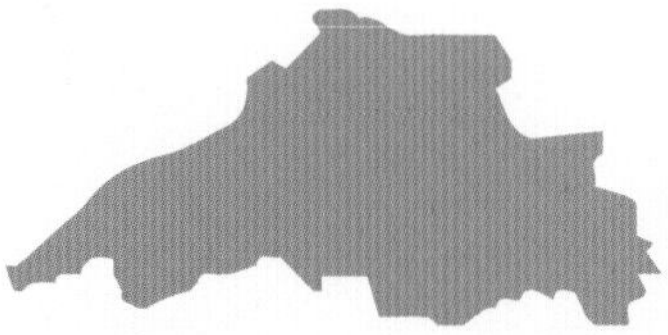

2. Lake Superior, North America
31,820 sq miles
(82,414 sq km)

LAND OF LAKES

There are more than 187,000 lakes in Finland, which gives the country the nickname "The Land of the Thousand Lakes."

The Amazon flows into the Atlantic Ocean

FASTEST-FLOWING RIVER

The Amazon is the fastest-flowing river in the world. Its waves are so strong that it is possible to surf down the river!

Mountains make up about one-fifth of the world's landscape.

1. Mount Tambora, Indonesia 1815 CE
2. Changbaishan Volcano, China 969 CE
3. Mount Thera, Santorini, Greece 1610 BCE

Three powerful volcanic eruptions

Many volcanoes are also mountains. These are three of the most powerful volcanic eruptions in history. When they erupt, volcanoes can cause great damage and change the landscape.

1. In which country would you find the Taj Mahal?
2. Atatürk was the first president of which country?
3. Which country is known for its Terra-cotta Army?
4. In which country would you find tents called ghers?

8. Rose mallow is the national flower of which country?
7. What is Japan's tallest structure called?
ASIA
Asia is the world's largest, most populated continent. China and India are big, bustling countries, where industry is growing rapidly. The main world religions all began in Asia. Many early civilizations flourished here, and the continent has many ancient sites.
6. Which country is the home of table tennis?
You can find all the answers and more quizzes on pages 120–121.
5. On which island would you find the Taipei 101 tower?

ASIA

Asia is the world's largest continent and home to more than half the world's population. Countries range from big, influential nations, such as China, to the tiny state of Qatar. The landscape includes dry deserts, green forests, snowy mountains, and vast expanses of wild, open countryside.

Dead Sea

The Dead Sea, on the borders of Israel, Jordan, and the West Bank, is a large salt lake. It gets its name because the water is too salty for any animal to live there. The salt, however, makes floating in the water easy. The salt is also used in skin and healthcare products.

SCALE

0 500 miles 1,000 miles

0 1,000 kilometers

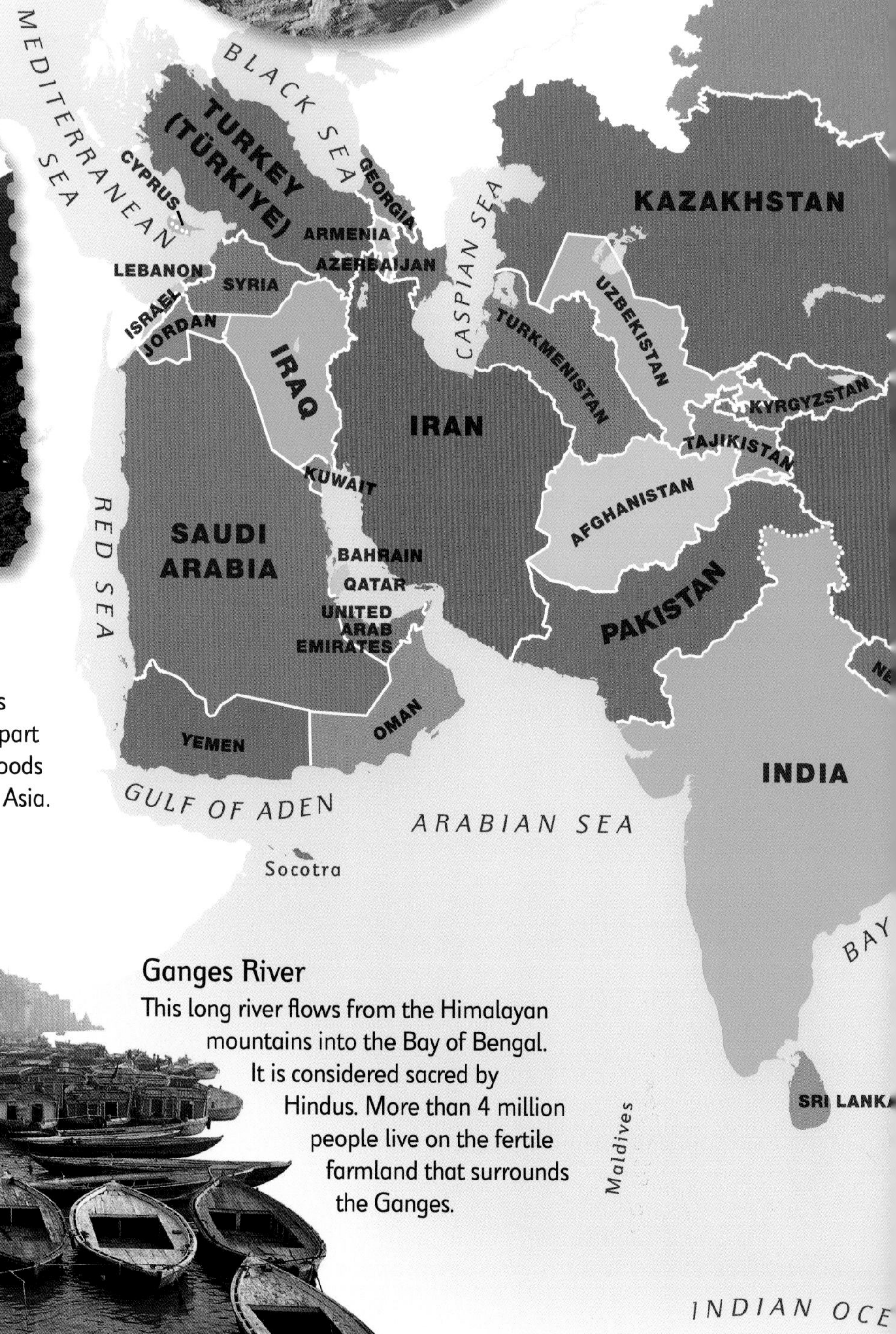

MEDITERRANEAN SEA
BLACK SEA
TURKEY (TÜRKIYE)
CYPRUS
GEORGIA
ARMENIA
AZERBAIJAN
CASPIAN SEA
KAZAKHSTAN
LEBANON
SYRIA
ISRAEL
JORDAN
IRAQ
UZBEKISTAN
TURKMENISTAN
KYRGYZSTAN
TAJIKISTAN
IRAN
KUWAIT
AFGHANISTAN
RED SEA
SAUDI ARABIA
BAHRAIN
QATAR
UNITED ARAB EMIRATES
PAKISTAN
YEMEN
OMAN
INDIA
GULF OF ADEN
ARABIAN SEA
Socotra
BAY
Maldives
SRI LANKA
INDIAN OCE

Khyber Pass

This high pass through the mountains between Afghanistan and Pakistan links central and southern Asia. It was a key part of the ancient Silk Road, along which goods were once traded between Europe and Asia.

Ganges River

This long river flows from the Himalayan mountains into the Bay of Bengal. It is considered sacred by Hindus. More than 4 million people live on the fertile farmland that surrounds the Ganges.

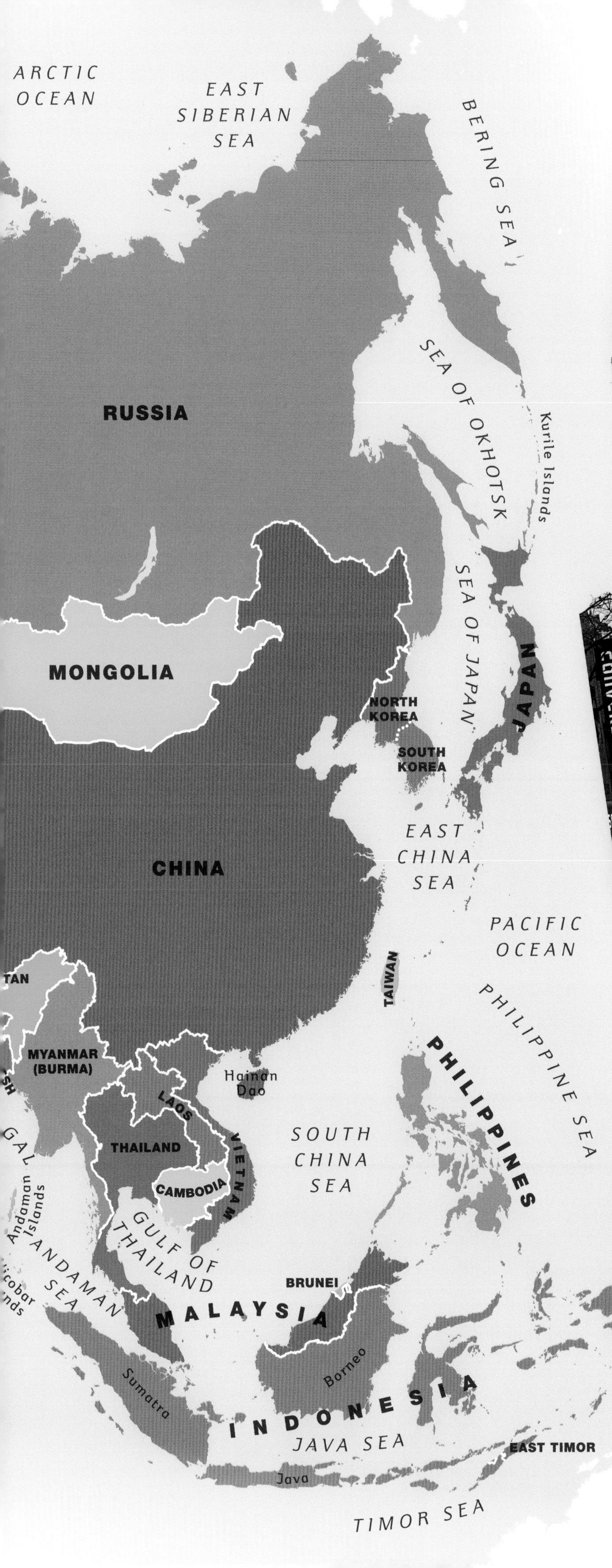
ARCTIC OCEAN
EAST SIBERIAN SEA
BERING SEA
SEA OF OKHOTSK
Kurile Islands
RUSSIA
SEA OF JAPAN
JAPAN
MONGOLIA
NORTH KOREA
SOUTH KOREA
EAST CHINA SEA
CHINA
PACIFIC OCEAN
TAIWAN
PHILIPPINE SEA
PHILIPPINES
MYANMAR (BURMA)
Hainan Dao
LAOS
THAILAND
VIETNAM
CAMBODIA
SOUTH CHINA SEA
Andaman Islands
GULF OF THAILAND
ANDAMAN SEA
BRUNEI
MALAYSIA
Borneo
Sumatra
INDONESIA
JAVA SEA
EAST TIMOR
Java
TIMOR SEA

Mongolian plains

Most of Mongolia is made up of wild, grassy plains. Around a third of the country's people live a nomadic life, roaming the plains on horseback and living in large tents called ghers.

CONVERSE
Mamonde
MIXXO

Seoul

This bustling city is the capital of South Korea. It is an exciting mix of the old and the new, with traditional street markets and ancient Buddhist temples alongside modern high-rise buildings and shops selling all the latest high-tech products.

Rice fields

Rice is grown in many parts of Asia, including China, India, and Southeast Asia. Farmers grow the rice in fields that are flooded with water, called paddy fields.

ASIAN RUSSIA AND KAZAKHSTAN

Asian Russia stretches from Europe's border to the Pacific Ocean. Much of the landscape is rugged, with few people living there. Kazakhstan lies to the southwest. This country also has large open spaces, including the vast plains of the Kazakh Steppe.

Presidential Palace
The Akorda Presidential Palace in Astana is the official workplace of the president of Kazakhstan and his staff. This impressive building opened in 2004.

Kazakhs hunting

Hunting with golden eagles
Many Kazakh people are skilled horse riders. Some hunt on horseback on the wide, open plains, using golden eagles to catch prey, such as foxes and hares.

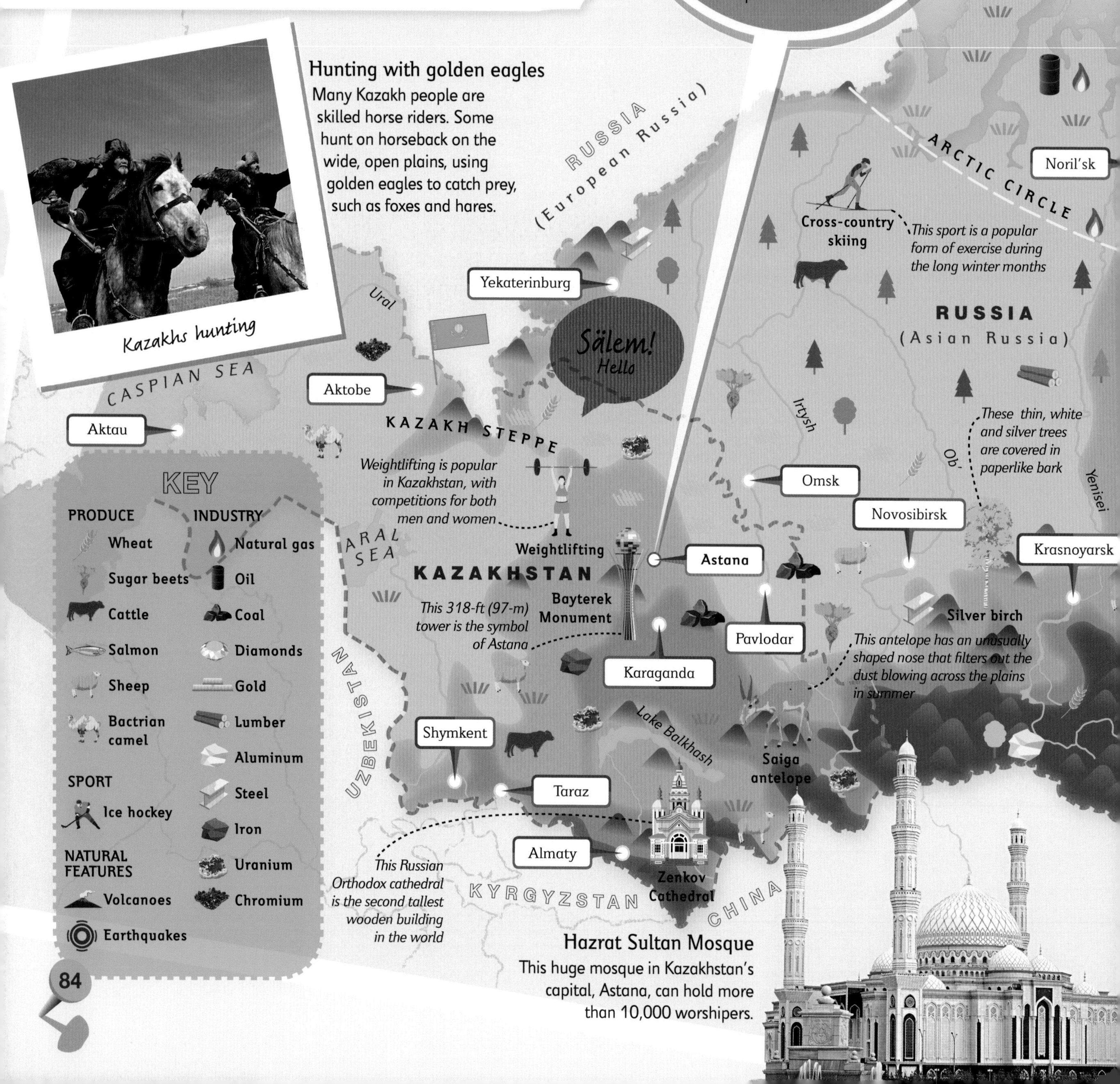

ARCTIC OCEAN
KARA S
ARCTIC CIRCLE
Noril'sk
RUSSIA (European Russia)
Cross-country skiing
This sport is a popular form of exercise during the long winter months
Yekaterinburg
Ural
RUSSIA (Asian Russia)
Sälem! Hello
CASPIAN SEA
Aktobe
Aktau
KAZAKH STEPPE
Irtysh
Ob'
Yenisei
These thin, white and silver trees are covered in paperlike bark
Weightlifting is popular in Kazakhstan, with competitions for both men and women
Omsk
Novosibirsk
Krasnoyarsk
ARAL SEA
Weightlifting
Astana
KAZAKHSTAN
Silver birch
This 318-ft (97-m) tower is the symbol of Astana
Bayterek Monument
Pavlodar
This antelope has an unusually shaped nose that filters out the dust blowing across the plains in summer
Karaganda
UZBEKISTAN
Lake Balkhash
Shymkent
Saiga antelope
Taraz
Almaty
This Russian Orthodox cathedral is the second tallest wooden building in the world
Zenkov Cathedral
KYRGYZSTAN
CHINA
KEY
PRODUCE
Wheat
Sugar beets
Cattle
Salmon
Sheep
Bactrian camel
INDUSTRY
Natural gas
Oil
Coal
Diamonds
Gold
Lumber
Aluminum
Steel
Iron
Uranium
Chromium
SPORT
Ice hockey
NATURAL FEATURES
Volcanoes
Earthquakes

Hazrat Sultan Mosque
This huge mosque in Kazakhstan's capital, Astana, can hold more than 10,000 worshipers.

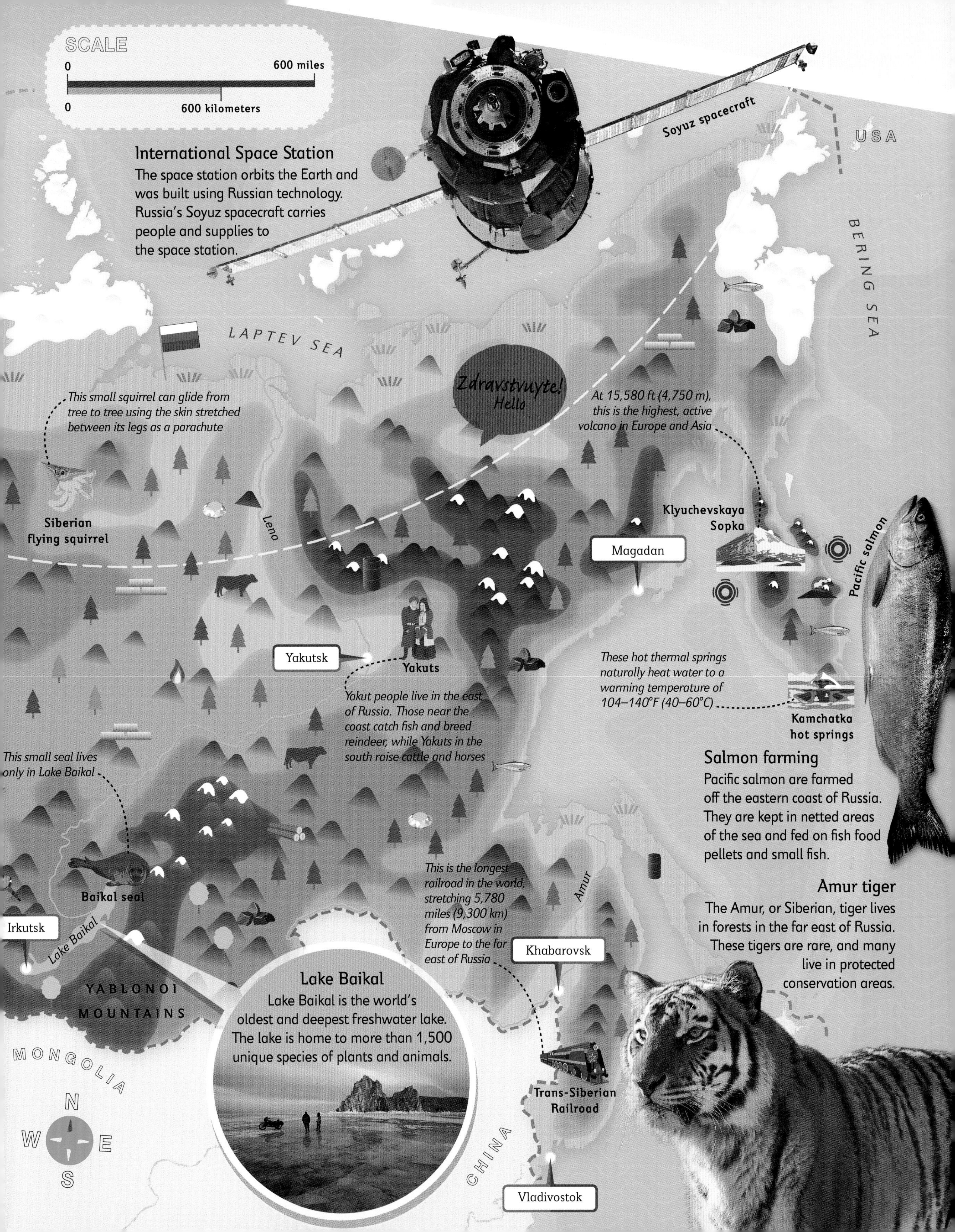

SCALE
0
600 miles
0
600 kilometers
Soyuz spacecraft
USA
BERING SEA
LAPTEV SEA
Zdravstvuyte!
Hello
This small squirrel can glide from tree to tree using the skin stretched between its legs as a parachute
Siberian flying squirrel
Lena
At 15,580 ft (4,750 m), this is the highest, active volcano in Europe and Asia
Klyuchevskaya Sopka
Magadan
Pacific salmon
Yakutsk
Yakuts
Yakut people live in the east of Russia. Those near the coast catch fish and breed reindeer, while Yakuts in the south raise cattle and horses
These hot thermal springs naturally heat water to a warming temperature of 104–140°F (40–60°C)
Kamchatka hot springs
This small seal lives only in Lake Baikal
Baikal seal
Irkutsk
Lake Baikal
This is the longest railroad in the world, stretching 5,780 miles (9,300 km) from Moscow in Europe to the far east of Russia
Amur
Khabarovsk
YABLONOI MOUNTAINS
MONGOLIA
N
W
E
S
Trans-Siberian Railroad
CHINA
Vladivostok

International Space Station

The space station orbits the Earth and was built using Russian technology. Russia's Soyuz spacecraft carries people and supplies to the space station.

Lake Baikal

Lake Baikal is the world's oldest and deepest freshwater lake. The lake is home to more than 1,500 unique species of plants and animals.

Salmon farming

Pacific salmon are farmed off the eastern coast of Russia. They are kept in netted areas of the sea and fed on fish food pellets and small fish.

Amur tiger

The Amur, or Siberian, tiger lives in forests in the far east of Russia. These tigers are rare, and many live in protected conservation areas.

TURKEY

Turkey (Türkiye) lies partly in Asia and partly in Europe and is influenced by both Eastern and Western culture. Istanbul, the historic city on the Bosphorus River, links the two continents. This huge country has a varied landscape, and its mountains, lakes, beaches, and ancient sites make it attractive to tourists.

Topkapı Palace

This grand palace was once home to the rulers of the Ottoman Empire. Today, it is a museum, containing many exhibition halls.

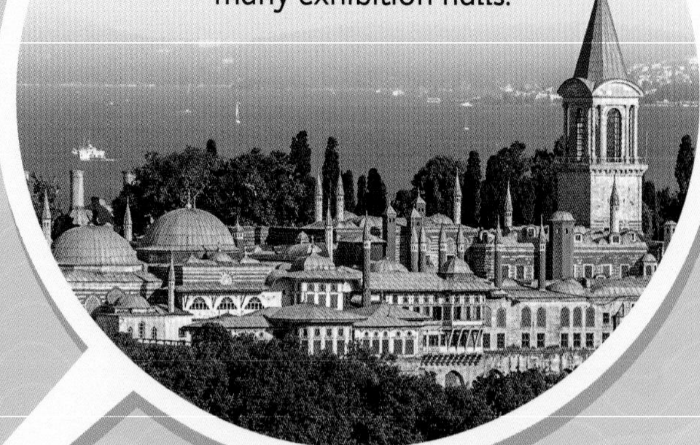

Wall tiles, Topkapi Palace

Iznik tiles

These beautiful painted tiles are named after the town where they were made. They decorate the walls of the Topkapi Palace in Istanbul.

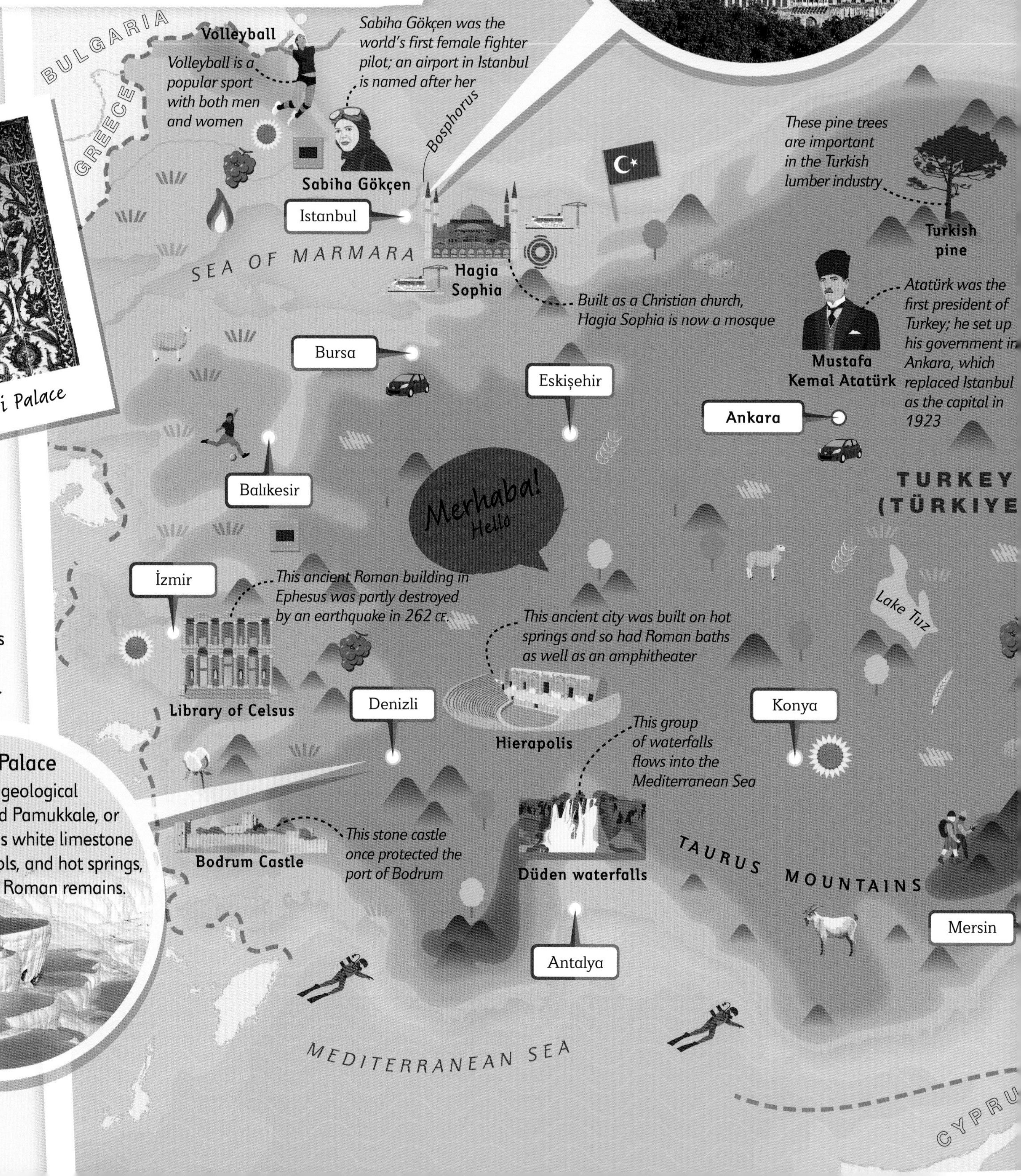

BULGARIA
GREECE
Volleyball
Volleyball is a popular sport with both men and women
Sabiha Gökçen was the world's first female fighter pilot; an airport in Istanbul is named after her
Sabiha Gökçen
Bosphorus
Istanbul
SEA OF MARMARA
Hagia Sophia
Built as a Christian church, Hagia Sophia is now a mosque
These pine trees are important in the Turkish lumber industry
Turkish pine
Atatürk was the first president of Turkey; he set up his government in Ankara, which replaced Istanbul as the capital in 1923
Mustafa Kemal Atatürk
Bursa
Eskişehir
Ankara
Balıkesir
Merhaba! Hello
TURKEY (TÜRKIYE
Lake Tuz
İzmir
This ancient Roman building in Ephesus was partly destroyed by an earthquake in 262 CE.
This ancient city was built on hot springs and so had Roman baths as well as an amphitheater
Library of Celsus
Denizli
Hierapolis
Konya
This group of waterfalls flows into the Mediterranean Sea
This stone castle once protected the port of Bodrum
Bodrum Castle
Düden waterfalls
TAURUS MOUNTAINS
Mersin
Antalya
MEDITERRANEAN SEA
CYPRU

Cotton Palace

This unique geological formation is called Pamukkale, or Cotton Palace. It has white limestone terraces, thermal pools, and hot springs, as well as Ancient Roman remains.

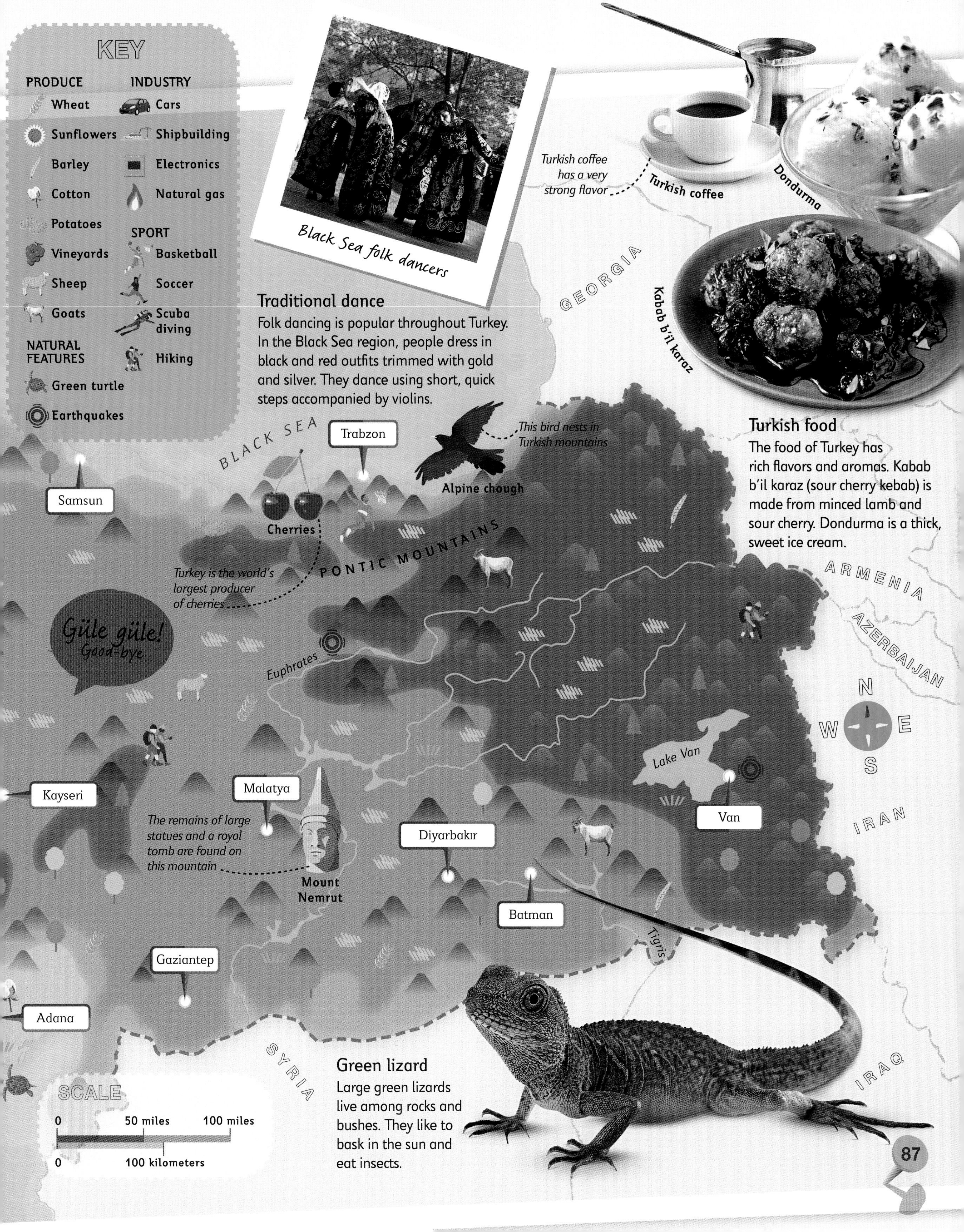
KEY
PRODUCE
Wheat
Sunflowers
Barley
Cotton
Potatoes
Vineyards
Sheep
Goats
INDUSTRY
Cars
Shipbuilding
Electronics
Natural gas
SPORT
Basketball
Soccer
Scuba diving
Hiking
NATURAL FEATURES
Green turtle
Earthquakes
Turkish coffee has a very strong flavor
Turkish coffee
Dondurma
Kabab b'il karaz
GEORGIA
BLACK SEA
Trabzon
Samsun
This bird nests in Turkish mountains
Alpine chough
Cherries
Turkey is the world's largest producer of cherries
PONTIC MOUNTAINS
ARMENIA
AZERBAIJAN
Güle güle!
Good-bye
Euphrates
Kayseri
Malatya
The remains of large statues and a royal tomb are found on this mountain
Mount Nemrut
Diyarbakır
Batman
Lake Van
Van
IRAN
N
W
E
S
Tigris
Gaziantep
Adana
SYRIA
IRAQ
SCALE
0
50 miles
100 miles
0
100 kilometers

Black Sea folk dancers

Traditional dance

Folk dancing is popular throughout Turkey. In the Black Sea region, people dress in black and red outfits trimmed with gold and silver. They dance using short, quick steps accompanied by violins.

Turkish food

The food of Turkey has rich flavors and aromas. Kabab b'il karaz (sour cherry kebab) is made from minced lamb and sour cherry. Dondurma is a thick, sweet ice cream.

Green lizard

Large green lizards live among rocks and bushes. They like to bask in the sun and eat insects.

SYRIA AND LEBANON

Syria is largely hot desert, but most people live in the cooler, fertile coastal areas by the Mediterranean Sea. Lebanon is a small, coastal country with a varied religious and cultural history. The land covered by Syria and Lebanon was once part of the Roman Empire.

Woman weaving on a loom

Carpet weaving

Beautiful, handwoven carpets are produced in Syria. Their highly detailed, traditional patterns come in a mix of colors, with red and black being particularly popular.

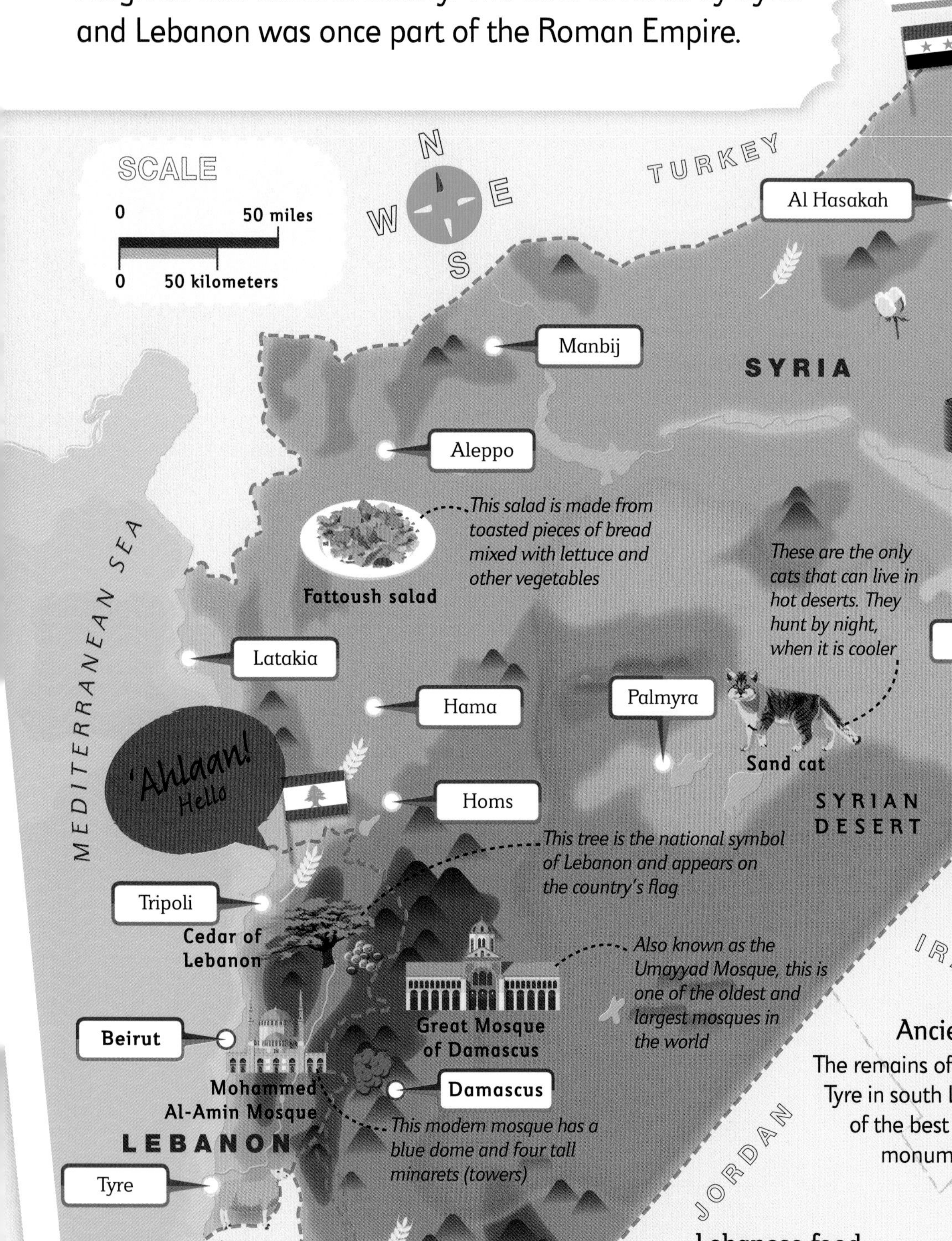

KEY
PRODUCE
Olives
Wheat
Vineyards
Sheep
Cotton
INDUSTRY
Oil
SCALE
0
50 miles
0
50 kilometers
N
E
S
W
TURKEY
Al Hasakah
Manbij
SYRIA
Aleppo
This salad is made from toasted pieces of bread mixed with lettuce and other vegetables
Fattoush salad
MEDITERRANEAN SEA
These are the only cats that can live in hot deserts. They hunt by night, when it is cooler
Abu Kamal
Latakia
Hama
Palmyra
Sand cat
'Ahlaan!
Hello
Homs
SYRIAN DESERT
This tree is the national symbol of Lebanon and appears on the country's flag
Tripoli
Cedar of Lebanon
Also known as the Umayyad Mosque, this is one of the oldest and largest mosques in the world
IRAQ
Great Mosque of Damascus
Beirut
Mohammed Al-Amin Mosque
Damascus
This modern mosque has a blue dome and four tall minarets (towers)
LEBANON
Tyre
JORDAN
ISRAEL

Mortuary statue

Umayyad dinar

Syrian artefacts

Archeologists have uncovered many ancient artifacts in Syria. These include gold coins, such as Umayyad dinars, and mortuary statues, used to mark graves.

Ancient architecture

The remains of the Roman city at Tyre in south Lebanon are some of the best preserved ancient monuments in the world.

Triumphal Arch at Tyre

Lebanese food

Lebanese food includes delicious snacks such as fatayer, which is a mini pie filled with meat, spinach, or cheese, and light dishes such as tabbouleh, a salad of bulgur wheat, tomatoes, onions, and herbs.

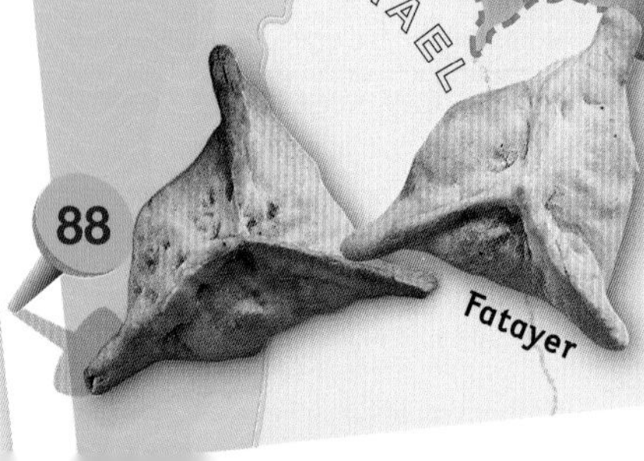

Fatayer

Tabbouleh

ISRAEL AND JORDAN

Israel, the Palestinian territories, and Jordan are part of an area known as the Holy Land, home to Jewish, Muslim, and Christian communities for thousands of years. While Israel and Jordan are recognized countries, the Palestinian people have been striving to create a country of their own for decades.

Bedouin brewing coffee

Bedouin hospitality

The Bedouin tribes that travel across the desert are known for their hospitality. Guests are welcomed and served food and drink, including freshly brewed coffee and spiced tea.

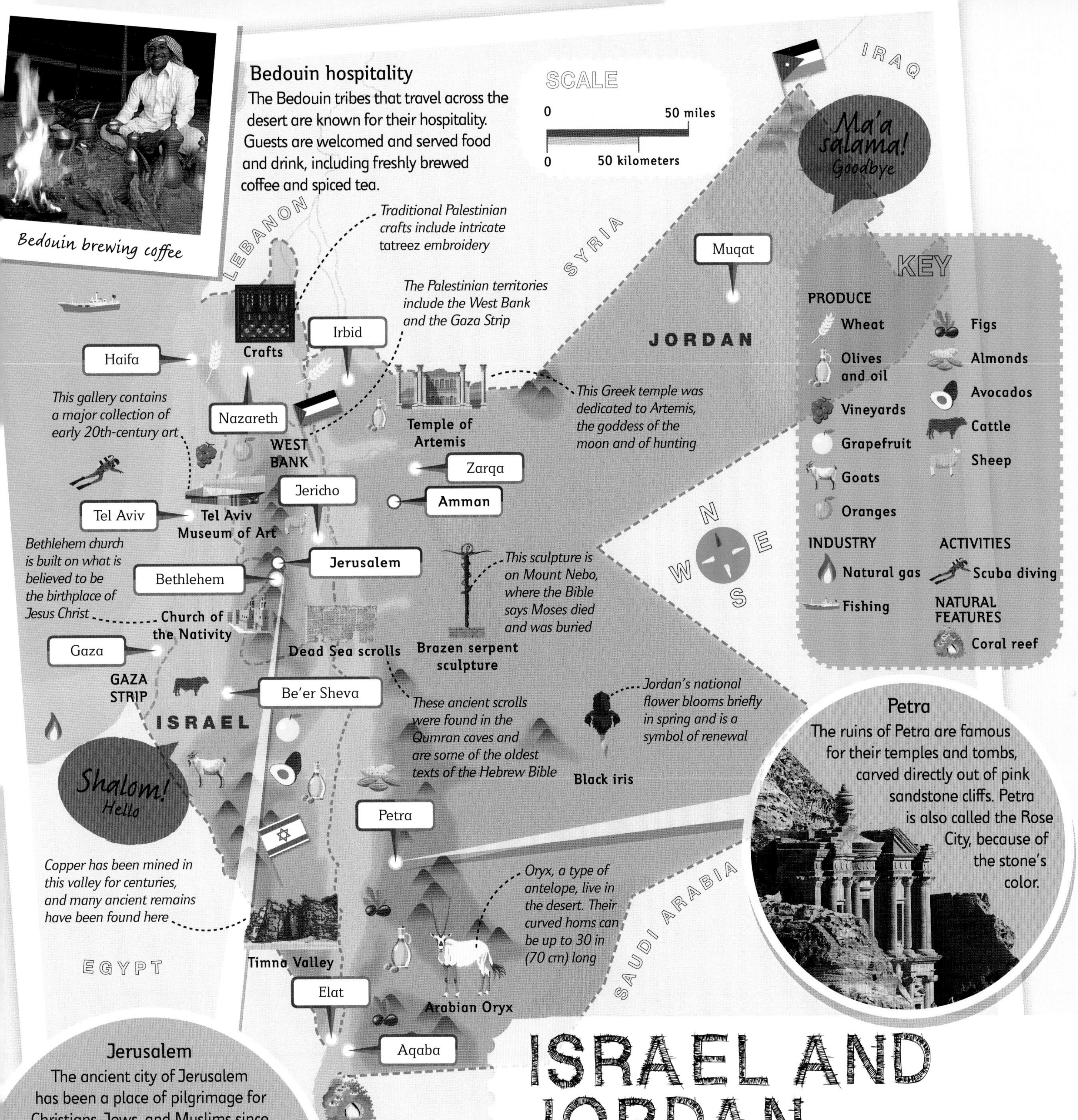

SCALE
0
50 miles
0
50 kilometers
IRAQ
SYRIA
LEBANON
EGYPT
SAUDI ARABIA
JORDAN
ISRAEL
WEST BANK
GAZA STRIP
Ma'a salama! Goodbye
Shalom! Hello
Muqat
Irbid
Haifa
Crafts
Nazareth
Temple of Artemis
Zarqa
Amman
Jericho
Tel Aviv
Tel Aviv Museum of Art
Jerusalem
Bethlehem
Church of the Nativity
Gaza
Dead Sea scrolls
Brazen serpent sculpture
Be'er Sheva
Black iris
Petra
Timna Valley
Elat
Aqaba
Arabian Oryx
Traditional Palestinian crafts include intricate tatreez embroidery
The Palestinian territories include the West Bank and the Gaza Strip
This gallery contains a major collection of early 20th-century art
This Greek temple was dedicated to Artemis, the goddess of the moon and of hunting
Bethlehem church is built on what is believed to be the birthplace of Jesus Christ
This sculpture is on Mount Nebo, where the Bible says Moses died and was buried
These ancient scrolls were found in the Qumran caves and are some of the oldest texts of the Hebrew Bible
Jordan's national flower blooms briefly in spring and is a symbol of renewal
Copper has been mined in this valley for centuries, and many ancient remains have been found here
Oryx, a type of antelope, live in the desert. Their curved horns can be up to 30 in (70 cm) long
N
E
S
W
KEY
PRODUCE
Wheat
Olives and oil
Vineyards
Grapefruit
Goats
Oranges
Figs
Almonds
Avocados
Cattle
Sheep
INDUSTRY
Natural gas
Fishing
ACTIVITIES
Scuba diving
NATURAL FEATURES
Coral reef

Petra

The ruins of Petra are famous for their temples and tombs, carved directly out of pink sandstone cliffs. Petra is also called the Rose City, because of the stone's color.

Jerusalem

The ancient city of Jerusalem has been a place of pilgrimage for Christians, Jews, and Muslims since biblical times.

IRAN, IRAQ, AND SAUDI ARABIA

Iran, Iraq, and Saudi Arabia all contain large areas of hot, sandy desert, with huge reserves of oil and natural gas. Some of the world's earliest civilizations flourished in these lands, and all three countries have many ancient ruins and other treasures.

Isfahan tile

Colorful tiles

The Safavid Empire ruled Persia (modern-day Iran) from the 14th to the 18th century. The capital of this empire was Isfahan, which was known for its fine art, including colorful tiles.

Fine foods

This region is noted for producing some of the world's most prized delicacies. These include high-quality dates, the delicate spice saffron, and the best and most expensive caviar (fish eggs).

Dates
Saffron
Caviar

Ur treasure

Ur was an important ancient city in what is now Iraq. Many treasures were found in tombs there. These include intricate gold jewelry and a lyre (type of harp) decorated with a golden bull's head.

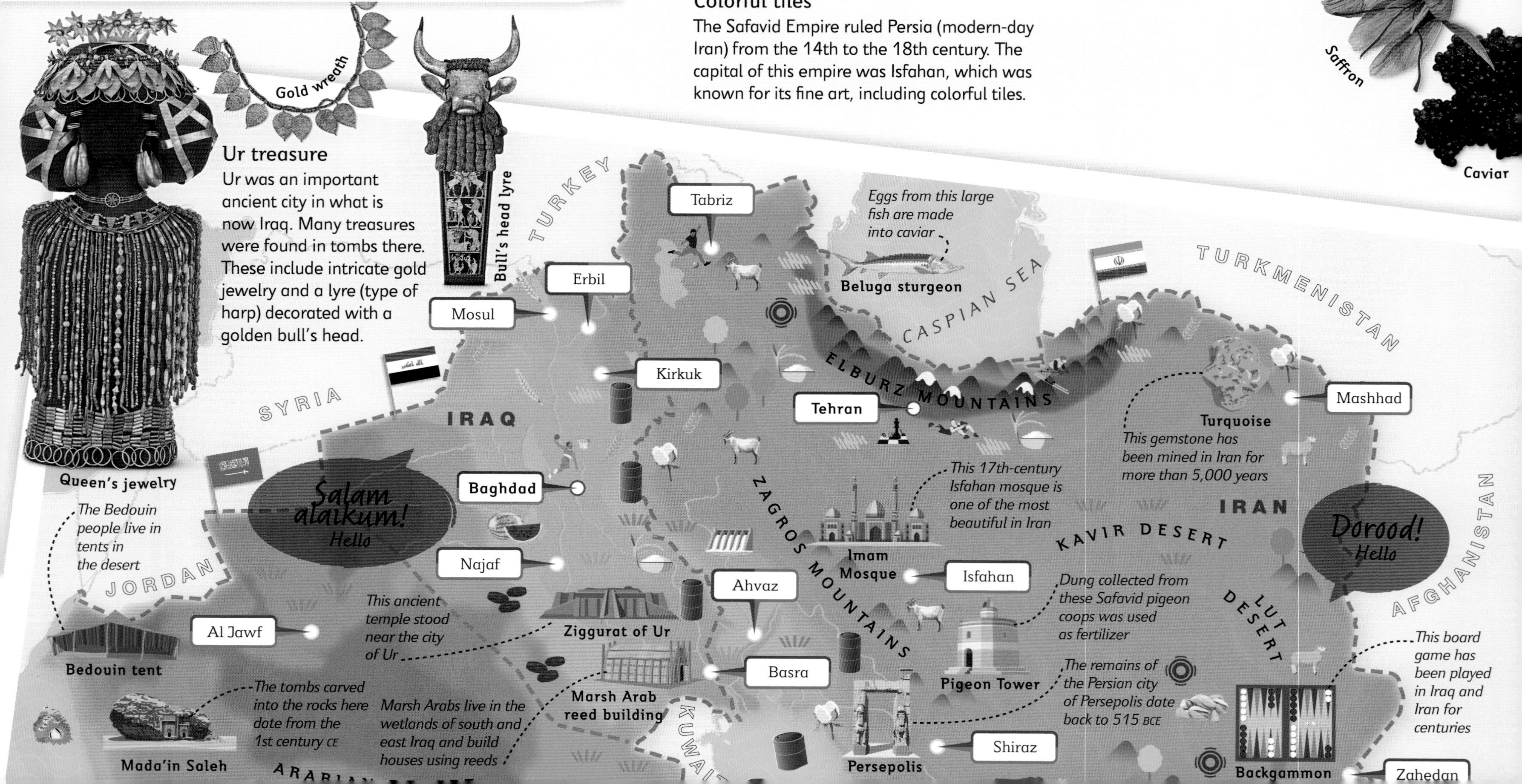

Queen's jewelry
Gold wreath
Bull's head lyre
TURKEY
SYRIA
JORDAN
IRAQ
KUWAIT
IRAN
TURKMENISTAN
AFGHANISTAN
CASPIAN SEA
ELBURZ MOUNTAINS
ZAGROS MOUNTAINS
KAVIR DESERT
LUT DESERT
Tabriz
Erbil
Mosul
Kirkuk
Tehran
Baghdad
Najaf
Ahvaz
Basra
Isfahan
Shiraz
Mashhad
Zahedan
Al Jawf
Salam alaikum! Hello
Dorood! Hello
Eggs from this large fish are made into caviar
Beluga sturgeon
Turquoise
This gemstone has been mined in Iran for more than 5,000 years
This 17th-century Isfahan mosque is one of the most beautiful in Iran
Imam Mosque
Dung collected from these Safavid pigeon coops was used as fertilizer
Pigeon Tower
The remains of the Persian city of Persepolis date back to 515 BCE
Persepolis
This board game has been played in Iraq and Iran for centuries
Backgammon
The Bedouin people live in tents in the desert
Bedouin tent
The tombs carved into the rocks here date from the 1st century CE
Mada'in Saleh
This ancient temple stood near the city of Ur
Ziggurat of Ur
Marsh Arabs live in the wetlands of south and east Iraq and build houses using reeds
Marsh Arab reed building

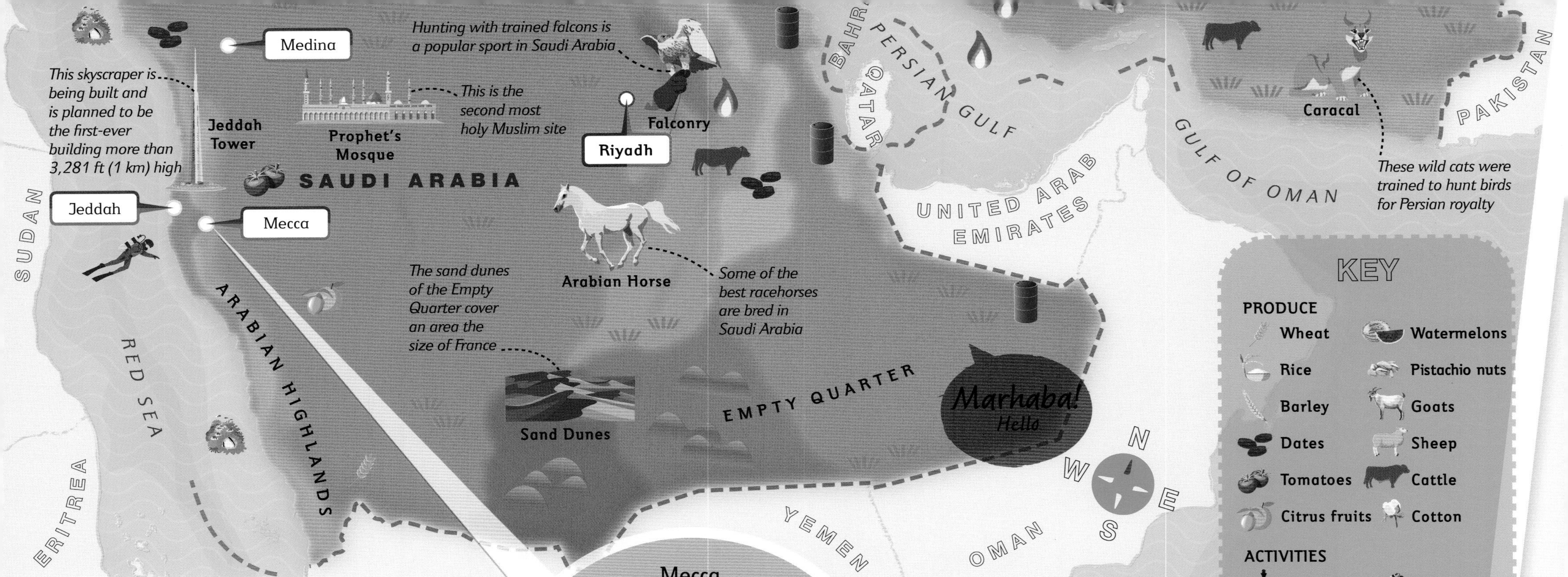

Medina
Hunting with trained falcons is a popular sport in Saudi Arabia
This skyscraper is being built and is planned to be the first-ever building more than 3,281 ft (1 km) high
Jeddah Tower
Prophet's Mosque
This is the second most holy Muslim site
Falconry
Riyadh
SAUDI ARABIA
Jeddah
Mecca
SUDAN
ARABIAN HIGHLANDS
RED SEA
ERITREA
ETHIOPIA
The sand dunes of the Empty Quarter cover an area the size of France
Arabian Horse
Some of the best racehorses are bred in Saudi Arabia
Sand Dunes
EMPTY QUARTER
Marhaba!
Hello
YEMEN
OMAN
N
W
E
S
ARABIAN SEA
BAHR
PERSIAN GULF
QATAR
UNITED ARAB EMIRATES
GULF OF OMAN
Caracal
These wild cats were trained to hunt birds for Persian royalty
PAKISTAN
KEY
PRODUCE
Wheat
Rice
Barley
Dates
Tomatoes
Citrus fruits
Watermelons
Pistachio nuts
Goats
Sheep
Cattle
Cotton
ACTIVITIES
Chess
Skiing
Basketball
Scuba diving
Wrestling
Soccer
INDUSTRY
Oil
Gas
Hydroelectric power
NATURAL FEATURES
Coral reef
Earthquakes
SCALE
0
100 miles
200 miles
0
200 kilometers

Nasir al-Mulk Mosque

Mecca

Mecca is the birthplace of the prophet Muhammad and is the holiest city in the Muslim world. Many Muslims travel here every year to pray at the sacred Kaaba shrine.

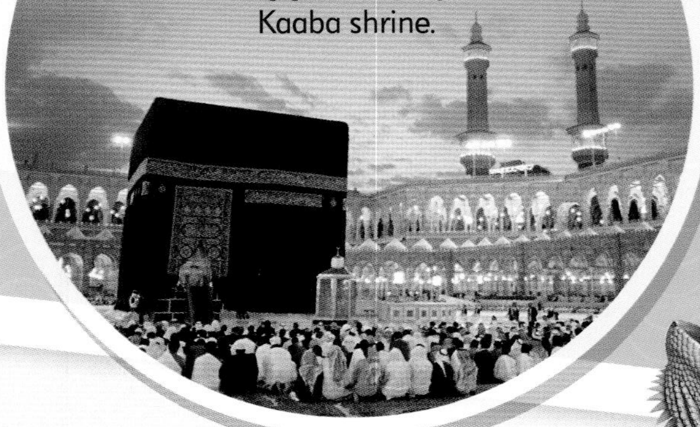

Stained glass

Stained glass is widely used in mosques. The windows of the Nasir al-Mulk Mosque in Shiraz, Iran are some of the most colorful. As sunlight streams through them, the building is flooded with dazzling colors.

Veiled chameleon

This chameleon is native to the southern part of Saudi Arabia, living in trees and bushes in the mountains and valleys. It catches insects by shooting out its long, sticky tongue.

AFGHANISTAN

Afghanistan lies between Central Asia and China. In ancient times, Chinese silk and other goods were traded along the Silk Road that passed through the Hindu Kush mountains. Temperatures in the deserts and mountains of Afghanistan vary from very hot in summer to freezing cold in winter.

Band-e Amir lakes

Six deep lakes lie side by side at Band-e Amir, in the Hindu Kush mountains. They are part of Afghanistan's first national park.

Citadel of Herat

This huge castle has 18 towers and 6½-ft (2-m) thick brick walls. It stands on the site of a fort built by Alexander the Great in 330 BCE.

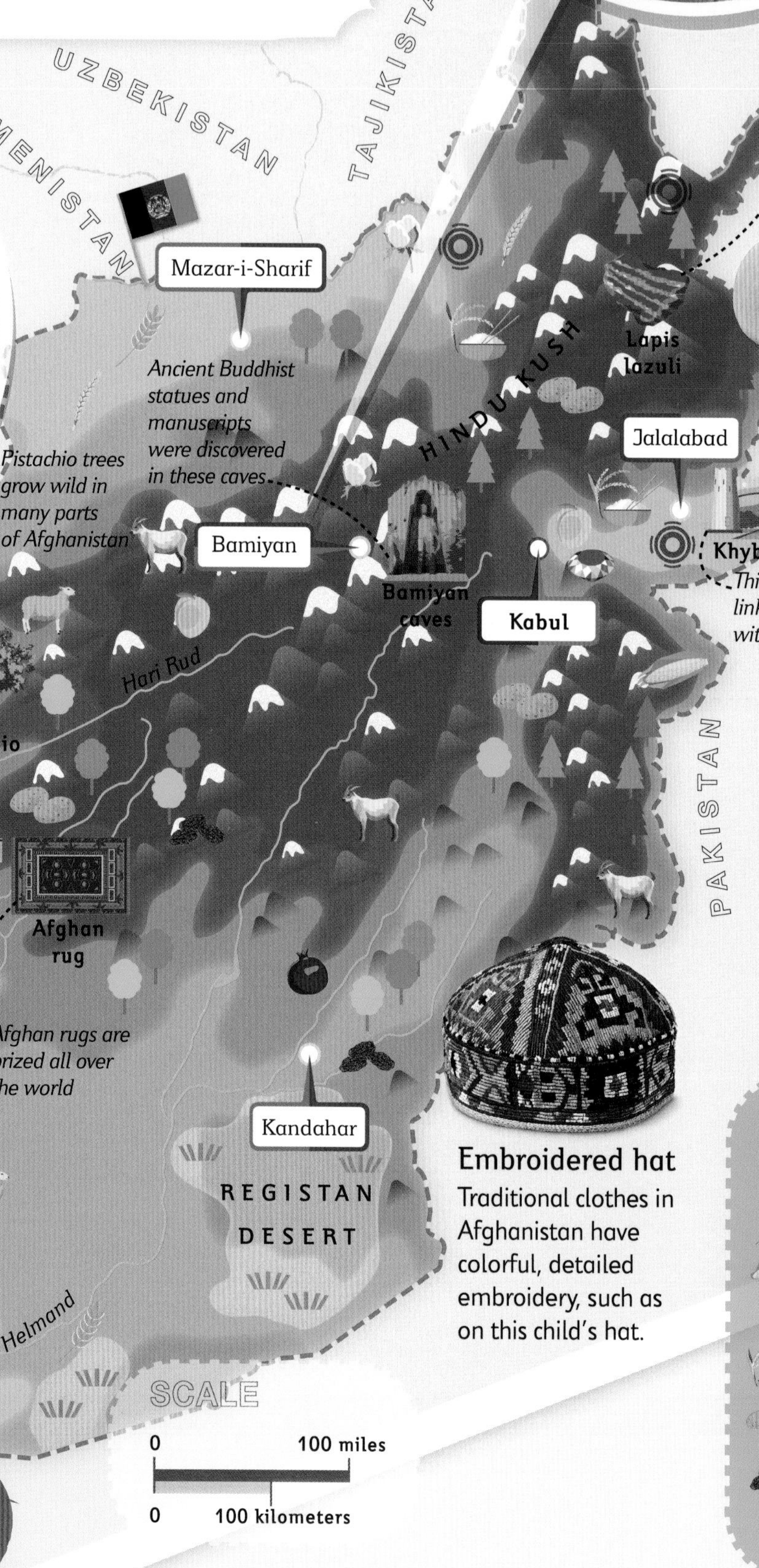
N
W
E
S
CHINA
TURKMENISTAN
UZBEKISTAN
TAJIKISTAN
IRAN
PAKISTAN
These unusual sheep have huge, spiraling horns, which can be up to 27 in (70 cm) long
Marco Polo sheep
This highly prized gemstone has been mined in Afghanistan for more than 5,000 years
Lapis lazuli
Mazar-i-Sharif
Ancient Buddhist statues and manuscripts were discovered in these caves
HINDU KUSH
Jalalabad
Pistachio trees grow wild in many parts of Afghanistan
Bamiyan
Bamiyan caves
Kabul
Khyber Pass
This mountain pass links Afghanistan with Pakistan
Hari Rud
Herat
Pistachio tree
Jama Masjid
This large mosque in Herat is covered in beautiful glazed tiles
Afghan rug
Afghan rugs are prized all over the world
Farah Rud
Kandahar
REGISTAN DESERT
Helmand
SCALE
0
100 miles
0
100 kilometers
Salaam!
Hello

Pistachios
Apricots
Pomegranates

Fruit and nuts

Afghanistan's farms produce some of the tastiest nuts and fruit in the world. These include large quantities of pistachio nuts, apricots, and pomegranates.

Embroidered hat

Traditional clothes in Afghanistan have colorful, detailed embroidery, such as on this child's hat.

Bactrian gold

This hoard of gold artifacts was discovered in ancient burial mounds in northern Afghanistan in 1978. It includes jewelry, coins, and figures.

KEY

PRODUCE
- Wheat
- Corn
- Barley
- Rice
- Potatoes
- Raisins
- Apricots
- Cotton
- Sheep
- Goats
- Pomegranates

NATURAL FEATURES
- Sapphires
- Earthquakes

PAKISTAN

Pakistan has the world's fifth largest population. Many people live along the Indus River and its tributaries (streams), which flow down through the middle of the country, providing water to irrigate the fertile farmland along the riverbanks. Farming is Pakistan's main source of income.

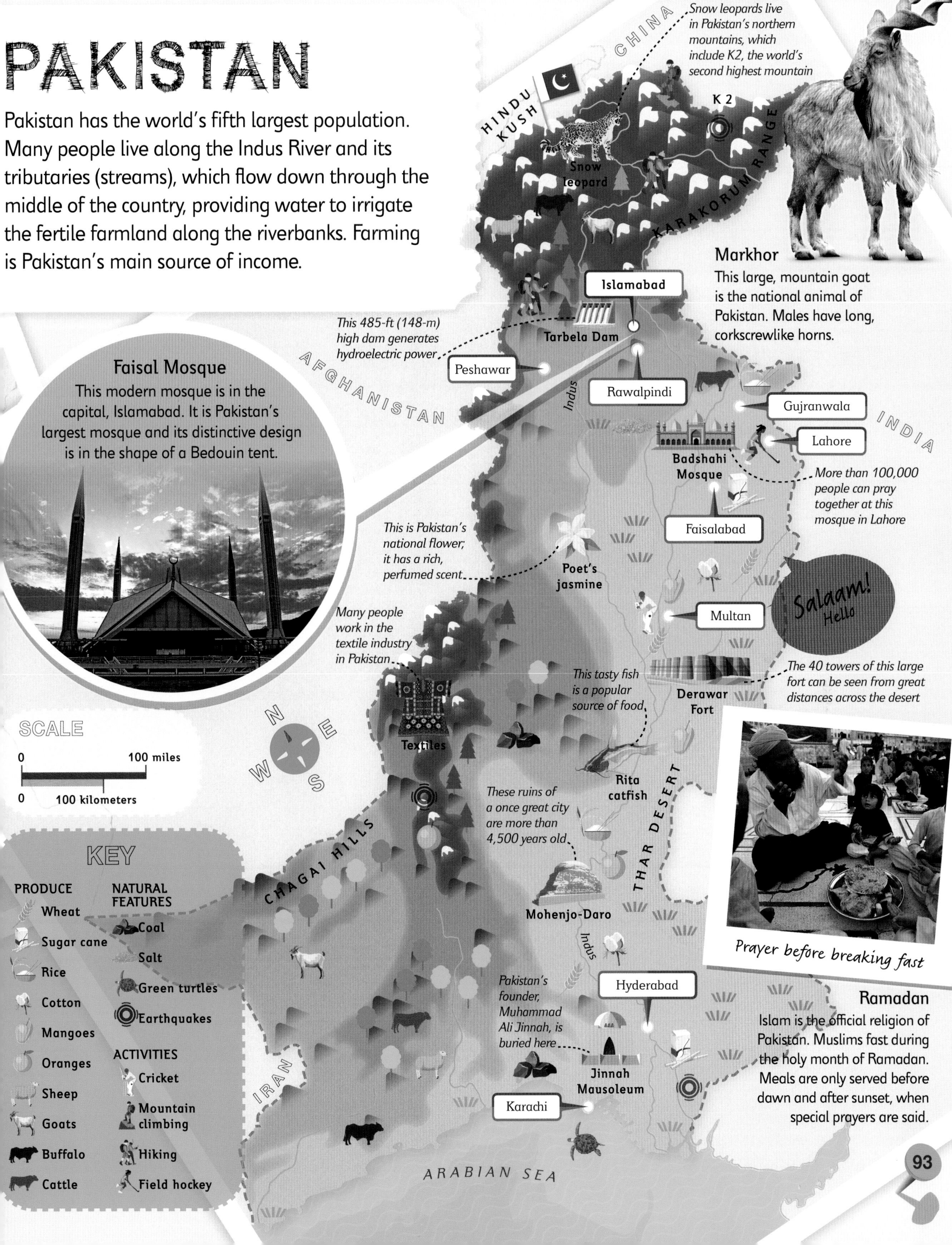

CHINA
HINDU KUSH
KARAKORUM RANGE
K 2
Snow leopards live in Pakistan's northern mountains, which include K2, the world's second highest mountain
Snow leopard
Islamabad
This 485-ft (148-m) high dam generates hydroelectric power
Tarbela Dam
Peshawar
AFGHANISTAN
Rawalpindi
Indus
Gujranwala
INDIA
Lahore
Badshahi Mosque
More than 100,000 people can pray together at this mosque in Lahore
Faisalabad
This is Pakistan's national flower; it has a rich, perfumed scent
Poet's jasmine
Multan
Salaam! Hello
Many people work in the textile industry in Pakistan
The 40 towers of this large fort can be seen from great distances across the desert
Derawar Fort
This tasty fish is a popular source of food
Textiles
Rita catfish
N
E
S
W
SCALE
0
100 miles
0
100 kilometers
These ruins of a once great city are more than 4,500 years old
THAR DESERT
CHAGAI HILLS
Mohenjo-Daro
Indus
KEY
PRODUCE
Wheat
Sugar cane
Rice
Cotton
Mangoes
Oranges
Sheep
Goats
Buffalo
Cattle
NATURAL FEATURES
Coal
Salt
Green turtles
Earthquakes
ACTIVITIES
Cricket
Mountain climbing
Hiking
Field hockey
Pakistan's founder, Muhammad Ali Jinnah, is buried here
Hyderabad
Jinnah Mausoleum
Karachi
IRAN
ARABIAN SEA

Markhor

This large, mountain goat is the national animal of Pakistan. Males have long, corkscrewlike horns.

Faisal Mosque

This modern mosque is in the capital, Islamabad. It is Pakistan's largest mosque and its distinctive design is in the shape of a Bedouin tent.

Prayer before breaking fast

Ramadan

Islam is the official religion of Pakistan. Muslims fast during the holy month of Ramadan. Meals are only served before dawn and after sunset, when special prayers are said.

INDIA AND SRI LANKA

India is a colorful and crowded country. It stretches from the snowy Himalayan mountains to the warm waters of the Indian Ocean. Sri Lanka is a tropical island that is known for its tea plantations.

Fragrant spices

Rich and flavorful spices are grown in India and Sri Lanka. Ginger adds warmth to sweet and savory dishes and several different spices are used in curries.

Ginger
Selection of spices

Throwing colored paint

Holi Festival

The Hindu spring festival celebrates color and love. People throw paint powder and get covered in bright colors.

Cricketers in Mumbai

Cricket

Cricket is the most popular sport in India. It is played across the country on grass cricket fields like this one in the city of Mumbai.

Peacock

The peacock is the national bird of India. The males have amazing tail feathers with swirled patterns that look like eyes.

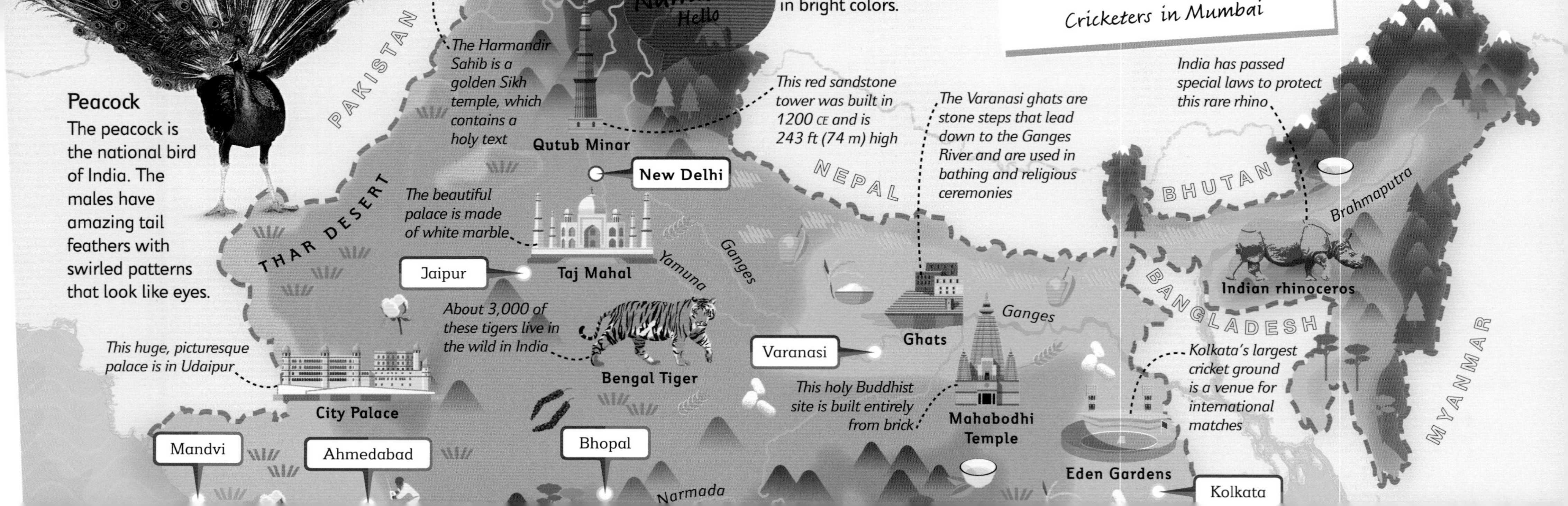

HIMALAYAS
Srinagar
Golden Temple
The Harmandir Sahib is a golden Sikh temple, which contains a holy text
Namaste!
Hello
Qutub Minar
This red sandstone tower was built in 1200 CE and is 243 ft (74 m) high
New Delhi
PAKISTAN
THAR DESERT
The beautiful palace is made of white marble
Taj Mahal
Jaipur
Yamuna
Ganges
About 3,000 of these tigers live in the wild in India
Bengal Tiger
This huge, picturesque palace is in Udaipur
City Palace
Mandvi
Ahmedabad
Bhopal
Narmada
NEPAL
The Varanasi ghats are stone steps that lead down to the Ganges River and are used in bathing and religious ceremonies
Ghats
Ganges
Varanasi
This holy Buddhist site is built entirely from brick
Mahabodhi Temple
CHINA
India has passed special laws to protect this rare rhino
BHUTAN
Brahmaputra
Indian rhinoceros
BANGLADESH
Kolkata's largest cricket ground is a venue for international matches
Eden Gardens
Kolkata
MYANMAR

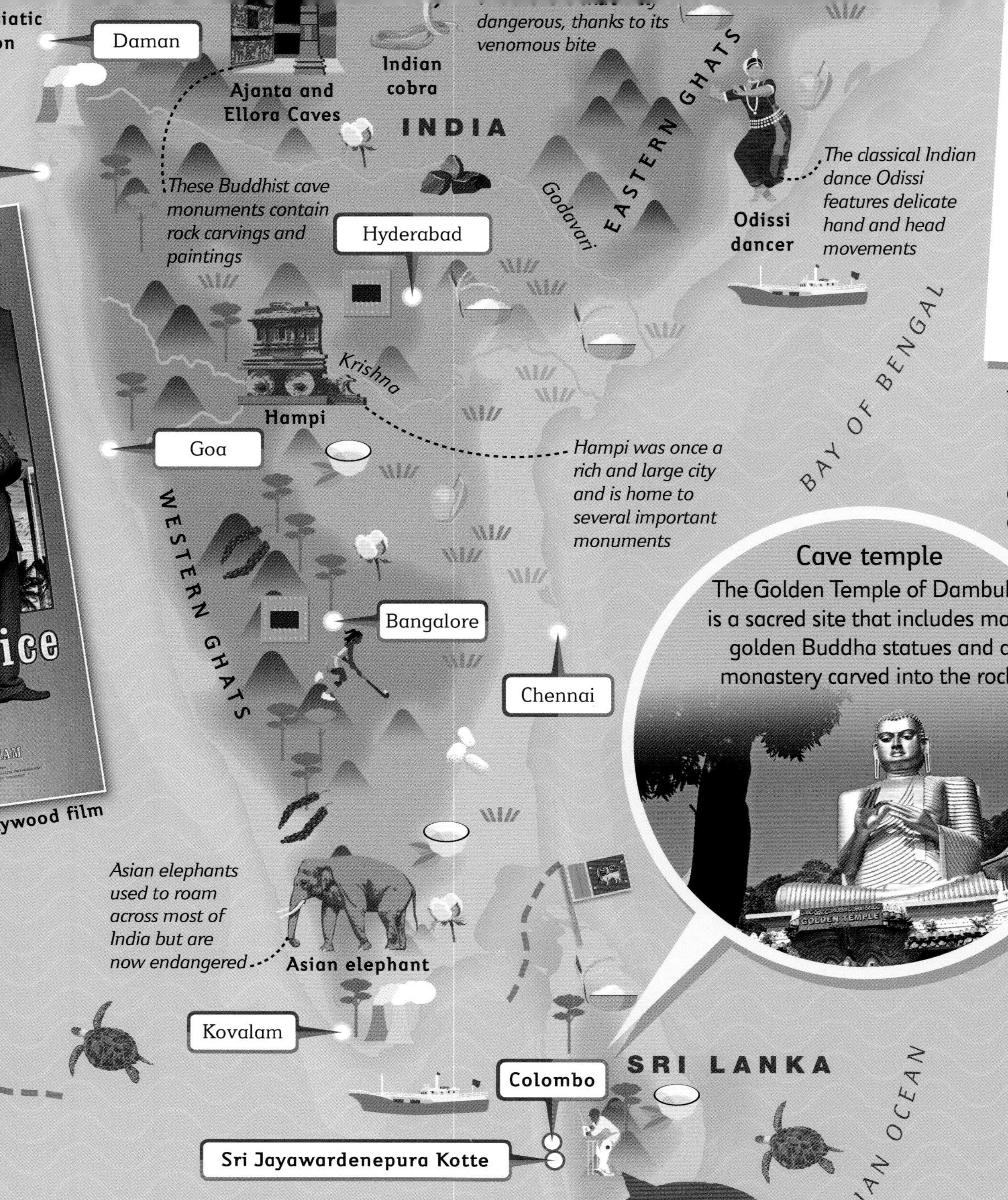
This lion is only found in the Gir Forest region of northwest India
Asiatic lion
Diu
Daman
Mumbai
ARABIAN SEA
Ajanta and Ellora Caves
These Buddhist cave monuments contain rock carvings and paintings
Indian cobra
dangerous, thanks to its venomous bite
INDIA
Hyderabad
Godavari
EASTERN GHATS
Odissi dancer
The classical Indian dance Odissi features delicate hand and head movements
Krishna
Hampi
Hampi was once a rich and large city and is home to several important monuments
Goa
WESTERN GHATS
Bangalore
Chennai
BAY OF BENGAL
Asian elephants used to roam across most of India but are now endangered
Asian elephant
Kovalam
Colombo
Sri Jayawardenepura Kotte
SRI LANKA
Kuhomadu!
Hello
INDIAN OCEAN
Andaman Islands
Nicobar Islands
N
W
E
S

SPECTACULAR, ROMANTIC, FUNNY AND SO SEXY.
Bride & Prejudice
BEND IT LIKE BECKHAM
Poster for a Bollywood film

Bollywood

Bollywood is one of the world's biggest film industries. It is based in Mumbai, and its movies are popular all over the world. The films feature songs, dancing, romance, and adventure. They are shot in bright, bold colors, like the posters that advertise them.

Kathakali performers

Kathakali

In Kerala state, South India, Kathakali performers wear face paint and costumes and perform dances that act out traditional stories.

Cave temple

The Golden Temple of Dambulla is a sacred site that includes many golden Buddha statues and a monastery carved into the rock.

KEY

PRODUCE
- Rice
- Cotton
- Tea
- Mangoes
- Black pepper
- Wheat

INDUSTRY
- Coal
- Silk
- Technology
- Nuclear power
- Fishing

SPORT
- Cricket
- Field hockey

NATURAL FEATURES
- Green turtle

SCALE

0 — 200 miles
0 — 200 kilometers

Gemstones

Precious gemstones are mined in Sri Lanka, including unique bright blue sapphires. The island has some of the richest gem fields in the world.

NEPAL AND BANGLADESH

Nepal and Bangladesh are two south Asian countries with very different landscapes. The high Himalayan mountains run through Nepal, while much of Bangladesh is only just above sea level, and large areas are flooded during the heavy monsoon rains.

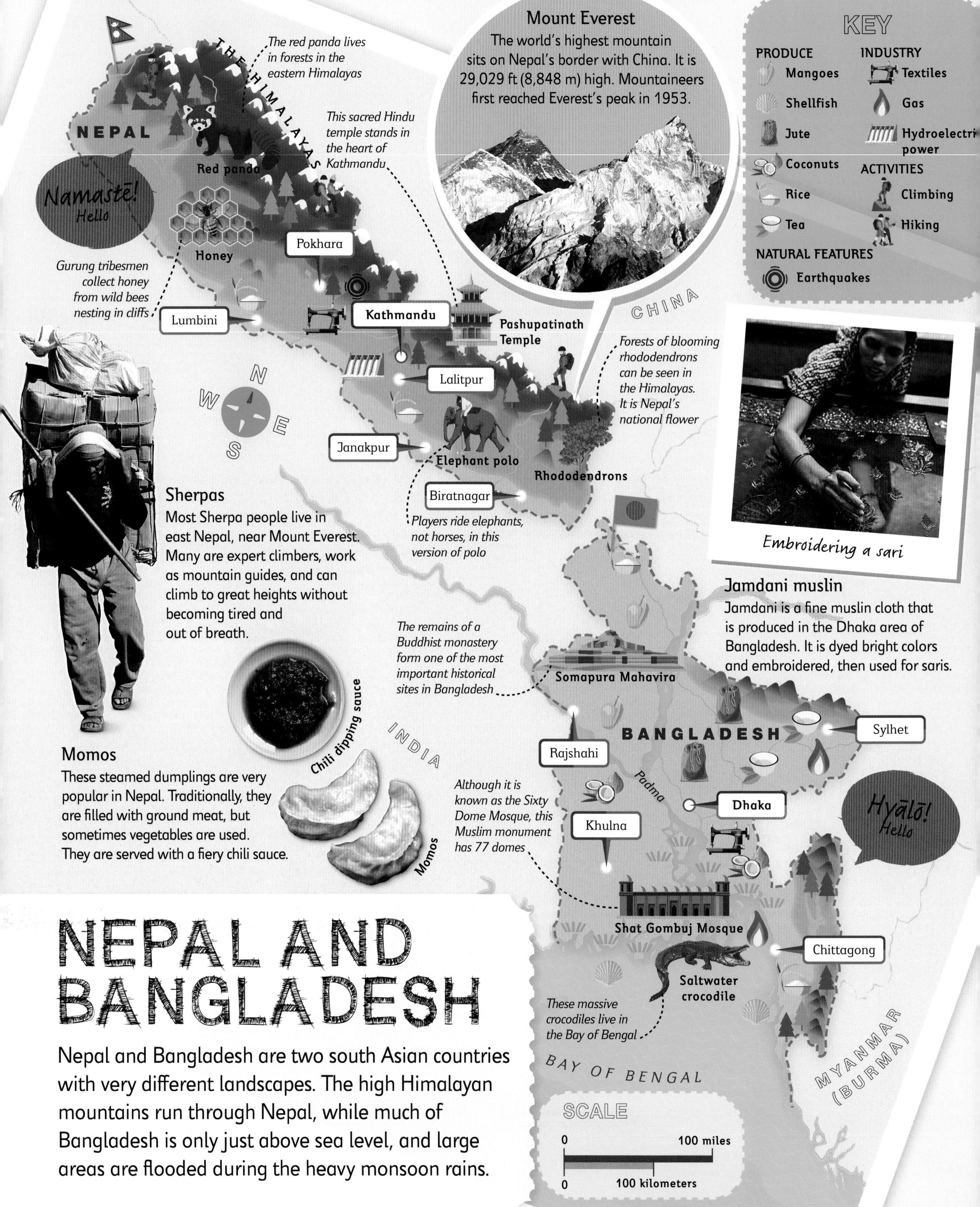

NEPAL
THE HIMALAYAS
The red panda lives in forests in the eastern Himalayas
Red panda
Namasté! Hello
Honey
Gurung tribesmen collect honey from wild bees nesting in cliffs
This sacred Hindu temple stands in the heart of Kathmandu
Pokhara
Lumbini
Kathmandu
Pashupatinath Temple
Lalitpur
Janakpur
Elephant polo
Biratnagar
Players ride elephants, not horses, in this version of polo
Rhododendrons
Forests of blooming rhododendrons can be seen in the Himalayas. It is Nepal's national flower
CHINA
N
W
E
S
INDIA
Chili dipping sauce
Momos
The remains of a Buddhist monastery form one of the most important historical sites in Bangladesh
Somapura Mahavira
BANGLADESH
Rajshahi
Sylhet
Padma
Dhaka
Khulna
Hyālō! Hello
Although it is known as the Sixty Dome Mosque, this Muslim monument has 77 domes
Shat Gombuj Mosque
Chittagong
Saltwater crocodile
These massive crocodiles live in the Bay of Bengal
BAY OF BENGAL
MYANMAR (BURMA)
SCALE
0
100 miles
0
100 kilometers
KEY
PRODUCE
Mangoes
Shellfish
Jute
Coconuts
Rice
Tea
INDUSTRY
Textiles
Gas
Hydroelectri power
ACTIVITIES
Climbing
Hiking
NATURAL FEATURES
Earthquakes

Mount Everest

The world's highest mountain sits on Nepal's border with China. It is 29,029 ft (8,848 m) high. Mountaineers first reached Everest's peak in 1953.

Embroidering a sari

Jamdani muslin

Jamdani is a fine muslin cloth that is produced in the Dhaka area of Bangladesh. It is dyed bright colors and embroidered, then used for saris.

Sherpas

Most Sherpa people live in east Nepal, near Mount Everest. Many are expert climbers, work as mountain guides, and can climb to great heights without becoming tired and out of breath.

Momos

These steamed dumplings are very popular in Nepal. Traditionally, they are filled with ground meat, but sometimes vegetables are used. They are served with a fiery chili sauce.

MYANMAR

Myanmar is a long, thin country that follows the Irrawaddy River and the coast of the Bay of Bengal. In the hills and forests of Myanmar, there are mines containing precious gemstones, such as jade and rubies. Its forests produce some of the world's finest teak wood, which is very strong and is used in shipbuilding and to make furniture.

Fire balloons

The Festival of Lights is held every year in Myanmar to mark the end of the rainy season in November. Hot-air balloons, called fire balloons, are released into the sky. They are lit by candles and come in various fun shapes.

Rooster fire balloon

Inle Lake

This lake in the mountains is home to some unique species of fish and snails. People live in houses raised on stilts around the edge of the lake.

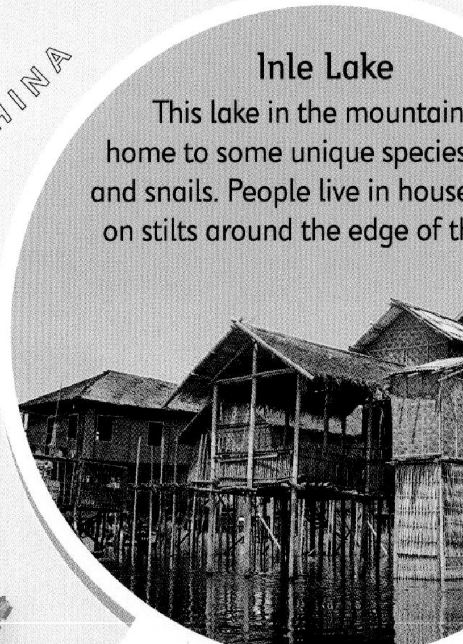

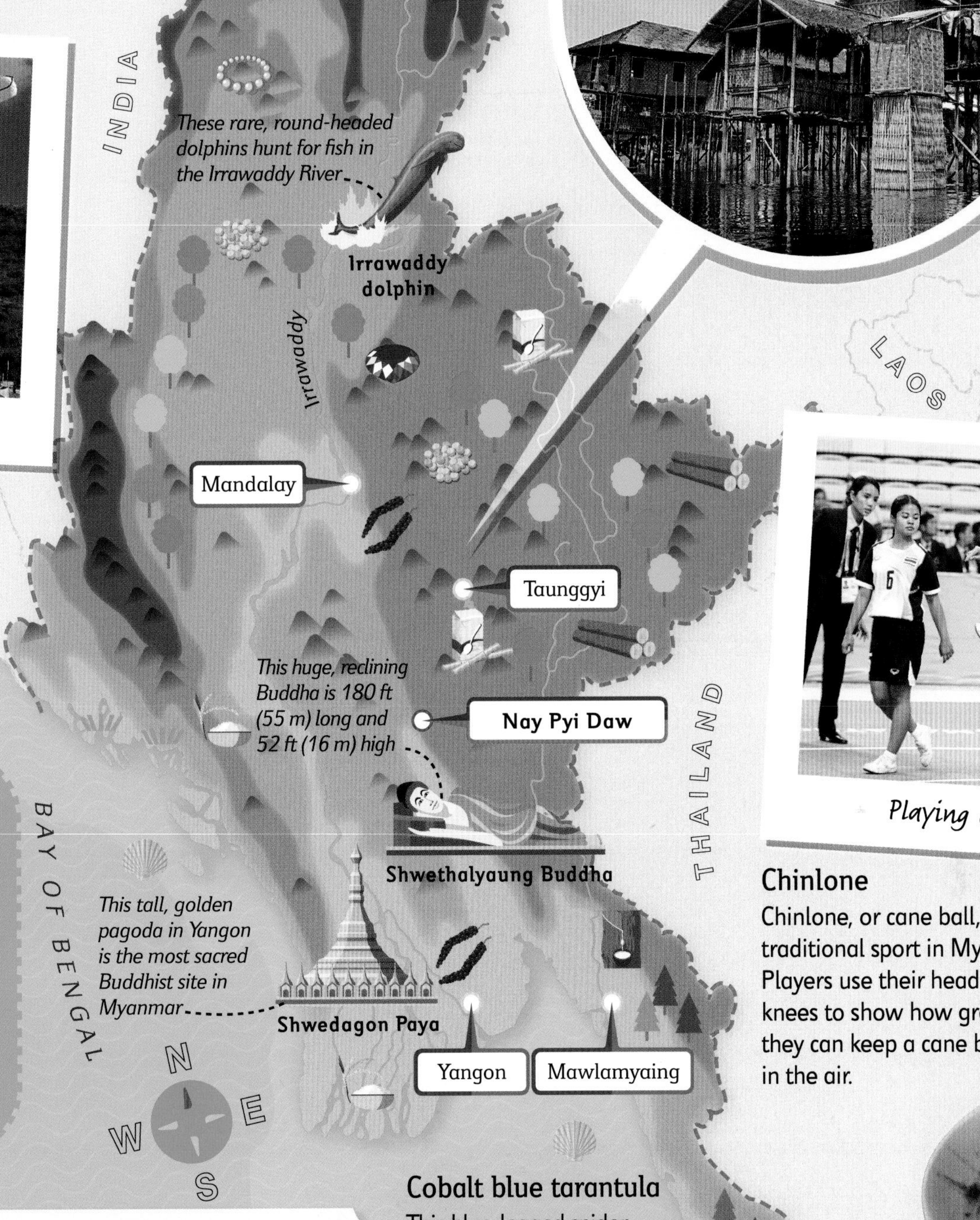
Maingalarpar!
Hello
CHINA
INDIA
LAOS
THAILAND
BAY OF BENGAL
These rare, round-headed dolphins hunt for fish in the Irrawaddy River
Irrawaddy dolphin
Irrawaddy
Mandalay
Taunggyi
Nay Pyi Daw
This huge, reclining Buddha is 180 ft (55 m) long and 52 ft (16 m) high
Shwethalyaung Buddha
This tall, golden pagoda in Yangon is the most sacred Buddhist site in Myanmar
Shwedagon Paya
Yangon
Mawlamyaing
N
E
S
W
SCALE
0
200 miles
0
200 kilometers
KEY
PRODUCE
Spices
Legumes
Shellfish
Sugar cane
Rice
INDUSTRY
Jade
Rubies
Rubber
Lumber
Fishing

Playing chinlone

Chinlone

Chinlone, or cane ball, is a traditional sport in Myanmar. Players use their head and knees to show how gracefully they can keep a cane ball in the air.

Cobalt blue tarantula

This blue-legged spider lives in Myanmar's tropical forests. It uses deadly venom to catch its prey, including mice and frogs.

Shan noodles

This popular dish uses flat rice noodles, which are served in a spicy broth with chicken or pork. It is served topped with mustard greens and chopped peanuts.

CHINA AND MONGOLIA

More than 1.4 billion people live in China. Most people live in the industrialized east of this vast country. Many work in thriving industries, such as technology. Mongolia has far fewer people. Much of the country is desert or grassland, called steppe.

Baby dinosaur fossils

Dinosaurs in the Gobi

Dinosaurs lived in Mongolia and China millions of years ago. Many well preserved dinosaur fossils have been found in the Gobi desert.

MONGOLIA
People use this two-humped camel to carry goods in the Gobi desert
Bactrian camel
Sain uu! Hello
Ni hăo! Hello
KAZAKHSTAN
KYRGYZSTAN
TAJIKISTAN
PAKISTAN
TAKLAMAKAN DESERT
Yak are kept for their milk, meat, and wool, and for transportation
Yak
PLATEAU OF TIBET
HIMALAYAS
Lhasa
Potala Palace
This Tibetan palace was the home of the Dalai Lama, the spiritual head of Tibetan Buddhism
NEPAL
BHUTAN
INDIA
MYANMAR (BURMA)

Tibetan monk

Buddhism

Buddhism is a religion and a philosophy based on the teachings of the Buddha. In Tibet, Buddhist monks wear red robes.

Tai Chi in the park

Tai Chi

This popular group exercise involves a series of slow, controlled movements. People practice Tai Chi for defensive training and to keep healthy.

Giant panda

The giant panda lives in the mountainous forests of south-central China. It feeds on bamboo and is one of the rarest bears in the world.

Chinese New Year

This is China's most important festival, when people celebrate the coming of spring. People hold parades led by a huge dancing dragon, a symbol of China that is believed to bring good luck.

Mongolian horses

There are more horses in Mongolia than people. The Mongol horse is small, but very strong and sturdy. Many children learn to ride by the age of three.

Porcelain

China is famous for its high-quality, durable pottery, called porcelain, which is made from kaolin, also known as China clay.

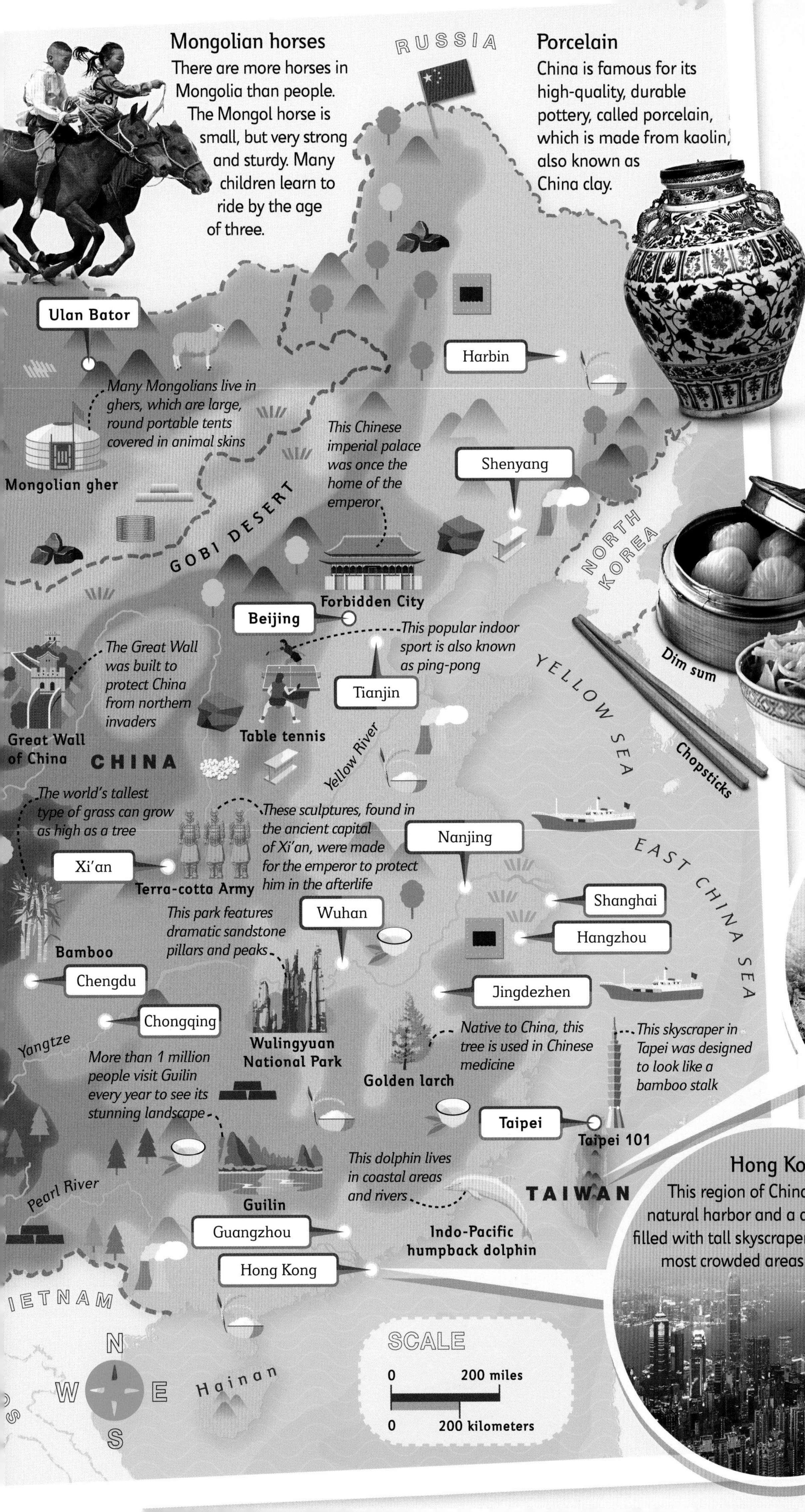
RUSSIA
KEY
PRODUCE
Sheep
Rice
Goats
Cotton
Tea
Millet
INDUSTRY
Coal
Copper
Iron
Tin
Steel
Gold
Lead
Nuclear power
Fishing
Electronics
Ulan Bator
Harbin
Many Mongolians live in ghers, which are large, round portable tents covered in animal skins
Mongolian gher
This Chinese imperial palace was once the home of the emperor
Shenyang
GOBI DESERT
NORTH KOREA
Forbidden City
Beijing
This popular indoor sport is also known as ping-pong
The Great Wall was built to protect China from northern invaders
Tianjin
Great Wall of China
Table tennis
CHINA
Yellow River
YELLOW SEA
Dim sum
Chopsticks
The world's tallest type of grass can grow as high as a tree
These sculptures, found in the ancient capital of Xi'an, were made for the emperor to protect him in the afterlife
Nanjing
Xi'an
Terra-cotta Army
EAST CHINA SEA
Shanghai
This park features dramatic sandstone pillars and peaks
Wuhan
Hangzhou
Bamboo
Chengdu
Jingdezhen
Chongqing
Native to China, this tree is used in Chinese medicine
This skyscraper in Tapei was designed to look like a bamboo stalk
Yangtze
Wulingyuan National Park
More than 1 million people visit Guilin every year to see its stunning landscape
Golden larch
Taipei
Taipei 101
This dolphin lives in coastal areas and rivers
Pearl River
TAIWAN
Guilin
Guangzhou
Indo-Pacific humpback dolphin
Hong Kong
IETNAM
N
W
E
S
Hainan
SCALE
0
200 miles
0
200 kilometers

Chinese food

Chinese cuisine is known for its variety of flavors. Meals often include rice or noodles and are eaten with chopsticks. Dim sum is a traditional Chinese food that consists of small, bite-sized portions.

Noodles with vegetables

Taroko Gorge

The Leehow River carved through marble rock near Taiwan's east coast, creating this gorge, which is also called Marble Gorge.

Hong Kong

This region of China has a deep natural harbor and a dynamic skyline filled with tall skyscrapers. It is one of the most crowded areas in the world.

NORTH AND SOUTH KOREA

Korea is a long peninsula that is divided into two countries: North Korea and South Korea, which are very different from each other. North Korea is mountainous and mostly rural. South Korea has many large cities and a thriving electronics industry.

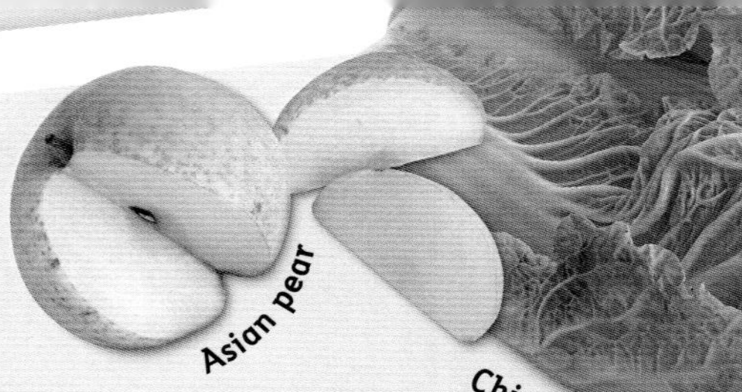

Asian pear
Chinese cabbage

Fruits and vegetables

The Asian pear is native to Korea and is commonly found in gardens. The pear has a yellow peel and a crisp texture. Chinese cabbage, a green-leaf vegetable, is grown in Korea.

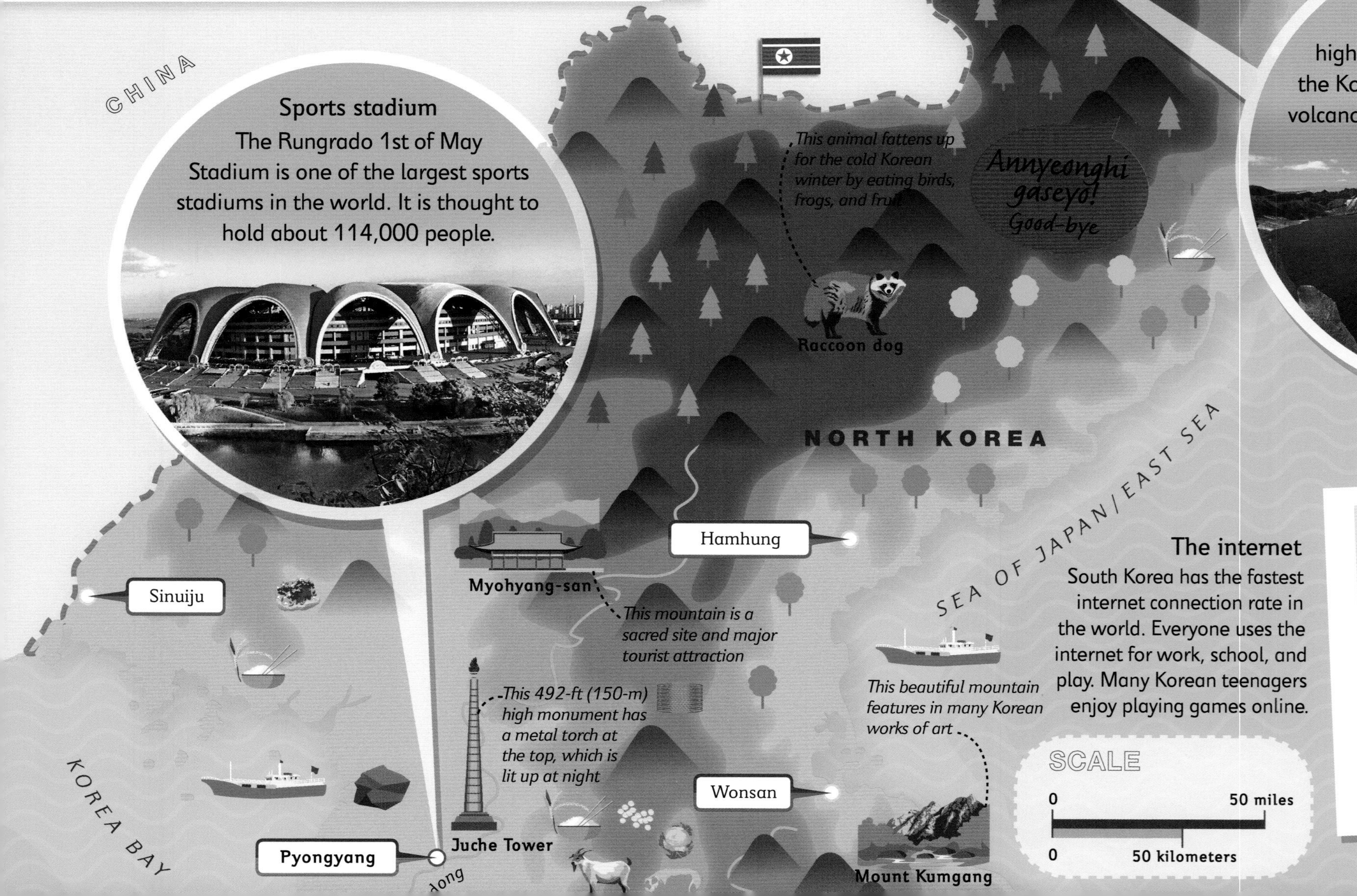

RUSSIA
CHINA
Chongjin
This animal fattens up for the cold Korean winter by eating birds, frogs, and fruit
Raccoon dog
Annyeonghi gaseyo! Good-bye
NORTH KOREA
SEA OF JAPAN/EAST SEA
Hamhung
Myohyang-san
This mountain is a sacred site and major tourist attraction
Sinuiju
This 492-ft (150-m) high monument has a metal torch at the top, which is lit up at night
Juche Tower
Wonsan
Pyongyang
KOREA BAY
This beautiful mountain features in many Korean works of art
Mount Kumgang
SCALE
0
50 miles
0
50 kilometers

Sports stadium

The Rungrado 1st of May Stadium is one of the largest sports stadiums in the world. It is thought to hold about 114,000 people.

Sacred mountain

Mount Paektu is Korea's highest mountain and is sacred to the Korean people. It is also an active volcano and has a large lake at the top.

The internet

South Korea has the fastest internet connection rate in the world. Everyone uses the internet for work, school, and play. Many Korean teenagers enjoy playing games online.

Using the internet

KEY

PRODUCE
- Rice
- Potatoes
- Soybeans
- Barley
- Cabbages
- Goats
- Pigs
- Electronics

INDUSTRY
- Fishing
- Shipbuilding
- Steel
- Iron
- Coal
- Cars
- Uranium
- Copper

ACTIVITIES
- Hiking
- Soccer
- Hot springs
- Scuba diving
- Baseball

NATURAL FEATURES
- Green turtle

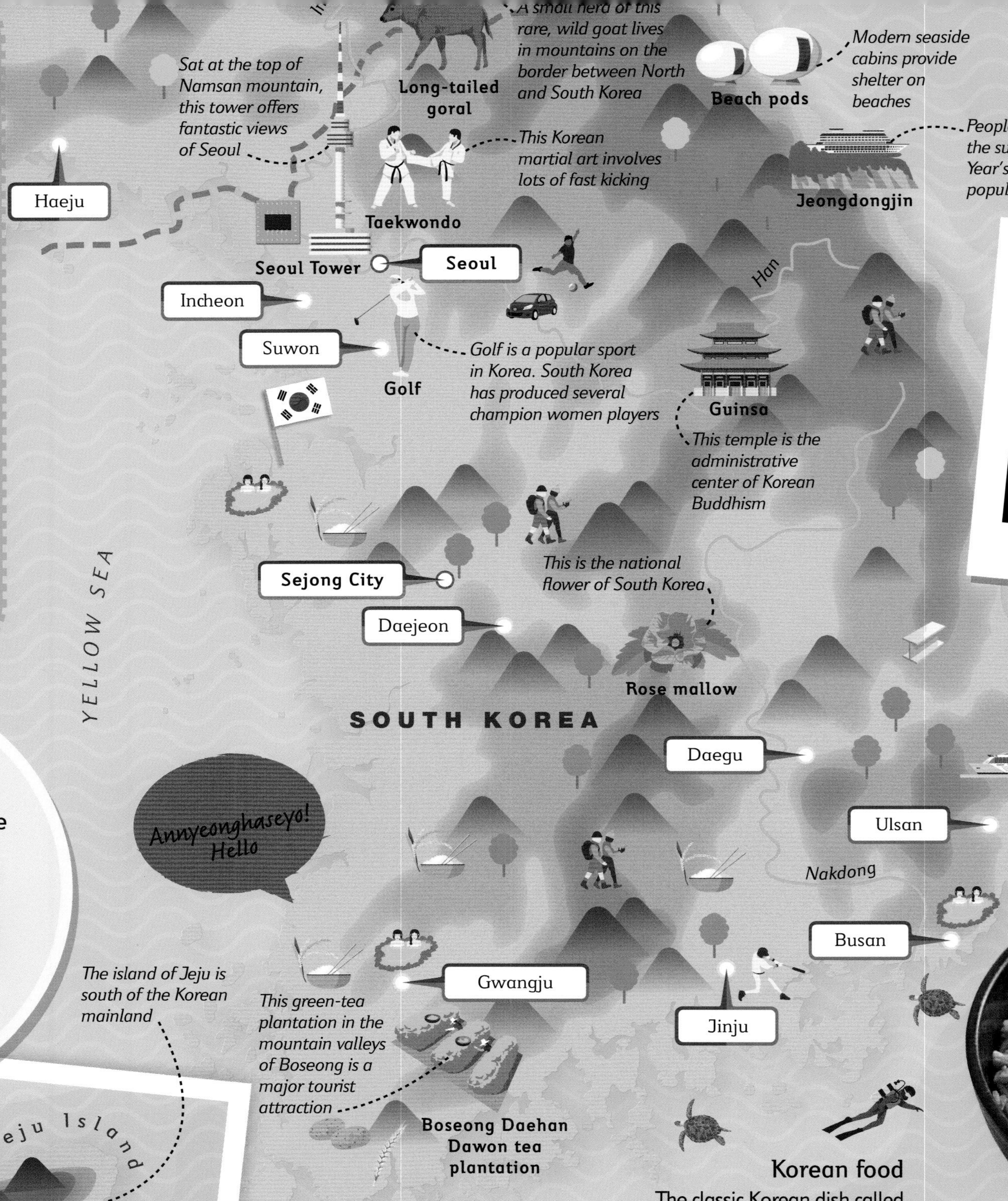

Haeju
Sat at the top of Namsan mountain, this tower offers fantastic views of Seoul
Long-tailed goral
A small herd of this rare, wild goat lives in mountains on the border between North and South Korea
Beach pods
Modern seaside cabins provide shelter on beaches
This Korean martial art involves lots of fast kicking
Taekwondo
Jeongdongjin
People go to watch the sunrise on New Year's Day at this popular tourist site
Seoul Tower
Seoul
Indheon
Suwon
Golf
Golf is a popular sport in Korea. South Korea has produced several champion women players
Han
Guinsa
This temple is the administrative center of Korean Buddhism
YELLOW SEA
Sejong City
Daejeon
This is the national flower of South Korea
Rose mallow
SOUTH KOREA
Daegu
Ulsan
Annyeonghaseyo! Hello
Nakdong
Busan
Gwangju
Jinju
The island of Jeju is south of the Korean mainland
This green-tea plantation in the mountain valleys of Boseong is a major tourist attraction
Boseong Daehan Dawon tea plantation

Jinju Lantern Festival

Floating festival

Every October, thousands of paper memorial lanterns, commemorating soldiers who died defending Korea, are lit and floated on the Nam River in Jinju.

Stone statues

Distinctive statues known as dol hareubang, or stone grandfathers, are found on the island of Jeju.

Jeju Island

Korean food

The classic Korean dish called bibimbap is a hot bowl of rice with vegetables, chili, meat, and egg. Kimchee is a traditional side dish made of seasoned vegetables, including Chinese cabbage.

Kimchee
Bibimbap

JAPAN

Japan is a modern, industrial country, but ancient traditions are still an important part of Japanese culture. Most people live in cities on one of the four main islands. Much of the country is mountainous, with many active volcanoes.

ねぶた愛好会

Lantern float

Aomori Nebuta festival

Festivals are held throughout Japan. Every summer, the city of Aomori holds a festival where huge paper lantern floats (nebutas), painted with pictures of mythical beasts and warriors, are carried through the streets.

Chawan
Chasen
Natsume
Chashaku

Tea ceremony

Matcha green tea is served in a special tea bowl (chawan) in a traditional ceremony that symbolizes friendship and respect between host and guest. Tea is placed in a small container (natsume). It is then added to hot water with a scoop (chashaku) and stirred with a bamboo whisk (chasen).

Kendo

Martial arts

Kendo is one of the most popular martial arts in Japan. Fighters use bamboo swords and wear protective armor.

そうだろ!

Anime

Manga and anime

Cartoon drawings are very popular in Japan. Comics in the distinctive hand-drawn style are called manga, while moving cartoons are known as anime.

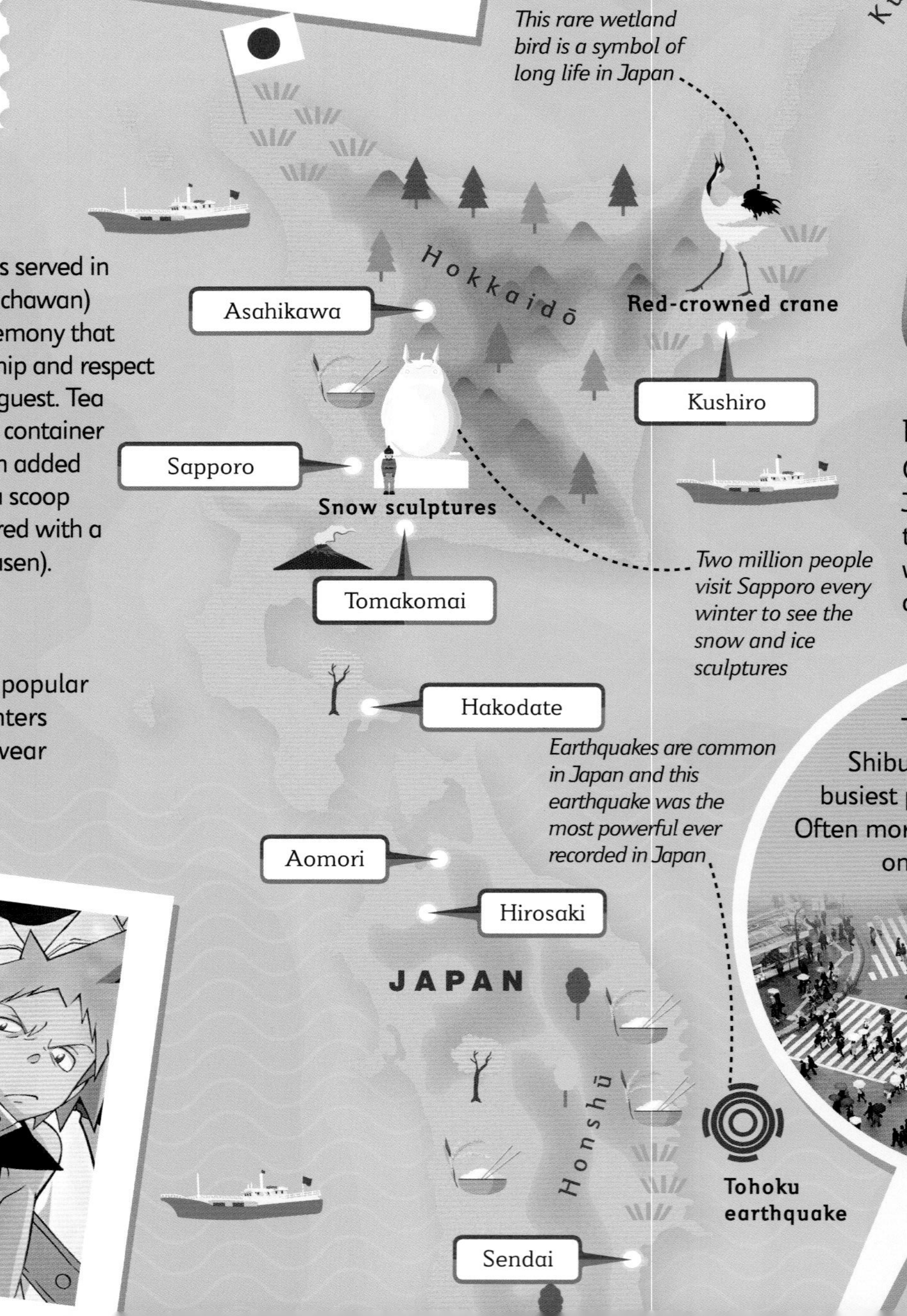

RUSSIA
Hokkaidō
Kurile Islands
Asahikawa
Sapporo
Snow sculptures
Tomakomai
Kushiro
Red-crowned crane
This rare wetland bird is a symbol of long life in Japan
Two million people visit Sapporo every winter to see the snow and ice sculptures
Hakodate
Aomori
Hirosaki
JAPAN
Honshū
Sendai
Earthquakes are common in Japan and this earthquake was the most powerful ever recorded in Japan
Tohoku earthquake

Pandas made from rice balls and pieces of seaweed

Bento

On special occasions, Japanese parents send their children to school with a lunch box, or bento, containing decorated food.

Tokyo

The crosswalk near Shibuya Station is one of the busiest places in this crowded city. Often more than 1,000 people will be on it at the same time.

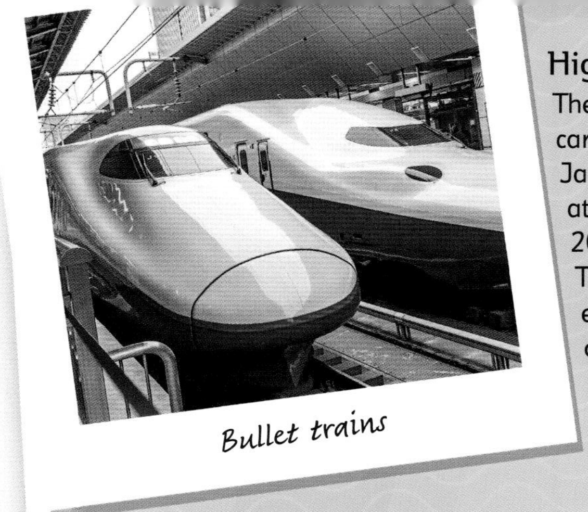

Bullet trains

High-speed trains

These superfast trains carry people between Japan's major cities at speeds of up to 200 mph (320 kph). Trains that travel even faster are on their way.

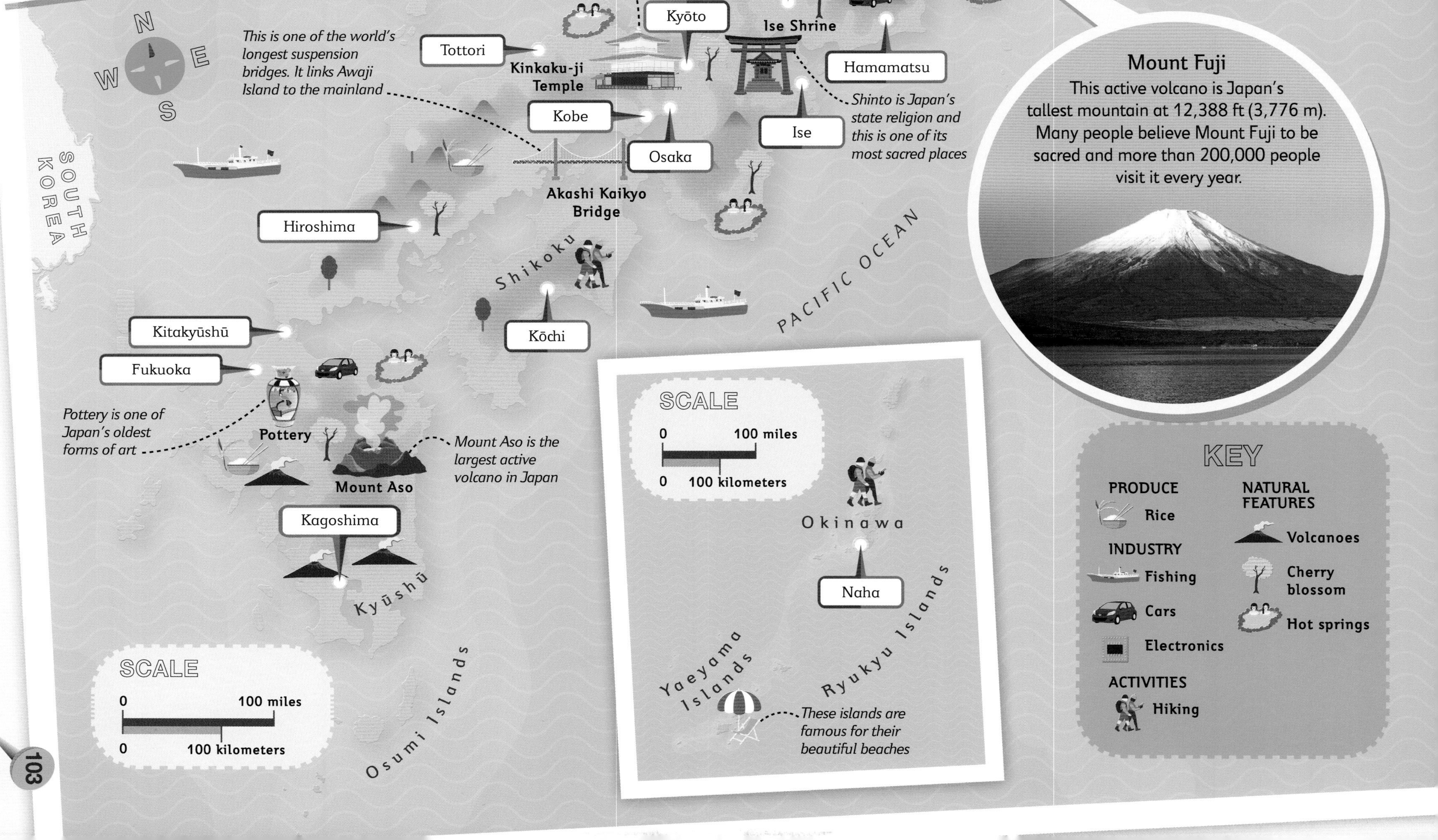

SEA OF JAPAN
EAST SEA
These monkeys are famous for keeping warm in hot springs.
Japanese macaque
Tokyo Skytree
Japan's tallest structure is the tower called Tokyo Skytree
Nagano
Saitama
Tokyo
Kawasaki
Yokohama
Kon'nichiwa!
Hello
Fuji
Nagoya
This popular tourist attraction in Kyōto is also known as the Golden Temple
Kyōto
Ise Shrine
Hamamatsu
Tottori
Kinkaku-ji Temple
This is one of the world's longest suspension bridges. It links Awaji Island to the mainland
N
E
W
S
Kobe
Osaka
Ise
Shinto is Japan's state religion and this is one of its most sacred places
SOUTH KOREA
Akashi Kaikyo Bridge
Hiroshima
Shikoku
PACIFIC OCEAN
Kōchi
Kitakyūshū
Fukuoka
Pottery is one of Japan's oldest forms of art
Pottery
Mount Aso
Mount Aso is the largest active volcano in Japan
Kagoshima
Kyūshū
Osumi Islands
SCALE
0
100 miles
0
100 kilometers
SCALE
0
100 miles
0
100 kilometers
Okinawa
Naha
Ryukyu Islands
Yaeyama Islands
These islands are famous for their beautiful beaches
KEY
PRODUCE
Rice
INDUSTRY
Fishing
Cars
Electronics
ACTIVITIES
Hiking
NATURAL FEATURES
Volcanoes
Cherry blossom
Hot springs

Mount Fuji

This active volcano is Japan's tallest mountain at 12,388 ft (3,776 m). Many people believe Mount Fuji to be sacred and more than 200,000 people visit it every year.

SOUTHEAST ASIA

Southeast Asia is a diverse region of many countries and small islands. Much of the mainland is mountainous and is covered with thick forests. The area is the home of fragrant spices and historic temples. The ancient architecture and sandy beaches make this region very popular with tourists.

Pho

Southeast Asian food

Southeast Asia has many unique dishes. These include Vietnamese pho, a soup with noodles, meat, and vegetables. Crunchy, fried crickets are also a delicacy.

Angkor Wat

This 12th-century temple is the world's largest religious monument. Today, it is a symbol of Cambodia and appears on the country's flag.

Making a moon kite

Malaysia's kite makers

Malaysia has a tradition of making colorful kites in complex shapes. One of the largest is the wau bulan, or moon kite, which is one of Malaysia's national symbols.

Ha Long Bay

This bay in northern Vietnam is famous for its dramatic landscape. More than 1,000 small islands, topped by trees, tower above the sea.

CHINA
LAOS
MYANMAR
VIETNAM
CAMBODIA
THAILAND
MALAYSIA
SINGAPORE
Hanoi
Vientiane
Chiang Mai
Da Nang
Bangkok
Phnom Penh
Ho Chi Minh
Phuket
George Town
Kuala Lumpur
Putrajaya
Medan
Kuching
Pontianak
Palembang
Jakarta
Andaman Islands
ANDAMAN SEA
Nicobar Islands
GULF OF THAILAND
Sumatra
INDIAN OCEAN
Thai kickboxing, known as Muay Thai, is a popular sport in Thailand
Muay Thai
Fried crickets
Tuk-tuk
These three-wheeled motor vehicles are used as taxis in Thailand
Wat Phra Kaew
This Bangkok temple houses a sacred statue, known as the Emerald Buddha
Water buffalo
These massive, strong animals are used to plow rice fields
Royal Palace
The king of Cambodia and his family live in this palace in Phnom Penh
Petronas Twin Towers
At 1,483 ft (452 m) this pair of skyscrapers are the tallest twin towers in the world
Badminton
Badminton is a popular sport in Indonesia, which has produced many top-class players
Rafflesia arnoldii flower
This rain forest flower is the largest in the world, measuring up to 3 ft (1 m) across
Borobudur Temple Compounds
This ancient site in Java is one of the world's greatest Buddhist monuments
SCALE
0
200 miles
0
200 kilometers

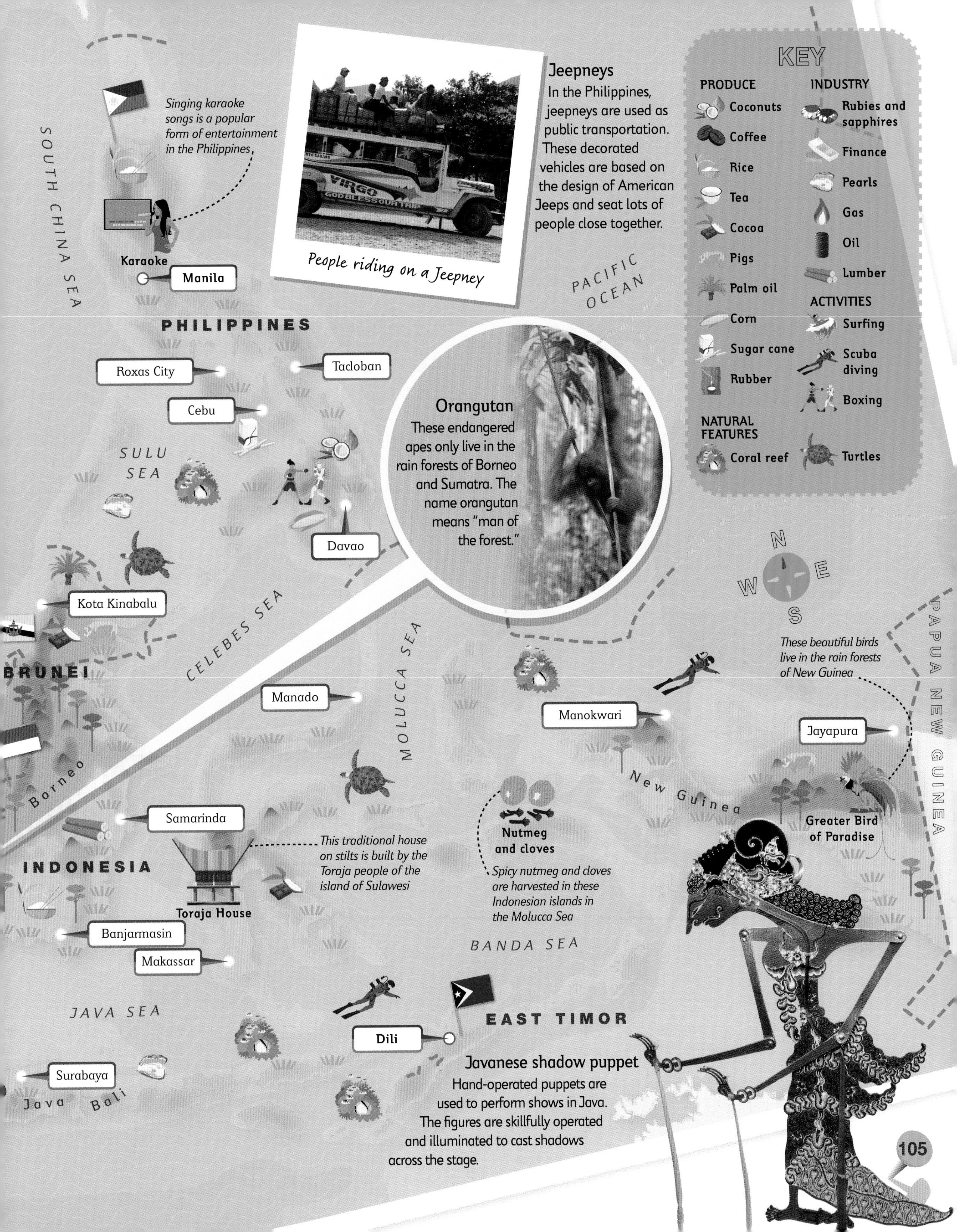
KEY
PRODUCE
Coconuts
Coffee
Rice
Tea
Cocoa
Pigs
Palm oil
Corn
Sugar cane
Rubber
NATURAL FEATURES
Coral reef
INDUSTRY
Rubies and sapphires
Finance
Pearls
Gas
Oil
Lumber
ACTIVITIES
Surfing
Scuba diving
Boxing
Turtles
Singing karaoke songs is a popular form of entertainment in the Philippines
Karaoke
Manila
SOUTH CHINA SEA
PACIFIC OCEAN
PHILIPPINES
Roxas City
Tacloban
Cebu
SULU SEA
Davao
Kota Kinabalu
CELEBES SEA
BRUNEI
MOLUCCA SEA
Manado
Manokwari
Jayapura
N
E
S
W
These beautiful birds live in the rain forests of New Guinea
PAPUA NEW GUINEA
New Guinea
Greater Bird of Paradise
Borneo
Samarinda
This traditional house on stilts is built by the Toraja people of the island of Sulawesi
Toraja House
INDONESIA
Nutmeg and cloves
Spicy nutmeg and cloves are harvested in these Indonesian islands in the Molucca Sea
Banjarmasin
Makassar
BANDA SEA
JAVA SEA
EAST TIMOR
Dili
Surabaya
Java
Bali

People riding on a Jeepney

Jeepneys

In the Philippines, jeepneys are used as public transportation. These decorated vehicles are based on the design of American Jeeps and seat lots of people close together.

Orangutan

These endangered apes only live in the rain forests of Borneo and Sumatra. The name orangutan means "man of the forest."

Javanese shadow puppet

Hand-operated puppets are used to perform shows in Java. The figures are skillfully operated and illuminated to cast shadows across the stage.

GREAT SITES

Throughout history, humans have built amazing structures and buildings. These great sites were often built to impress people and as a display of power. In the past, cathedrals and castles were among the largest and most awe-inspiring buildings. Today's spectacular buildings and structures include towering skyscrapers and long bridges.

OLDEST BUILDING

The Megalithic Temples of Malta were constructed 5,500 years ago and are among the oldest buildings that still stand today. They were used for religious ceremonies.

Six of the tallest buildings

Tall skyscrapers are built in cities, where land is expensive. Each of these buildings is the tallest on their respective continents. The Burj Khalifa in Asia is the tallest building in the world. It has 163 floors and contains apartments, restaurants, hotel rooms, and offices.

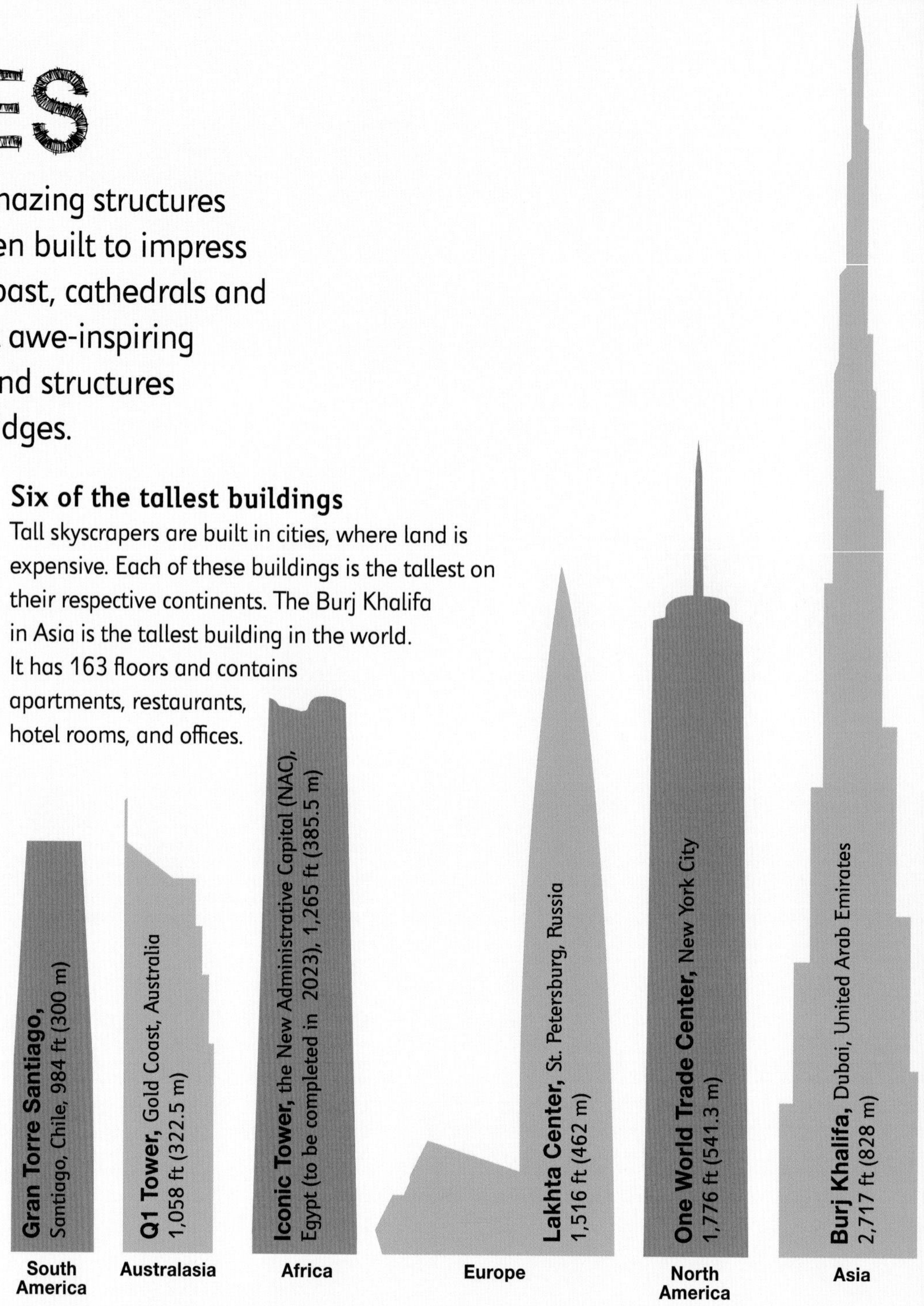

Gran Torre Santiago, Santiago, Chile, 984 ft (300 m)
South America
Q1 Tower, Gold Coast, Australia 1,058 ft (322.5 m)
Australasia
Iconic Tower, the New Administrative Capital (NAC), Egypt (to be completed in 2023), 1,265 ft (385.5 m)
Africa
Lakhta Center, St. Petersburg, Russia 1,516 ft (462 m)
Europe
One World Trade Center, New York City 1,776 ft (541.3 m)
North America
Burj Khalifa, Dubai, United Arab Emirates 2,717 ft (828 m)
Asia

Five of the longest bridges

Long bridges are built across rivers, lakes, harbors, valleys, and even swamps and are an important way of connecting communities. These bridges are the longest in their respective continents.

Macleay Valley Bridge, New South Wales, Australia 10,500 ft (3,200 m)
Australasia

Vasco da Gama Bridge, Lisbon, Portugal, 40,500 ft (12,345 m)
Europe

Rio–Niterói Bridge, Rio de Janeiro, Brazil 8.26 miles (13.29 km)
South America

6th October Bridge, Cairo, Egypt 12.7 miles (20.5 km)
Africa

Lake Pontchartrain Causeway, New Orleans, USA 23.83 miles (38.35 km)
North America

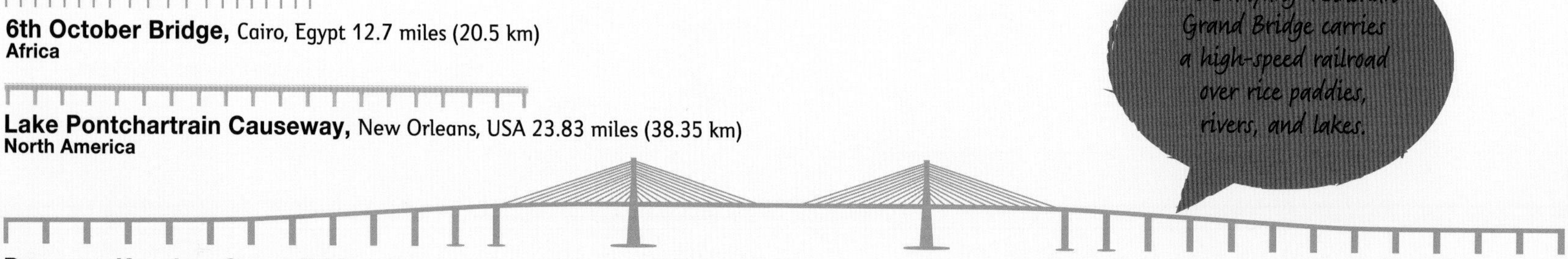

The Danyang–Kunshan Grand Bridge carries a high-speed railroad over rice paddies, rivers, and lakes.

Danyang–Kunshan Grand Bridge, Jiangsu, China, 102.4 miles (164.8 km)
Asia

Ten popular tourist attractions

These 10 great sites are some of the most popular places for tourists to visit. They include historic buildings, religious sites, and ancient monuments.

Golden Gate Bridge,
San Francisco, USA

Forbidden City,
Beijing, China

Angkor Wat,
Siem Reap, Cambodia

Eiffel Tower,
Paris, France

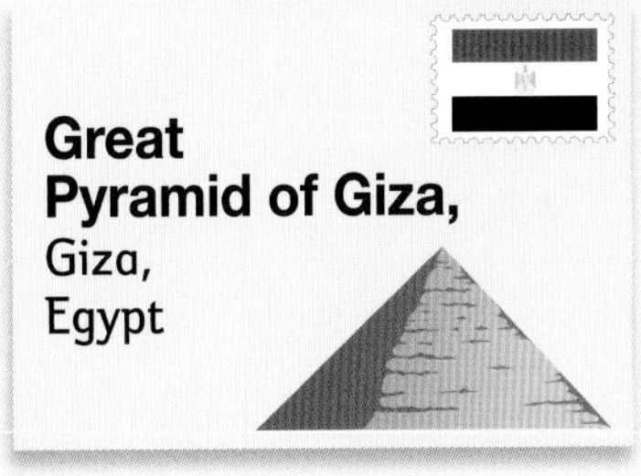
Great Pyramid of Giza,
Giza, Egypt

La Sagrada Família,
Barcelona, Spain

Hagia Sophia,
Istanbul, Turkey

Uluru,
Northern Territory, Australia

Machu Picchu,
Andes, Peru

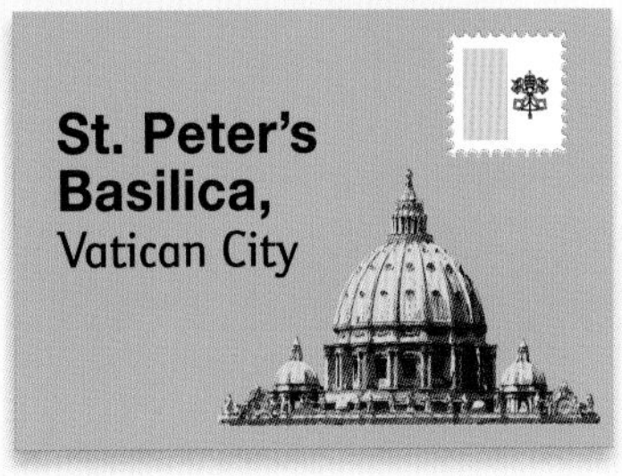
St. Peter's Basilica,
Vatican City

New Seven Wonders of the World

In 2007, a worldwide survey voted the great sites shown here as being the New Seven Wonders of the World. The original Seven Wonders of the Ancient World included the Great Pyramid at Giza, Egypt.

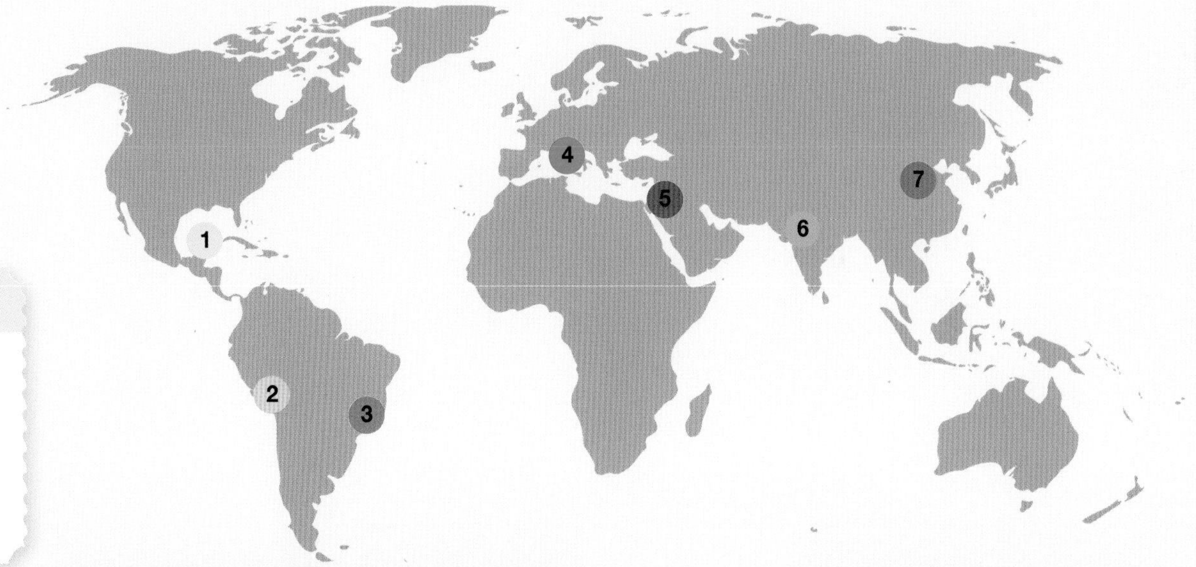
1
2
3
4
5
6
7

1. CHICHEN ITZA, Mexico

This ancient city was built by the Mayans. It has many great stone buildings, including this pyramid, called El Castillo.

2. MACHU PICCHU, Peru

Nestled in the Andes, this stone city built by the Incas is now in ruins. The name Machu Picchu means "old mountain."

3. CHRIST THE REDEEMER, Brazil

This huge statue of Jesus Christ is 100 ft (30 m) tall. It is carved out of soapstone and looms over Rio de Janeiro in Brazil.

4. COLOSSEUM, Italy

The Romans built this massive, oval-shaped stadium. It could seat more than 50,000 people. Gladiators fought in it.

5. PETRA, Jordan

The ancient city of Petra was carved out of rocky cliffs. It is also known as the "Rose City," because of the rock's pink color.

6. TAJ MAHAL, India

Taj Mahal means "crown of palaces." It was built as a tomb for Mumtaz Mahal, wife of the Mogul emperor Shah Jahan.

7. GREAT WALL OF CHINA, China

The longest human-made structure, the Great Wall is an amazing sight as it winds its way through the mountains of China.

4. What is the name of this rock formation in Australia?
3. Flying doctors travel across the deserts of which country?
04
2. Nelson Falls is found on which remote island?
1. Which fox lives in the far north of the world?

5. Which Arctic people cut holes in the ice to catch fish?

6. In which country is this building shaped like a beehive?

AUSTRALASIA AND THE POLAR REGIONS

The countries of Australia, New Zealand, and the Pacific Island nations make up Australasia, in the southern half of the world. At the extreme north and south are the polar regions of the Arctic and Antarctic, where few people live because it is so cold.

7. Penguins are found in which polar region?

8. What is the coral reef off Australia's coastline called?

You can find all the answers and more quizzes on pages 120–121.

AUSTRALASIA

The vast region of Australasia contains a wide variety of different landscapes, ranging from the desert that covers most of Australia to tropical islands dotted around the Pacific Ocean, which are fringed with golden, sandy beaches and coral reefs. There are also large areas of dense rain forest in eastern Australia, Tasmania, Papua New Guinea, and New Zealand.

The dotted lines show where these island groups are, as many are too small to show up on this map
PHILIPPINE SEA
Northern Mariana Islands
(UNITED STATES)
Guam
(UNITED STATES)
PALAU
MICRONESIA
PAPUA NEW GUINEA
ARAFURA SEA
TIMOR SEA
Christmas Island
(AUSTRALIA)
Cocos (Keeling) Islands
(AUSTRALIA)
Ashmore and Cartier Islands
(AUSTRALIA)
Coral Sea Islar
(AUSTRALIA)
COF
SE
INDIAN OCEAN
Northern Territory
AUSTRALIA
Queensland
Western Australia
South Australia
New South Wales
Victoria
Tasmania

Perth

This coastal city is the capital of the state of Western Australia. Its center is filled with modern, high-rise buildings. Although it is one of the world's most isolated cities, Perth is home to people from many different countries and cultures.

Uluru

This unique, sandstone rock formation rises up majestically from the desert of Australia's Northern Territory and is of great spiritual and cultural importance to Australia's First Nations.

SCALE

0 | 500 miles | 1,000 miles

0 | 1,000 kilometers

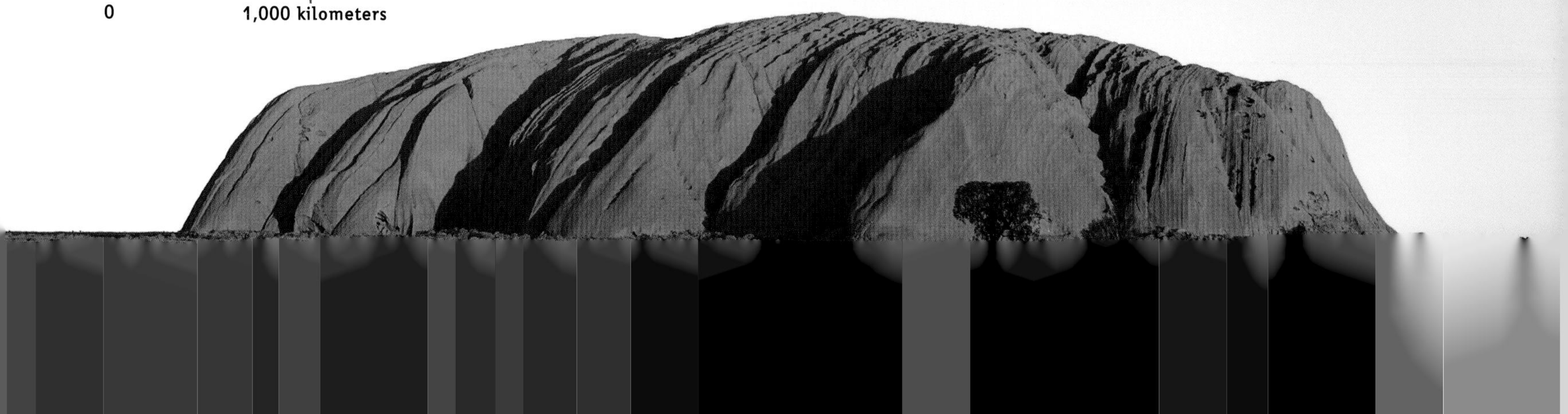

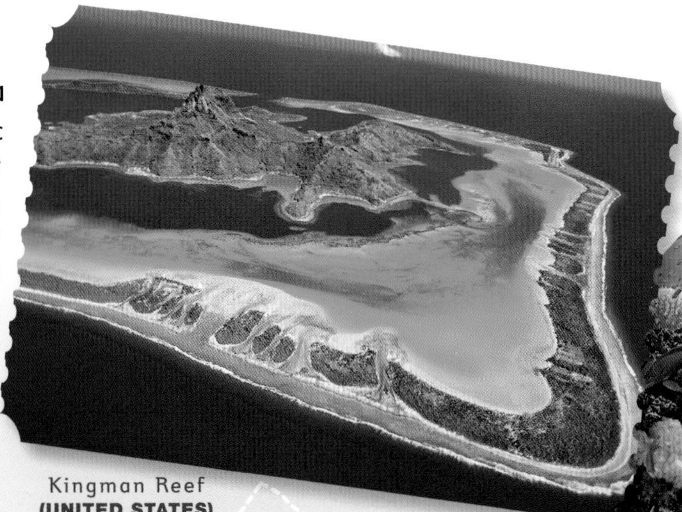

French Polynesia

A group of 118 far-flung Pacific islands makes up this territory that is governed by France, although it is a long way from Europe. The islands have beautiful beaches and coral reefs.

Coral reefs

Some of the world's most colorful corals and tropical fish live in the warm waters of the Pacific Ocean. The most amazing coral reef is the Great Barrier Reef off the northeast coast of Australia.

Wake Island
(UNITED STATES)
MARSHALL ISLANDS
Kingman Reef
(UNITED STATES)
Palmyra Atoll
(UNITED STATES)
Baker and Howland Islands
(UNITED STATES)
NAURU
Jarvis Island
(UNITED STATES)
KIRIBATI
OLOMON SLANDS
TUVALU
Tokelau
(NEW ZEALAND)
Wallis and Futuna
(FRANCE)
SAMOA
American Samoa
(UNITED STATES)
VANUATU
Cook Islands
(NEW ZEALAND)
FIJI
Niue
(NEW ZEALAND)
French Polynesia
(FRANCE)
TONGA
New Caledonia
(FRANCE)
Pitcairn, Henderson, Ducie, and Oeno Islands
(UNITED KINGDOM)
Norfolk Island
(AUSTRALIA)
owe Island
STRALIA)
Kermadec Islands
(NEW ZEALAND)
PACIFIC OCEAN
NEW ZEALAND
MAN
A
Chatham Islands
(NEW ZEALAND)
Bounty Islands
(NEW ZEALAND)
Antipodes Islands
(NEW ZEALAND)
Auckland Islands
(NEW ZEALAND)
Campbell Islands
(NEW ZEALAND)
uarie Island
USTRALIA)

Milford Sound

The waters of this beautiful fjord, on the southwest coast of New Zealand's South Island, flow almost 9 miles (15 km) inland from the Tasman Sea. Majestic cliffs sweep up 3,900 ft (1,200 m) on either side. Every year, nearly a million people visit this stunning site.

AUSTRALIA

Australia is a huge island between the Indian and Pacific oceans. The middle of Australia is a vast desert known as the Outback, which is extremely hot and dry. Most Australians live around the coastal areas, where it is cooler. Here, many people enjoy outdoor activities, such as surfing.

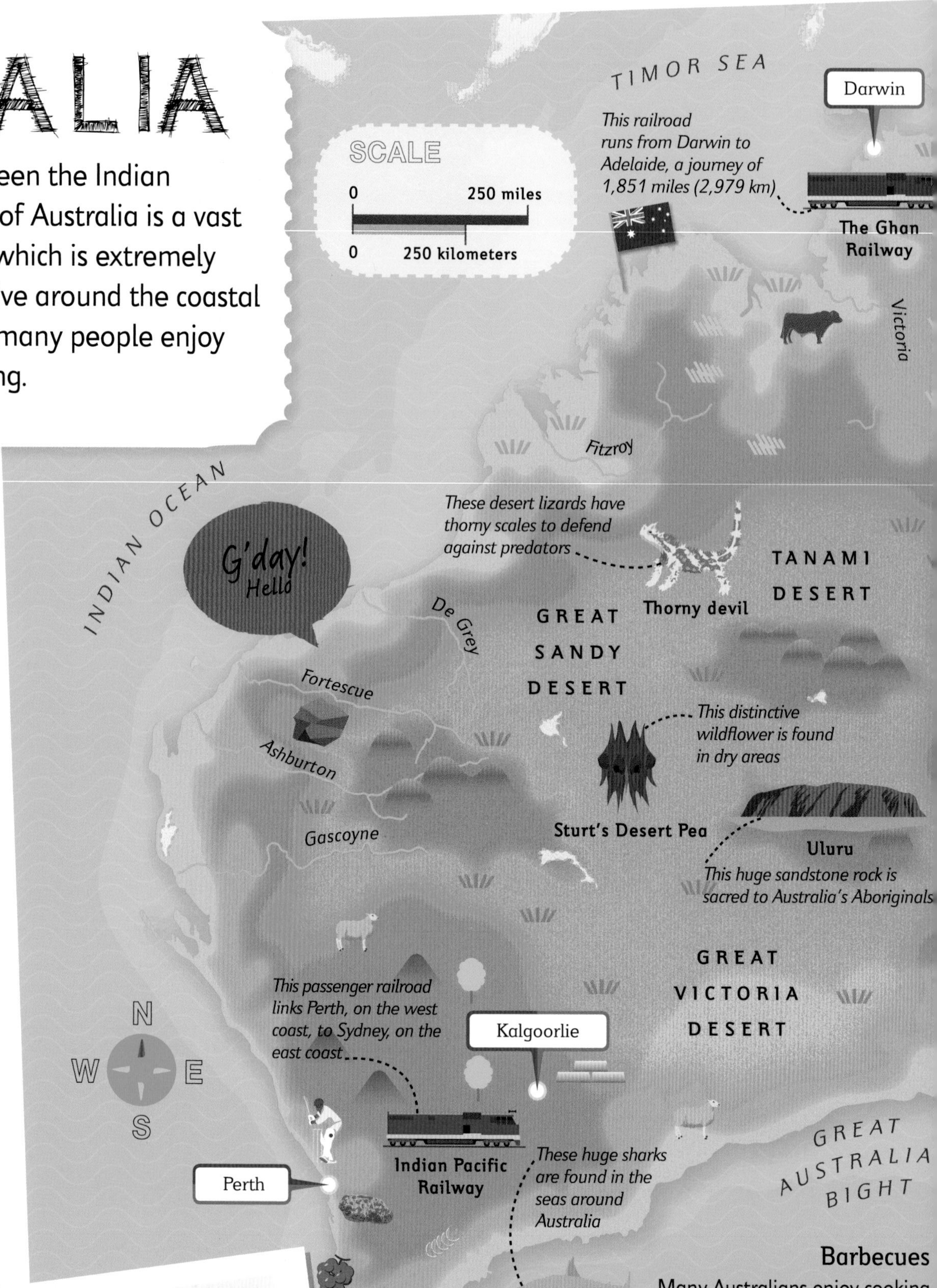

TIMOR SEA
Darwin
SCALE
0
250 miles
0
250 kilometers
This railroad runs from Darwin to Adelaide, a journey of 1,851 miles (2,979 km)
The Ghan Railway
Victoria
Fitzroy
INDIAN OCEAN
G'day! Hello
These desert lizards have thorny scales to defend against predators
Thorny devil
TANAMI DESERT
De Grey
GREAT SANDY DESERT
Fortescue
Ashburton
This distinctive wildflower is found in dry areas
Sturt's Desert Pea
Gascoyne
Uluru
This huge sandstone rock is sacred to Australia's Aboriginals
GREAT VICTORIA DESERT
This passenger railroad links Perth, on the west coast, to Sydney, on the east coast
Kalgoorlie
N
W
E
S
Indian Pacific Railway
Perth
These huge sharks are found in the seas around Australia
GREAT AUSTRALIA BIGHT
Great white shark

KEY
PRODUCE
Cotton
Vineyards
Cattle
Sheep
Bananas
Wheat
Sugar cane
RESOURCES
Coal
Iron Ore
Bauxite
Gold
Silver
Uranium
Lumber
ACTIVITIES
Surfing
Skiing
Scuba diving
Cricket
Rugby

Kangaroos

Australia is home to many unique animals, including the kangaroo. Kangaroos, like other marsupials, have a pouch in which they carry their young. They move by hopping on their back legs.

A baby kangaroo is called a joey

Surfing

Sun, sand, surf

Australia has long stretches of sandy beaches. People enjoy surfing on some of the world's biggest waves.

Barbecues

Many Australians enjoy cooking and eating outside. Barbecuing is a great way to cook tasty food, like these juicy shrimp.

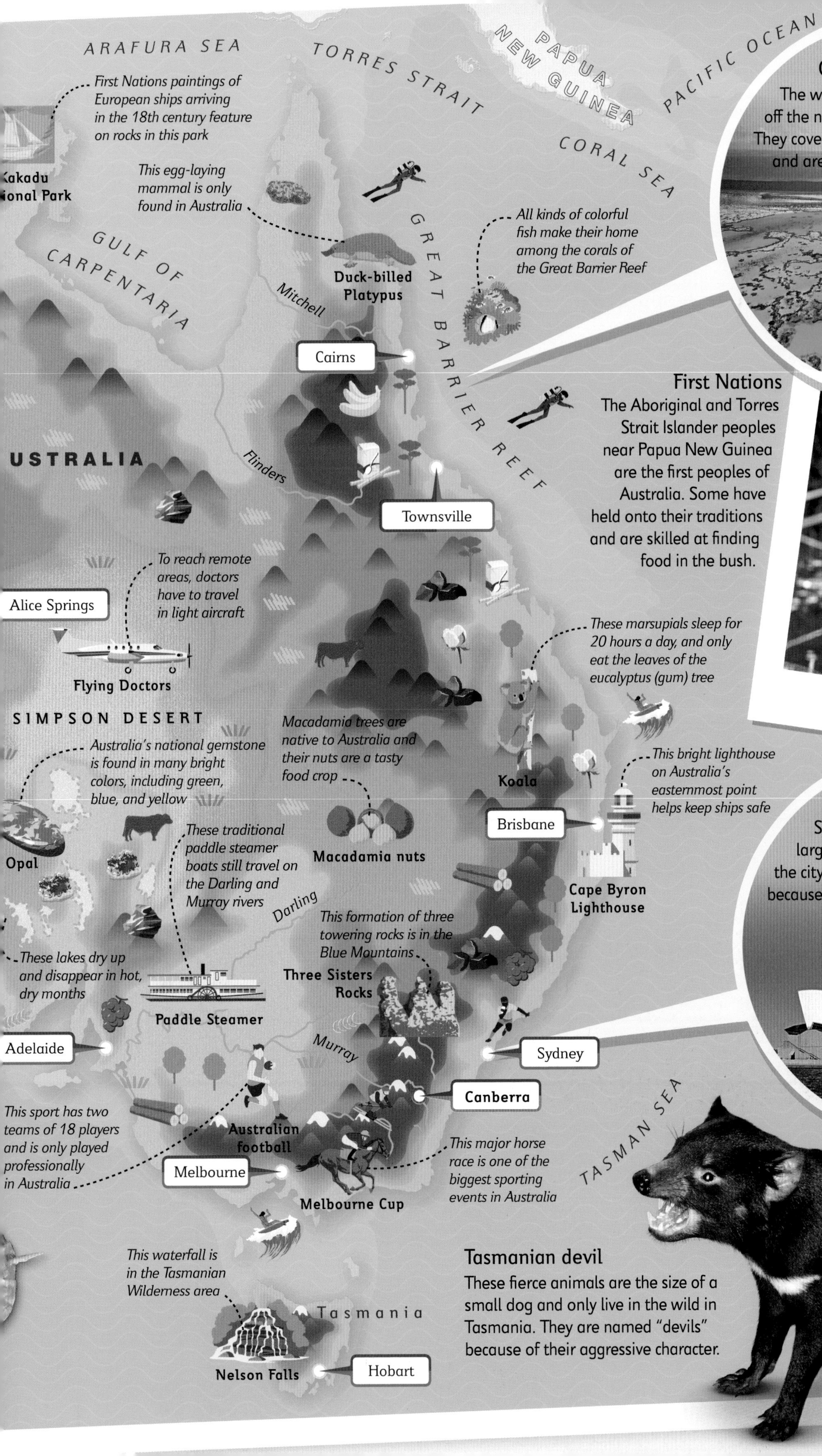
ARAFURA SEA
TORRES STRAIT
PAPUA NEW GUINEA
PACIFIC OCEAN
CORAL SEA
First Nations paintings of European ships arriving in the 18th century feature on rocks in this park
Kakadu
ional Park
This egg-laying mammal is only found in Australia
Duck-billed Platypus
GULF OF CARPENTARIA
GREAT BARRIER REEF
All kinds of colorful fish make their home among the corals of the Great Barrier Reef
Mitchell
Cairns
USTRALIA
Flinders
Townsville
To reach remote areas, doctors have to travel in light aircraft
Alice Springs
Flying Doctors
SIMPSON DESERT
These marsupials sleep for 20 hours a day, and only eat the leaves of the eucalyptus (gum) tree
Koala
Australia's national gemstone is found in many bright colors, including green, blue, and yellow
Opal
Macadamia trees are native to Australia and their nuts are a tasty food crop
Macadamia nuts
This bright lighthouse on Australia's easternmost point helps keep ships safe
Brisbane
Cape Byron Lighthouse
These traditional paddle steamer boats still travel on the Darling and Murray rivers
Darling
This formation of three towering rocks is in the Blue Mountains
Three Sisters Rocks
These lakes dry up and disappear in hot, dry months
Paddle Steamer
Adelaide
Murray
Sydney
Canberra
This sport has two teams of 18 players and is only played professionally in Australia
Australian football
Melbourne
This major horse race is one of the biggest sporting events in Australia
Melbourne Cup
TASMAN SEA
This waterfall is in the Tasmanian Wilderness area
Tasmania
Nelson Falls
Hobart

Great Barrier Reef

The world's largest coral reefs are off the northeastern coast of Australia. They cover about the same area as Japan and are a great site for scuba divers.

First Nations

The Aboriginal and Torres Strait Islander peoples near Papua New Guinea are the first peoples of Australia. Some have held onto their traditions and are skilled at finding food in the bush.

Gathering water lilies

Opera House

Sydney is Australia's oldest and largest city. Its opera house stands in the city's harbor. It is instantly recognizable because of its dramatic shape. The roofs look like the sails of a ship.

Tasmanian devil

These fierce animals are the size of a small dog and only live in the wild in Tasmania. They are named "devils" because of their aggressive character.

Kiwi

This flightless bird is native to New Zealand. It is the country's national symbol and appears on coins and badges. New Zealanders are often referred to as "Kiwis."

PACIFIC OCEAN
N
E
S
W
The Māori people built wooden meeting houses, often with detailed carving on the outside
Carved meeting house
Whangarei
Kauri
This huge tree only grows on New Zealand's North Island. It can be up to 165 ft (50 m) tall with a 16 ft (5 m) diameter trunk
Auckland
BAY OF PLENTY
Hamilton
Rotorua
Gisborne
Waikato
Lake Taupo
North Island
Hawke Bay
Napier
Art Deco building
Napier has many Art Deco buildings, which were built after an earthquake in the 1930s
New Plymouth
Mt Taranaki
This active volcano last erupted in the mid-19th century
TASMAN SEA
Palmerston North
The government works in this building. It is known as "the Beehive" because of its shape
"Beehive" Parliament building
Wellington
Nelson
Blenheim

The haka

All Blacks rugby team

The All Blacks is the nickname of the national men's rugby union team. It is one of the best rugby teams in the world. The men perform a haka, a traditional Māori war dance, before each international match.

Pohutu Geyser

"Pohutu" means explosion or big splash. Hot water from this geyser spurts up into the air about 20 times a day, reaching heights of around 100 ft (30 m).

KEY

PRODUCE
- Sheep
- Cattle
- Vineyards
- Apples and pears
- Peaches
- Wheat

INDUSTRY
- Hydrolectric power
- Oil
- Gas
- Coal
- Gold

ACTIVITIES
- Skiing
- Hiking
- Fishing
- Mountain biking
- White-water rafting
- Sailing
- Hot springs

NATURAL FEATURES
- Earthquakes
- Volcanoes

SCALE

0 — 50 miles

0 — 50 kilometers

Māori club

Māori warriors used short-handled clubs to strike their enemies in battle. They were made from wood, whale bone, hard volcanic rock, or iron. Some were elaborately carved

NEW ZEALAND

New Zealand is one of the world's most isolated countries, being nearly 930 miles (1,500 km) from its nearest neighbor, Australia. It is made up of two large islands and several smaller ones. Farmland and forests cover much of the country. Volcanic activity has created many high mountains and hot springs.

Hiking on Franz Josef glacier

Glaciers

New Zealand has many glaciers, mostly on South Island. One of the largest is the Franz Josef glacier, named after an Austrian emperor by a German explorer. This massive block of ice is 7½ miles (12 km) long.

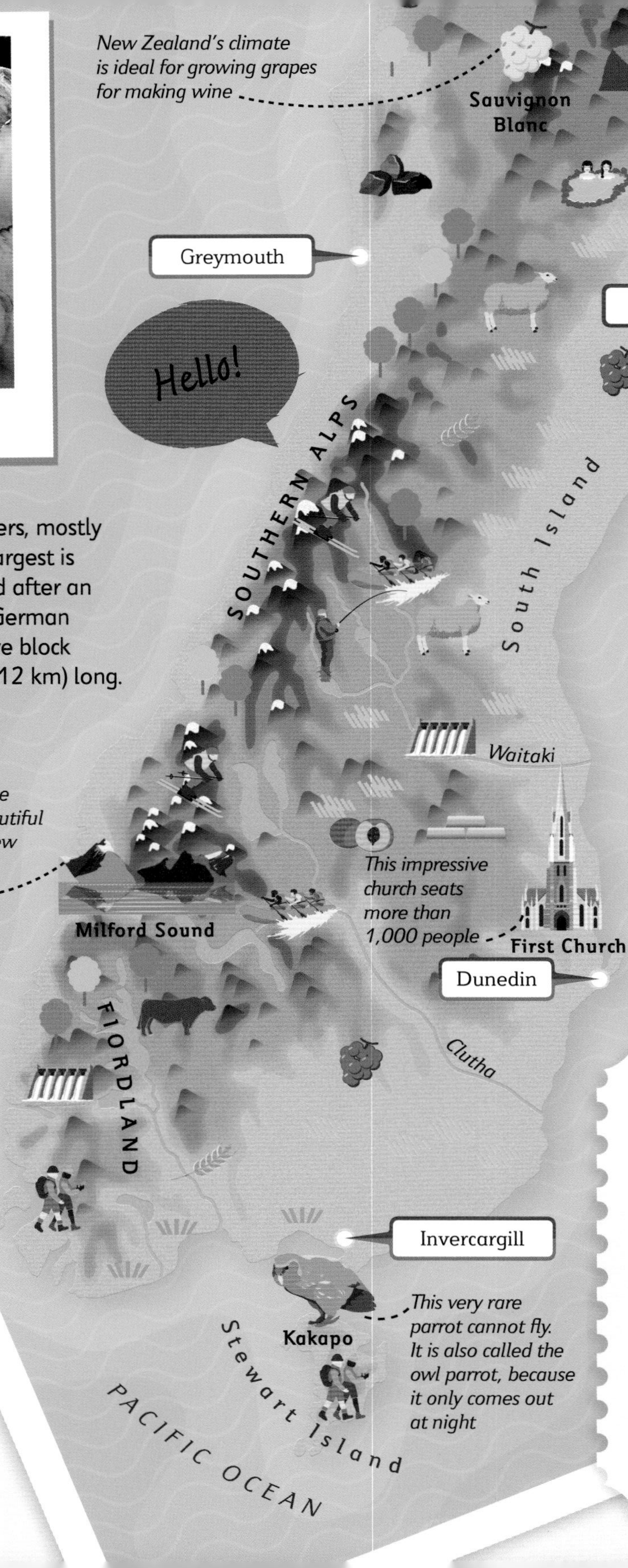

New Zealand's climate is ideal for growing grapes for making wine
Sauvignon Blanc
Large numbers of sperm whales feed in the waters near Kaikoura
Kaikoura
Sperm whale
Greymouth
Christchurch
Hello!
SOUTHERN ALPS
South Island
Waitaki
Despite its remote location, this beautiful fjord is one of New Zealand's most visited sites
Milford Sound
This impressive church seats more than 1,000 people
First Church
Dunedin
FIORDLAND
Clutha
Invercargill
This very rare parrot cannot fly. It is also called the owl parrot, because it only comes out at night
Kakapo
Stewart Island
PACIFIC OCEAN

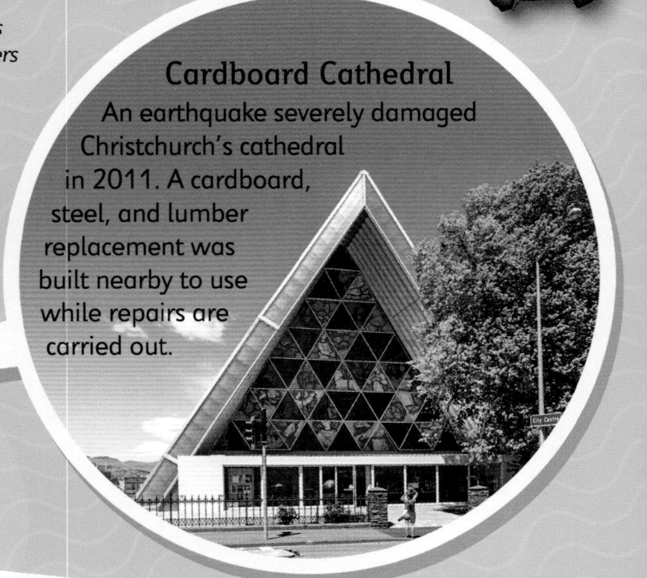

Cardboard Cathedral

An earthquake severely damaged Christchurch's cathedral in 2011. A cardboard, steel, and lumber replacement was built nearby to use while repairs are carried out.

Māori dancers

Māori

Māoris were the first people to arrive in New Zealand, nearly 1,000 years ago. Today, they make up less than a quarter of the population, but interest in their culture is growing. Children can now learn the Māori language in school.

Green-lipped mussels

Kiwi fruit

Farming and fishing

New Zealand exports its produce all over the world. It is famous for its lamb and juicy, green-fleshed kiwi fruit. Large, green-lipped mussels live around the coast and are also farmed.

ANTARCTICA

Antarctica is the coldest and driest continent on Earth. More than 99 percent of the land is covered by a huge ice sheet, which is up to 2¾ miles (4.5 km) thick in places. No people live there permanently, but scientists and tourists visit to study this icy world and its unique animals and plants.

Krill

The cold waters of the Southern Ocean are full of krill. These little shrimplike animals are the main source of food for many birds and whales.

British Antarctic Survey
NATURAL ENVIRONMENT RESEARCH COUNCIL

Halley VI dining unit

Antarctic stations

Scientists live and work in Antarctica in research stations. *Halley VI* is a British station that has eight units, which can be moved independently. Each unit sits above the ice on stilts with skis.

Larsen B Ice Shelf

This huge area of ice on the edge of the Weddell Sea melted and broke up in 2002 as a result of global climate change.

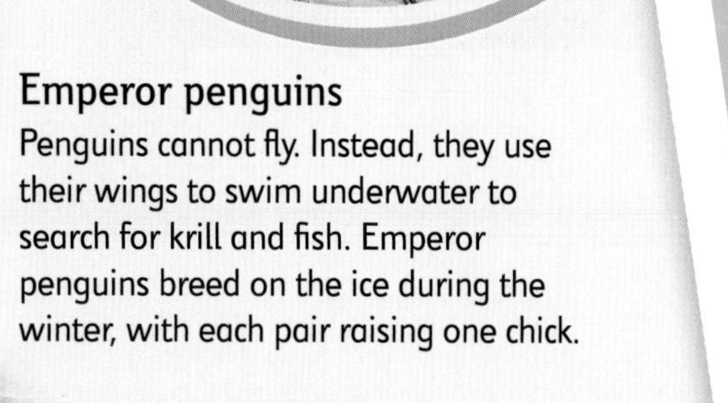

Emperor penguins

Penguins cannot fly. Instead, they use their wings to swim underwater to search for krill and fish. Emperor penguins breed on the ice during the winter, with each pair raising one chick.

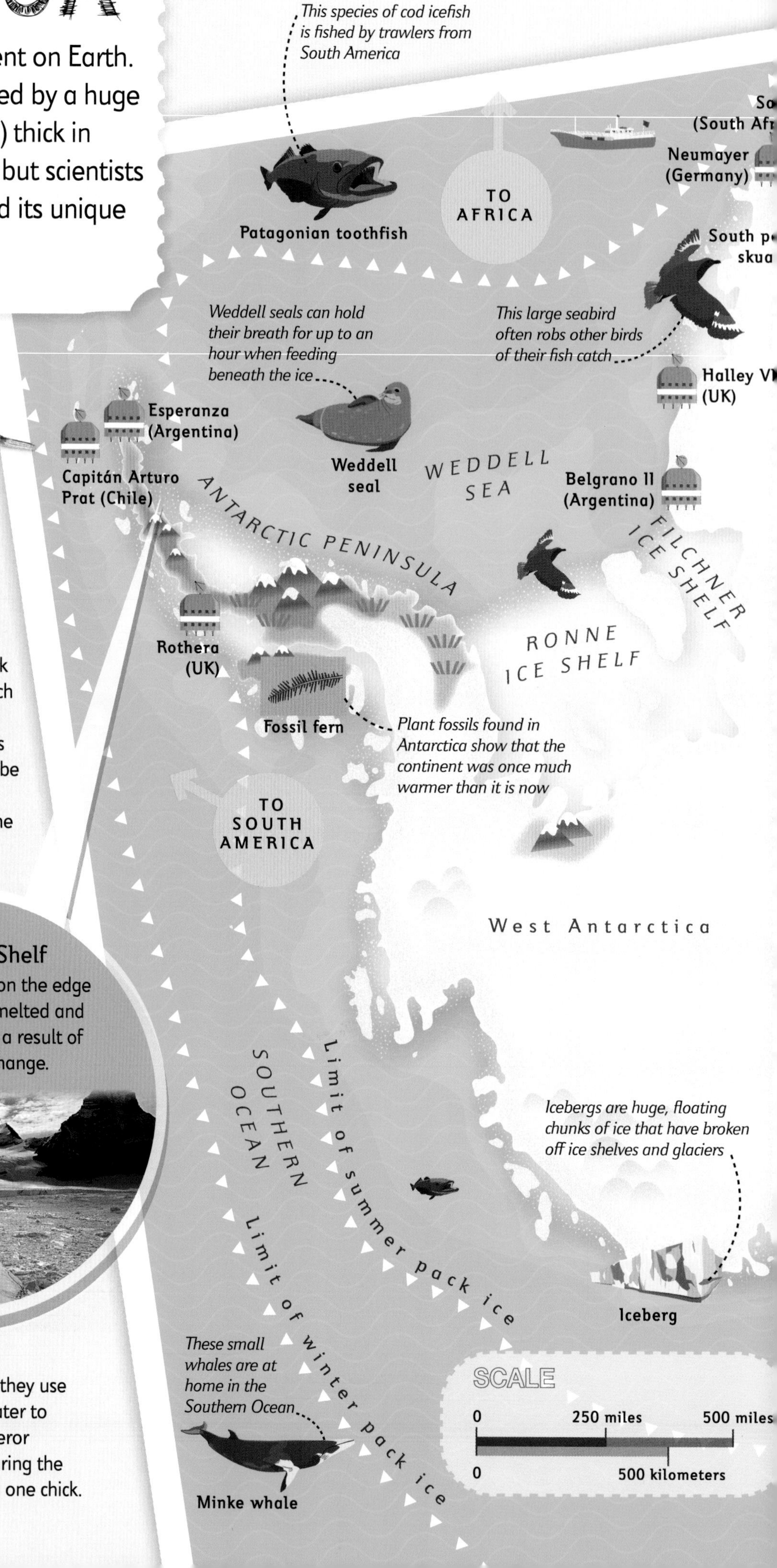

This species of cod icefish is fished by trawlers from South America
Patagonian toothfish
TO AFRICA
Sa
(South Afr
Neumayer
(Germany)
South p
skua
This large seabird often robs other birds of their fish catch
Weddell seals can hold their breath for up to an hour when feeding beneath the ice
Weddell seal
Halley VI
(UK)
Esperanza
(Argentina)
Capitán Arturo Prat (Chile)
WEDDELL SEA
Belgrano II
(Argentina)
ANTARCTIC PENINSULA
FILCHNER ICE SHELF
RONNE ICE SHELF
Rothera
(UK)
Fossil fern
Plant fossils found in Antarctica show that the continent was once much warmer than it is now
TO SOUTH AMERICA
West Antarctica
SOUTHERN OCEAN
Limit of summer pack ice
Limit of winter pack ice
Icebergs are huge, floating chunks of ice that have broken off ice shelves and glaciers
Iceberg
These small whales are at home in the Southern Ocean
Minke whale
SCALE
0
250 miles
500 miles
0
500 kilometers

These ships can break through ice up to 3 ft (1 m) thick
Research ship
Maitri (India)
Syowa (Japan)
SOUTHERN OCEAN
The wandering albatross is found across the Southern Ocean
Wandering albatross
Zhongshan (China)
Davis (Australia)
Taishan (China)
The snow petrel is one of the few birds to have been seen at the South Pole
Snow petrel
East Antarctica
Amundsen–Scott (USA)
South Pole
Vostok (Russia)
NSANTARCTIC MOUNTAINS
South Geomagnetic Pole
Every summer, Scott station rugby club plays a game on the snow against a team from McMurdo station
ROSS ICE SHELF
Rugby
The Ice Marathon has been held every summer since 2006, and even the penguins have been known to join in!
Scott (NZ)
McMurdo (USA)
Ice Marathon
ROSS SEA
Mario Zucchelli (Italy)
Dumont d'Urville (France)
This powerful seal eats krill, penguins, and other seals
More than 2 million pairs of Adélie penguins breed around Antarctica every year, nesting on ice-free areas of rock
TO AUSTRALIA
TO NEW ZEALAND
Adélie penguin
Leopard seal

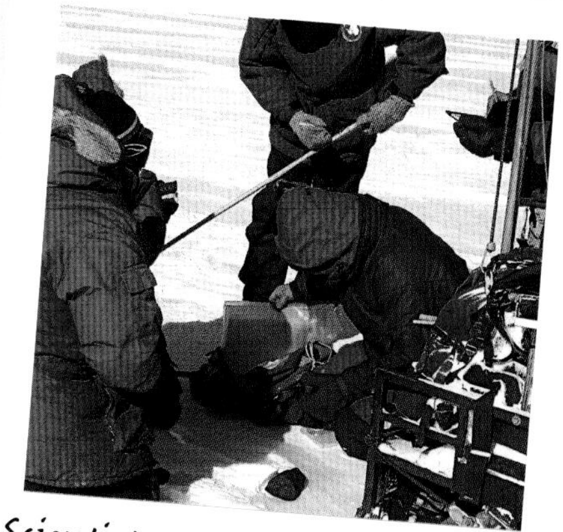

Scientists examining a meteorite

Meteorites

Rocks from space that land on the Earth's surface are called meteorites. Thousands of meteorites have been collected from Antarctica, including ones from the Moon and the planet Mars.

Roald Amundsen

Race to the South Pole

Explorers competed to be the first people to reach the South Pole, the southernmost point on Earth. Norwegian adventurer Roald Amundsen led the first successful team there in 1911.

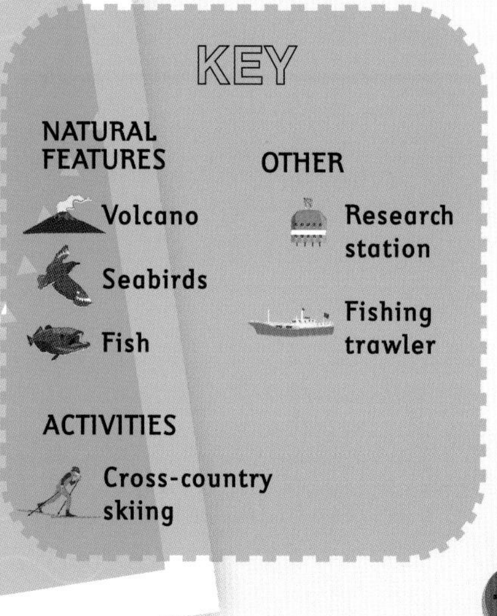
KEY
NATURAL FEATURES
Volcano
Seabirds
Fish
OTHER
Research station
Fishing trawler
ACTIVITIES
Cross-country skiing

THE ARCTIC

The extreme northern edges of the countries of Europe, Asia, and North America lie within the Arctic region. At its center lies the North Pole. Most of the Arctic is ice, floating above the Arctic Ocean. In summer, the ice shrinks and chunks break off into the ocean. In winter, the ice expands.

Polar bear
The polar bear's thick fur helps it keep warm in freezing Arctic temperatures. It hunts mainly seals, which it catches through holes in the ice. It is also a very good swimmer.

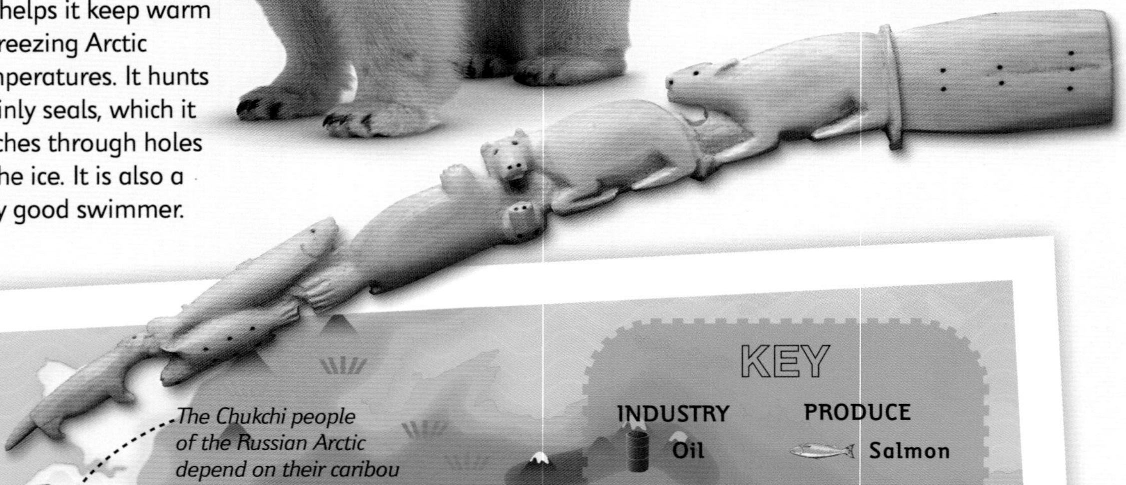

Inuit carving
The Inuit are an Indigenous people who live in the Arctic regions of the USA, Canada, and Greenland. Art is important in Inuit culture, and craftworkers make sculptures out of natural materials like rock and bone.

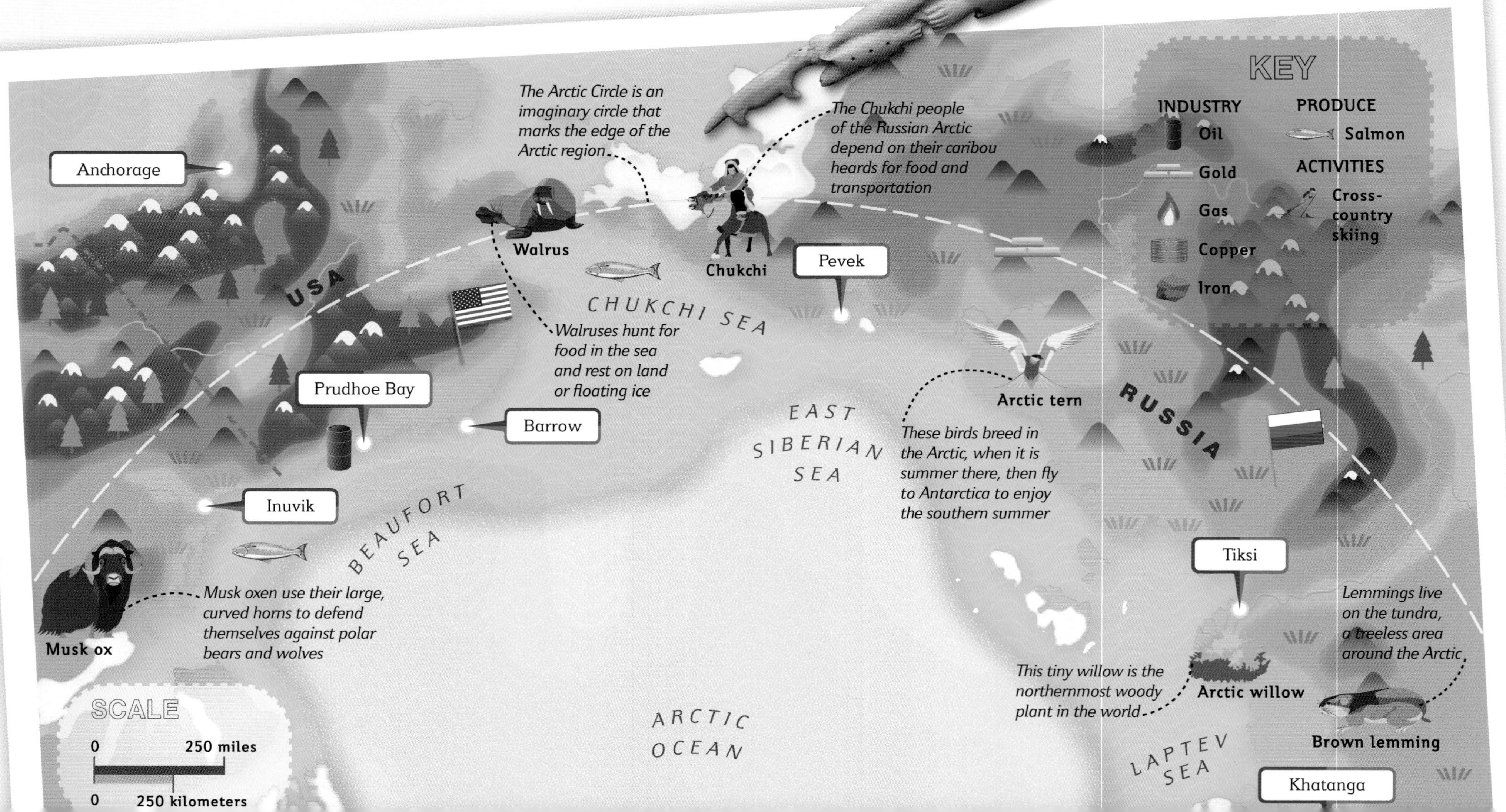

KEY
INDUSTRY
Oil
Gold
Gas
Copper
Iron
PRODUCE
Salmon
ACTIVITIES
Cross-country skiing
Anchorage
USA
Prudhoe Bay
Inuvik
Barrow
Musk ox
Musk oxen use their large, curved horns to defend themselves against polar bears and wolves
BEAUFORT SEA
Walrus
Walruses hunt for food in the sea and rest on land or floating ice
The Arctic Circle is an imaginary circle that marks the edge of the Arctic region
CHUKCHI SEA
Chukchi
The Chukchi people of the Russian Arctic depend on their caribou heards for food and transportation
Pevek
EAST SIBERIAN SEA
Arctic tern
These birds breed in the Arctic, when it is summer there, then fly to Antarctica to enjoy the southern summer
RUSSIA
Tiksi
Arctic willow
This tiny willow is the northernmost woody plant in the world
Lemmings live on the tundra, a treeless area around the Arctic
Brown lemming
Khatanga
LAPTEV SEA
ARCTIC OCEAN
SCALE
0 250 miles
0 250 kilometers

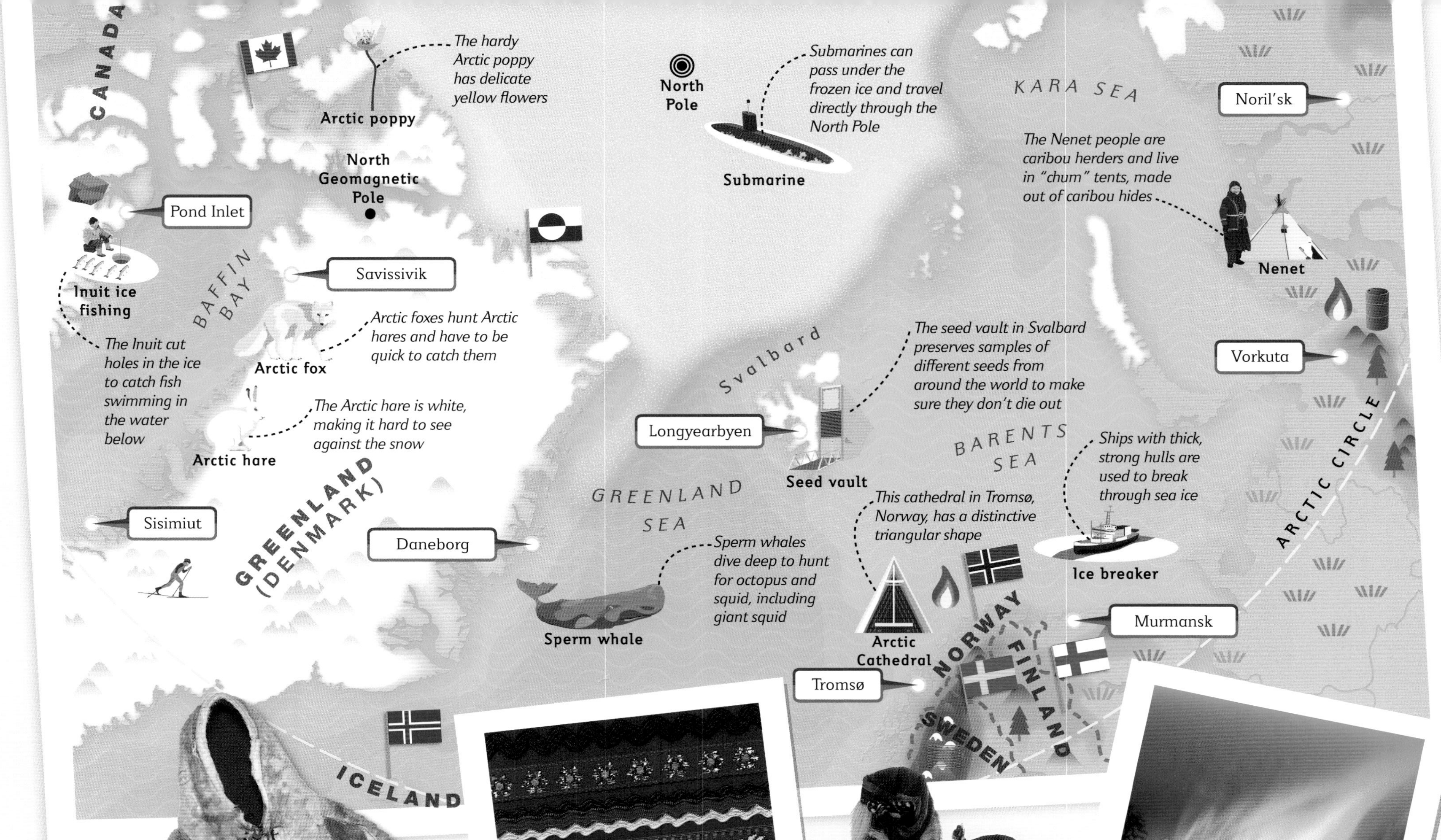
CANADA
The hardy Arctic poppy has delicate yellow flowers
Arctic poppy
North Geomagnetic Pole
Pond Inlet
Inuit ice fishing
The Inuit cut holes in the ice to catch fish swimming in the water below
BAFFIN BAY
Savissivik
Arctic foxes hunt Arctic hares and have to be quick to catch them
Arctic fox
The Arctic hare is white, making it hard to see against the snow
Arctic hare
Sisimiut
GREENLAND (DENMARK)
Daneborg
ICELAND
North Pole
Submarines can pass under the frozen ice and travel directly through the North Pole
Submarine
Svalbard
Longyearbyen
Seed vault
The seed vault in Svalbard preserves samples of different seeds from around the world to make sure they don't die out
GREENLAND SEA
Sperm whales dive deep to hunt for octopus and squid, including giant squid
Sperm whale
BARENTS SEA
This cathedral in Tromsø, Norway, has a distinctive triangular shape
Arctic Cathedral
Tromsø
NORWAY
SWEDEN
FINLAND
Ships with thick, strong hulls are used to break through sea ice
Ice breaker
Murmansk
KARA SEA
Noril'sk
The Nenet people are caribou herders and live in "chum" tents, made out of caribou hides
Nenet
Vorkuta
ARCTIC CIRCLE

Inuit coat

The Inuit need thick, warm clothing to survive in the freezing Arctic winters. Coats are traditionally made from animal furs, which help trap heat.

Sami embroidery

Sami embroidery and shoes

The Sami are the Indigenous people of Lapland. Traditional Sami crafts include colorful embroidery and fur clothing, including footwear.

Northern Lights

Dark nights

The Arctic has long, dark nights in winter, and for many days the Sun does not rise at all. Some nights, the colorful Northern Lights, or Aurora Borealis, can be seen flashing across the sky.

ATLAS PICTURE QUIZ

NAME THE COUNTRY

Here are the outlines of some of the countries that appear in this atlas. Can you name them? Look at the clues to help you. The answers are on page 121.

This huge island has a vast hot and dry area in the middle known as the Outback

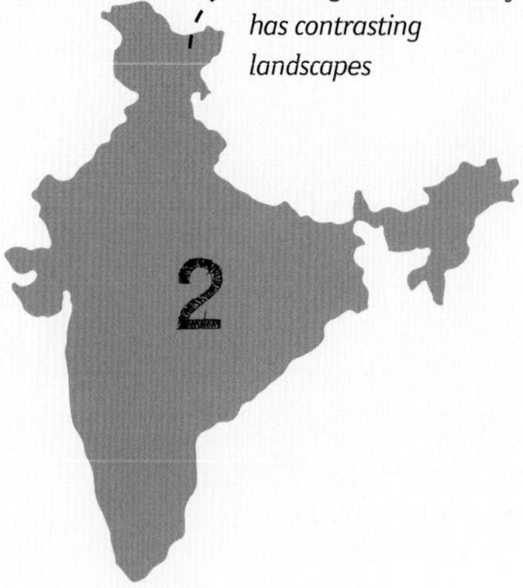

This large Asian country has contrasting landscapes

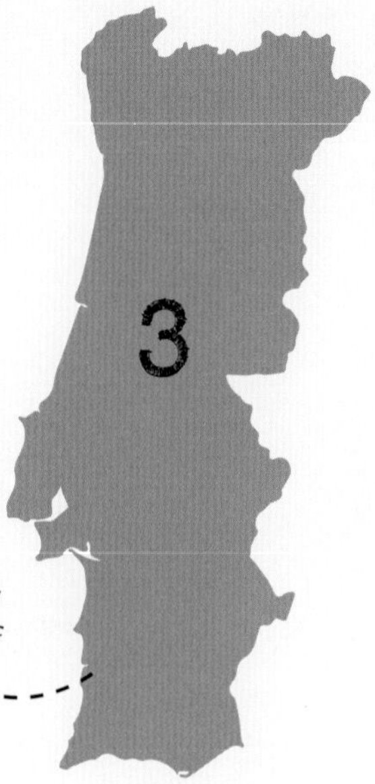

This sunny country lies on the edge of Western Europe

This long, thin South American country has mountains and deserts

This icy country is in the far north of Europe

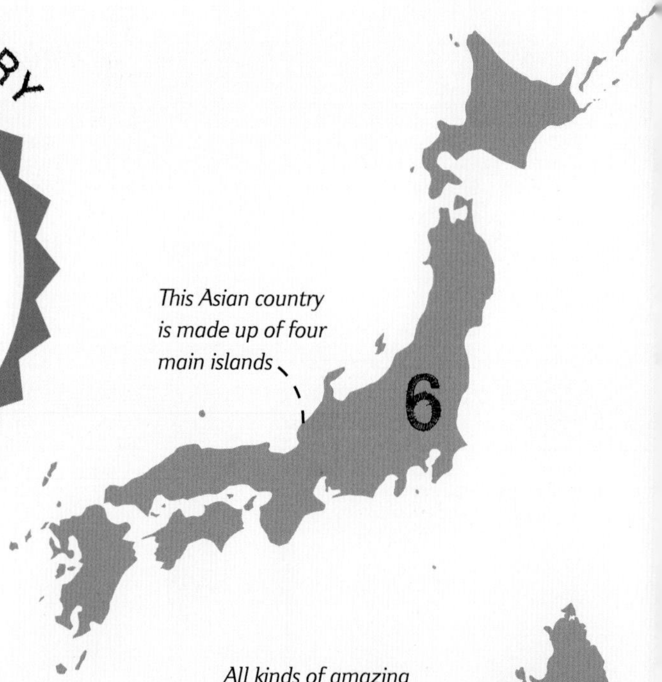

This Asian country is made up of four main islands

This fertile country in the southern hemisphere is made up of two main islands

This North American country is the second biggest in the world

This long, thin country is shaped like a boot

All kinds of amazing animals are unique to this African island

GUESS THE ICON

All these colorful icons appear somewhere in this book. See if you can answer these questions about them. The answers are at the bottom of the page.

1. In which country would you find the Atacama desert?

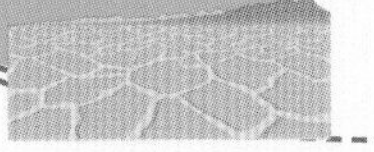

2. In which North African country is this ancient theater?

3. In which country does the kakapo make its home?

4. Which animal is this okapi related to?

5. In which region would you find this hare?

6. Which country did the artist Vincent van Gogh come from?

7. Which Asian country is the black iris the symbol of?

8. Where would you find a poppy with yellow flowers?

9. In which country would you find the Forbidden City?

10. Where would you find stars embedded in the sidewalk?

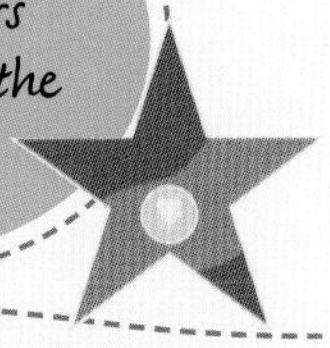

11. In which country would you find Mt. Taranaki?

12. In which mountainous country does the llama live?

13. This seal lives in which huge lake in Russia?

14. In which country would you find the Shwethalyaung Buddha?

15. In which Asian country would you find the ziggurat of Ur?

16. In which country would you find this Odissi dancer?

17. On which continent is the Ice Marathon held?

18. In which African country is Nshima eaten?

19. What's the name of this Italian leaning tower?

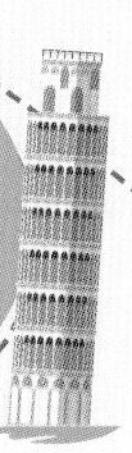

20. In which country would you find the Little Mermaid?

21. The gymnast Nadia Comăneci came from which country?

22. Which city in the US is famous for its cable cars?

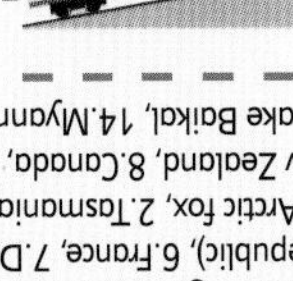

23. What's the name of this strange-looking fish?

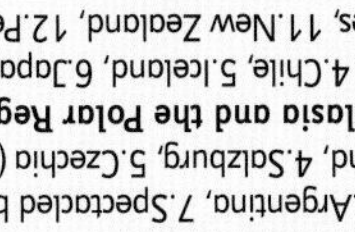

Answers: Pages 8–9 North America: 1.Mount Rushmore, 2.Dominican Republic, 3.Toronto, 4.Mexico, 5.New York, 6.Colorado River, 7.Inuit, 8.Panama Canal. **Pages 22–23 South America:** 1.Rio de Janeiro, 2.Andes, 3.Colombia, 4.Chile, 5.Brazil, 6.Argentina, 7.Spectacled bear, 8.Peru. **Pages 34–35 Africa:** 1.Tuareg, 2.Kenya, 3.Libya, 4.Feluccas, 5.Congo, 6.South Africa, 7.Zambia, 8.Madagascar. **Pages 50–51 Europe:** 1.Corsica, 2.St. Basil's Cathedral, 3.England, 4.Salzburg, 5.Czechia (Czech Republic), 6.France, 7.Danube River, 8.Spain. **Pages 80–81 Asia:** 1.India, 2.Turkey (Türkiye), 3.China, 4.Mongolia, 5.Taiwan, 6.China, 7.Tokyo Skytree, 8.South Korea **Pages 108–109 Australasia and the Polar Regions:** 1.Arctic fox, 2.Tasmania, 3.Australia, 4.Uluru (Ayers Rock), 5.Inuit, 6. New Zealand, 7.Antarctica, 8.Great Barrier Reef. **Pages 120 Name the Country:** 1.Australia, 2.India, 3.Portugal, 4.Chile, 5.Iceland, 6.Japan, 7.New Zealand, 8.Canada, 9.Italy, 10.Madagascar. **Pages 121 Guess the Icon:** 1.Chile, 2.Algeria, 3.New Zealand, 4.Giraffe, 5.Arctic, 6.Netherlands, 7.Jordan, 8.Arctic, 9.China, 10.Los Angeles, 11.New Zealand, 12.Peru, 13.Lake Baikal, 14.Myanmar, 15.Iraq, 16.India, 17.Antarctica, 18.Zambia, 19.Tower of Pisa, 20.Denmark, 21.Romania, 22.San Francisco, 23.Patagonian toothfish.

GLOSSARY

Aboriginals
Original or first-known inhabitants of a country

annexation
When a state declares sovereignty or power over another territory

artifact
Human-made object, generally of historic or cultural interest, such as a painting or a vase

canyon
Deep, narrow valley with very steep, rocky sides. A stream or river usually flows through it

capital
Country's most important city. It is where the government usually meets and passes laws

climate
Normal weather pattern during the year in any part of the world

continents
Seven large areas of land that the world is divided into: Africa, Antarctica, Asia, Australasia, Europe, North America, and South America

coral reef
Rocklike structure formed by a group of corals (simple sea animals) in the warm waters along tropical coasts.

country
Area of Earth that is governed by the same leaders and has the same flag. Most continents are made up of many different countries

crops
Plants grown to feed people and animals. Crops need the right soil and climate to grow well

culture
Way of life and beliefs of the people of a region or country

delta
Flat land formed from material deposited by a river around the area where it enters the sea or flows into a lake. Soil in a delta area is usually very fertile

desert
Dry region that gets 10 in (25 cm) or less of rainfall in a year. Deserts can be hot or cold. Only a few animals and plants are able to live in desert areas

dunes
Mounds or ridges of sand that are formed by the wind or flowing water pushing the sand together. They are usually found along beaches or in sandy deserts

earthquake
Movement of large blocks of rock beneath the Earth's surface. Cracks may open up in the ground, causing buildings to collapse

endangered
Word used to describe a species of plant or animal with only a few living members left

equator
Imaginary line around the Earth, which is exactly halfway between the North and South Poles. Countries close to the equator are hotter than countries that are farther away from it

ethnic group
Group of people who share the same racial, religious, or cultural background

exports
Goods or services that are sold to another country

extinct
Word used to describe a plant or animal species that has no living members. All dinosaurs, for example, are now extinct

fertile land
Land where the soil is particularly good for growing crops on

fjord
Long, narrow bay or inlet, with steep, high, rocky sides. The word is Norwegian and was first used to describe the many deep inlets along Norway's rocky coast

fossil
Remains or shape of a prehistoric plant or animal that have been preserved in rock

game reserve
Area where wild animals are protected from hunters, or where hunting is limited by law. Africa has many game reserves

geyser
Fountain of hot water and steam that shoots up out of the ground. Geysers form when an underground stream flows over hot, volcanic rocks

glacier
Huge, thick sheet of ice moving very slowly, either down the side of a mountain or over an area of land. Glaciers help to shape and form the landscape

grasslands
Open land covered in grass and a few small bushes. Larger plants, such as trees, rarely grow on grasslands. Grasslands are called prairies in the United States

gulf
Large area of sea that is almost enclosed by land, such as the Gulf of Mexico and Persian Gulf

hot (thermal) spring
Place where hot water, heated by volcanic activity, flows out of cracks in the ground

hurricane
Very violent storm with extremely strong winds that can cause a great deal of damage

hydroelectric power
Electricity created by machinery driven by fast-flowing water. Water forced under high pressure through dams built across rivers is often used for this purpose

iceberg
Massive piece of ice that has broken off from a glacier or ice sheet and floated out to sea

imports
Goods or services bought from another country

Indigenous
Original people from a land or country

irrigation
Supplying water to dry areas of land, so that crops can grow there. The water is carried or pumped along pipes or ditches

island
Piece of land that has water all around it. Islands occur in oceans, seas, lakes, and rivers

migrate
Move from one country or region to go and live in another. People migrate for many reasons, such as to find work or escape war

mine
Place where naturally occurring resources (such as coal, iron ore, copper, and gold) and gemstones (such as diamonds and rubies) are dug out of the ground

mineral
Natural substance found in the Earth's rocks, such as metals and precious gemstones, which are removed by mining

monsoon
Strong wind that blows across south and Southeast Asia. It changes direction as the seasons change, causing very heavy rain from May to September

mountain
Area of land that rises up much higher than the land around it to form a peak at the top. Some mountaintops are so high that they reach the icy cold air far above Earth, and so have snow on them even in summer

national park
Area of countryside that has been preserved in its natural state by the government of a country to protect the wildlife there and for people to enjoy

native
Person linked to a place by birth, or whose family are from the original inhabitants of an area.

nomads
People who do not live in one fixed place, but move around an area to graze their animals, make a living, and to find the best seasonal sources of food

oasis
Area of fertile land in the desert. Plants can grow easily there, unlike in the rest of the desert, because water lies on or very close to the surface

ocean
Very large sea. There are five oceans: Pacific Ocean, Atlantic Ocean, Indian Ocean, Arctic Ocean, and Southern Ocean

pampas
Name given to the vast grasslands found in part of South America

peninsula
Strip of land that is surrounded by water on three of its sides

plain
Area of flat, open land with very few trees. Plains are often covered with grass

plateau
Large area of high, flat land. Some mountains, such as Table Mountain in Cape Town, South Africa, have a plateau at the top

polar region
Area near to the North or South Pole. Polar regions are covered in a thick layer of ice for most of the year and are extremely cold

population
Total number of people living in a given area of land

port
Town or city on the coast with a harbor, where boats and ships can load or unload goods and let passengers board or get off

province
Officially recognized area of a country or state. Provinces often have their own leaders, although they are still governed by the laws of the country they are part of

rain forest
Dense forest with very high rainfall. Most are near the equator and are also very hot

rapids
Part of a river that is moving at great speed, because it is flowing over very steep ground.

reservoir
Large natural or artificial lake, where water is collected and stored for people to use in homes, businesses, industry, and farming

river
Large stream of water that flows from a high place to a lower place. Rivers start as small streams high up in the mountains and flow down into the sea

safari
Journey that involves looking at wild animals in their natural surroundings. It usually refers to trips taken in Africa

savanna
Name given to open grasslands in tropical and subtropical countries

sea
Large body of saltwater. Seas (including oceans) cover most of the Earth's surface

sea level
Average level of the surface of the world's seas and oceans. The height of land is given as how far it is above sea level. The depth of a sea or ocean is given as how far it is below sea level

shrubland
Area of land covered in lots of small trees and bushes, as well as different types of grass

species
Distinct group of animals or plants that share similar features

state
Nation or territory that is organized as a community under one government

steppe
Name given to the vast, grassy plains that stretch from Eastern Europe right across central Asia

terrain
Area of land, usually with a particular feature, such as mountains or grassy plains

territory
Area of land that belongs to a particular country or state

tornado
Spinning cloud of very strong wind. Tornadoes will destroy almost anything in their path

tribe
Group of people who share the same culture and history. It usually refers to people who live together in traditional communites, far from cities and towns

tropical
Conditions found in areas near the Equator. Tropical weather, for example, is very hot and wet

valley
Low area of land between hills or mountains

vegetation
Type of plants found in an area of land

volcano
Mountain or hill that may erupt, pouring out hot lava (molten rock) from a crater in its top

wetlands
Land with wet, spongy soil, such as a marsh or swamp. Many animals and plants specialize in living in wetlands

wildlife
Wild animals that live in an area of land

INDEX

Lantern Festival (Jinju) 101
Ramadan 93
tea ceremony (Japan) 102
Thanksgiving (USA) 15
Fiji 111
Finland 52, 54–5, 79
fish, *see* wildlife
fjords 54
flags 4
food
baking (Germany) 63
barbecues (Australia) 112
beef (Argentina) 31
bento (Japan) 102
bibimbap (Korea) 101
blinis (Russia) 77
bobotie (South Africa) 46
bunny chow (South Africa) 46
café culture (France) 59
Caribbean 19
cheese (France/Poland) 58
Chlebičky (Czech Republic) 69
chocolates (Belgium) 60
curries (India and Sri Lanka) 94
dim sum (China) 99
Dobos cake (Hungary) 70
enerja (Ethiopia) 41
fatayer (Lebanon) 88
fish and chips (Britain) 56
goulash (Hungary) 70
ice cream (Italy/Turkey) 66, 87
jollof rice and suya (Nigeria) 42
kebabs (Greece/Turkey) 87
kimchee (Korea) 101
momos (Nepal) 96
musssels and fries (Belgium) 60
pasta (Italy) 67
pho (Vietnam) 104
pizza (Italy) 67
rollmops (Northern Europe) 54
Sachertorte (Austria) 61
sausages (Slovakian) 69
shan noodles (Myanmar) 97
shchi (Russia) 76
tabbouleh (Lebanon) 88
tacos (Mexico) 17
tagines (North Africa) 38
tapas (Spain) 65
tzatziki (Greece) 75
forests 5
Northern European 52
rain forest 24, 28, 44, 48
fossils 98
France 53, 58–9
French Polynesia 111
fruit, *see* produce
Fuji, Mount (Japan) 103

G

Ganges, River 78, 82
Gaza Strip 89
Germany 53, 62–3
Ghana 43
glaciers 115
global warming 20
Gobi Desert 49, 98
Grand Canyon (USA) 48
Great Barrier Reef (Australia) 48, 111, 113
Greece 74–5
Greenland 119
Guatemala 18

H

Ha Long Bay (Vietnam) 104
habitats 5
Haiti 19
Hamburg (Germany) 62
Hawaii (USA) 10, 14
High Tatra Mountains (Poland/Slovakia) 69
Himalayan Mountains 78, 82, 94, 96
Hindu Kush Mountains 92
historic sites
Ambohimanga (Madagascar) 47
Angkor Wat (Cambodia) 104, 107
Astronomical Clock (Prague) 68
Big Ben (London) 57
Bran Castle (Romania) 72
Brandenburg Gate (Berlin) 62
Charles Bridge (Prague) 68
Château de Chenonceau (France) 58
Chichén Itzá (Mexico) 107
Citadel of Herat (Afghanistan) 92
Colosseum (Rome) 67, 107
Eiffel Tower (Paris) 52, 107
El Jem (Tunisia) 39
Forbidden City (Beijing) 107
Great Pyramid of Giza (Egypt) 40, 107
Great Wall of China 107
Houses of Parliament (London) 57
Machu Picchu (Peru) 27, 107
Market Square (Kraków) 69
Megalithic Temples (Malta) 106
Palenque (Mexico) 17
Parthenon (Athens) 75
Petra (Jordan) 89, 107
Pula Amphitheatre (Croatia)
pyramids 40, 107
Rhine Valley castles (Germany) 63
San Agustín Park (Colombia) 26
Széchenyi Baths (Budapest) 70
Taj Mahal (India) 107
Tassili n'Ajjer (Algeria) 39
Topkapi Palace (Istanbul) 86
Triumphal Arch (Tyre) 88
Ur (Iraq) 90
Vasa Museum (Stockholm) 55
Vianden Castle (Luxembourg) 60
Holy Land 89
Honduras 18
Hong Kong (China) 99
Hungary 70

I

Iceland 54
Iguaçu Falls (Brazil/Argentina) 29
India 94–5
population 32, 33
Indonesia 32, 105
Indus, River 93
industry
cobalt mining 44
fishing 75, 115
oil 12, 42
salmon farming 85
Inle Lake (Myanmar) 97
insects, *see* wildlife
internet 100
Iran 90–1
Iraq 90
Ireland 56–7
Irrawaddy, River 97
Isfahan (Iran) 90
Islam 91, 93
Islamabad (Pakistan) 93
Israel 89
Istanbul (Turkey) 86, 107
Italy 53, 66–7
Ivory Coast 43

J

Jamaica 19
Japan 102–3
Java 104, 105
Jeju Island (Korea) 101
Jerusalem (Israel) 89
Jinju (South Korea) 101
Jordan 89

K

K2 (Pakistan) 78
Kalahari Desert 49
Kangchenjunga (India/Nepal) 78
Kazakhstan 84
Kebili (Tunisia) 21
Kenya 41
keys, map 5
Khyber Pass (Afghanistan/Pakistan) 82
Kiev (Ukraine) 71
Kilauea (Hawaii) 10
Kim Il-sung 100
Kiribati 111
Klinck (Greenland) 21
Korea 100–1
Kraków (Poland) 69
Krka National Park (Croatia) 70

L

lakes
Baikal (Russia) 85
Band-e Amir lakes (Afghanistan) 92
Bled (Slovenia) 70
Caspian Sea 79
Finland 79
Inle Lake (Myanmar) 97
largest 79
Nasser (Egypt) 40
Superior (Canada/USA) 79
Titicaca (Bolivia/Peru) 24
Victoria (Africa) 79
language 4
Laos 104
Lapland (Norway/Sweden/Finland) 54
Larsen B Ice Shelf (Antarctica) 116
Latvia 76
Lebanon 88
Leehow, River 99
Lhotse (Nepal) 78
Libya 38, 39
Liechtenstein 52, 53
Lisbon (Portugal) 64
Lithuania 76
Loire Valley (France) 58
London (England) 57
Los Angeles (USA) 14
Low Countries 60
Luxembourg 60
Luxor (Egypt) 21
Lysefjord (Norway) 54

M

Madagascar 47
Madeira (Portugal) 64
Makalu (China/Nepal) 78
Malaysia 104
Malmö (Sweden) 55
Malta 106
maps, how to read 4–5
markets
Christmas market (Dresden, Germany) 63
craft market (San Pedro, Peru) 27
Market Square (Kraków, Poland) 69
medina (Marrakesh, Morocco) 38
outdoor markets (France) 59
street market (Chichicastenango, Guatemala) 18
West Africa 36
Marrakesh (Morocco) 38
Marshall Islands 111
Matterhorn (Italy/Switzerland) 61
Mauritania 36
Mawsynram (Meghalaya, India) 21
Mecca (Saudi Arabia) 91
Mediterranean climate 20
Mediterranean Sea 52
Megalithic Temples (Malta) 106
meteorites 117
Mexico 16–17
Mexico City 10, 16, 17, 33
Micronesia 110
Milford Sound (New Zealand) 111
Mississippi, River 78–9

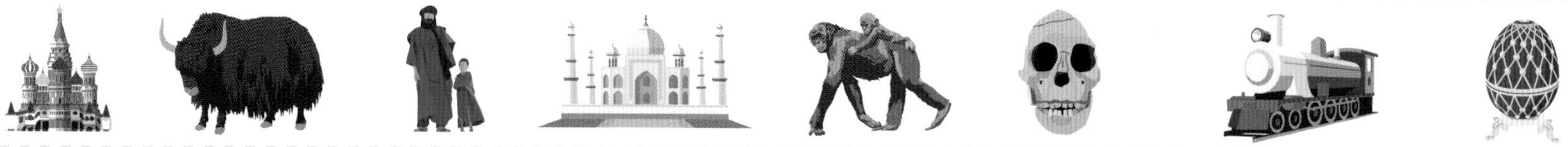

modern sites
- Akorda Presidential Palace (Astana) 84
- Aswan Dam (Egypt) 40
- Burj Khalifa (Dubai) 106
- Carlton Centre (Johannesburg) 106
- Christ the Redeemer (Rio de Janeiro) 29, 107
- Eden Project (England) 57
- Federation Towers (Moscow) 106
- Gran Torre Santiago (Santiago, Chile) 106
- Halley VI Antarctic station 116
- International Space Station 85
- Kumsusan Palace of the Sun (Pyongyang) 100
- One World Trade Center (New York) 106
- Sydney Opera House (Australia) 113
- *see also* bridges

Mohenjo-daro (Pakistan) 21
Monaco 53, 59
Mongolia 32, 83, 98–9
monsoons 21
Mont Blanc (France/Italy) 53
Montréal 13
Monument Valley (USA) 10
Morocco 38
Moscow (Russia) 33, 53
mosques, *see* religious sites
mountains 5, 78–9
- The Alps 53, 61
- Andes 24, 27, 30
- Carpathian Mountains (Romania) 72, 73
- High Tatra (Poland/Slovakia) 69
- Himalayan Mountains 78, 82, 94, 96
- Hindu Kush 92
- K2 (Pakistan) 78
- Kangchenjunga (India/Nepal) 78
- Lhotse (Nepal) 78
- Makalu (China/Nepal) 78
- Mount Everest (Nepal) 48, 78, 96
- Mount Fuji (Japan) 103
- Mount Paektu (North Korea) 100
- Pirin Mountains (Bulgaria) 73
- Rocky Mountains 10
- Sugar Loaf Mountain (Rio de Janeiro, Brazil) 29, 48
- Table Mountain (South Africa) 37, 46
- *see also* volcanoes

Muhammad, the Prophet 91
Mumbai (India) 94, 95
mummies 40
music, *see* culture and the arts
Myanmar 97

N

Nasser, Lake (Egypt) 40
natural wonders 48–9
- Blyde River Canyon (South Africa) 46
- Cliffs of Moher (Ireland) 57
- Copper Canyon (Mexico) 16
- Cotton Palace (Turkey) 86
- Death Valley (California, USA) 21
- Franz Josef glacier (New Zealand) 115
- Grand Canyon (USA) 48
- Great Barrier Reef (Australia) 48, 111, 113
- Ha Long Bay (Vietnam) 104
- Milford Sound (New Zealand) 111
- Monument Valley (USA) 10
- Northern Lights (Aurora Borealis) 48, 119
- Pohutu Geyser 114
- Pulpit Rock (Norway) 54
- Rio de Janeiro Harbour (Brazil) 48
- Taroko Gorge (Taiwan) 99
- Uluru (Australia) 107, 110
- *see also* caves; lakes; mountains; rivers; volcanoes; waterfalls

Nepal 78, 96
Netherlands 60
New Seven Wonders of the World 107
New York (USA) 11, 15
New Zealand 109, 110, 111, 114–15
Niagara Falls (Canada/USA) 13
Nicaragua 18
Nigeria 42
nights, Arctic 119
Nile, River 37, 40
North Africa 38–9
North America 6, 8–19
North Korea 100–1
North Pole 118
Northern Europe 52, 54–5
Northern Ireland 56
Northern Lights (Aurora Borealis) 48, 119
Norway 52, 54–5
nuts, *see* produce

O

orchids 47
Orinoco, River 78
Oymyakon (Russia) 21

P

Pacific Islands 109, 110, 111
paddy fields 83
Paektu, Mount (North Korea) 100
Pakistan 93
palaces, *see* historic sites; modern sites
Palenque (Mexico) 17
Palestinian territories 89
Pampas 25, 31
Pamukkale (Turkey) 86
Panama 18
Papua New Guinea 105, 110
Parícutin Volcano (Mexico) 48
Paris (France) 52, 107
Patagonia 31
people
- Native Americans 9, 14
- Aztecs 16
- Bedouin tribes 89
- First Nations 110, 113
- First people 12
- gauchos 31
- gladiators 67, 70
- Haida 12
- Inuits 118, 119
- Maasai 41
- Māoris 114, 115
- Mayans 16, 17, 18, 107
- Native Americans 9, 14
- Navajo tribe 14
- Quechua 27
- Romans 39, 67, 70, 86, 88
- Safavid dynasty 90
- Sami 54, 119
- sapeurs 44
- sherpas 96
- Umayyad Caliphate 88
- Vikings 55
- Yanomami tribe 28
- Yoruba tribe 42
- Zulus 46

Perth (Australia) 110, 112
Peru 24, 27
Petra (Jordan) 89, 107
Philadelphia (USA) 15
Philippines 105
Pirin Mountains (Bulgaria) 73
Pohutu Geyser 114
Poland 68–9
polar regions 109, 116–19
- climate 20

Polynesia, French 111
population 32–3
Portugal 64
Prague (Czech Republic) 68
produce
- apricots 92
- Asian pears 100
- avocados 19
- blackcurrants 69
- canola oil 13
- cassavas 45
- caviar 90
- Chinese cabbage 100
- cocoa beans 43
- coconuts 18
- coffee 28, 41, 61, 67, 87, 89
- cotton 40
- dates 90
- flax 13
- gooseberries 69
- grapes 30, 58
- green-lipped mussels 115
- honey 71
- kiwi fruit 115
- limes 19
- maple syrup 13
- okra 43
- olive oil 65
- oranges 28
- peaches 30
- pineapples 18
- pistachios 92
- plantains 43
- pomegranates 92
- potatoes 27
- raspberries 69, 77
- rice 83
- roses 73
- saffron 90
- spices 94
- sunflowers 58
- sweet potatoes 45
- tea 56, 89
- vanilla 47
- walnuts 71
- wine 30, 58

Puerto Rico 19
Pula (Croatia) 70
Pyongyang (North Korea) 100

Q

Q1 Tower (Gold Coast, Australia) 106
Qatar 82

R

rainfall 21
rain forest
- Amazonian 24, 28, 48
- Congo 44

Ramnefjellsfossen (Norway) 49
religious sites
- Cardboard Cathedral (Christchurch) 115
- Church of St George (Ethiopia) 41
- Faisal Mosque (Islamabad) 93
- Golden Temple of Dambulla (Sri Lanka) 95
- Haghia Sophia (Istanbul) 107
- Hassan II Mosque (Casablanca) 38
- Hazrat Sultan Mosque (Astana) 84
- Horezu Monastery (Romania) 72
- Jerusalem (Israel) 89
- Metéora monasteries (Greece) 74
- Nasir al-Mulk Mosque (Shiraz) 91
- La Sagrada Familia (Barcelona) 107
- St Basil's Cathedral (Moscow) 53
- St Peter's Basilica (Rome) 107
- Sultan Ahmed (Blue) Mosque (Istanbul) 86
- Trinity Church (Zhovka, Ukraine) 71

Rhine, River 62, 63
Rio de Janeiro (Brazil) 29, 48, 107

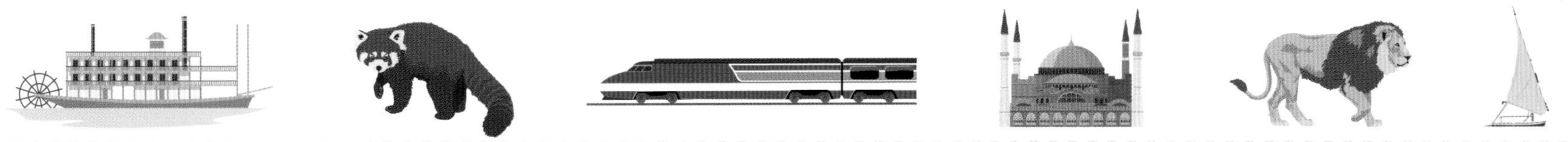

rivers 78–9
Amazon 24, 78–9
Congo 44, 78
Ganges 78, 82
Indus 93
Irrawaddy 97
Mississippi 78–9
Nile 37, 40, 78–9
Orinoco 78
Rhine 62, 63
Yangtze 78–9
Yenisei 78–9
Zambezi 45
Rocky Mountains 10
Romania 72–3
Rome (Italy) 67, 107
roses 73
Russia 52
Asian 84–5
European 76–7
Ryukyu Islands (Japan) 103

S

Sahara Desert 36, 39, 49
San Antonio de Ureca (Equatorial Guinea) 21
San Francisco (USA) 14, 107
sand dunes 39
São Paulo (Brazil) 25, 33
Sardinia (Italy) 67
Saudi Arabia 90–1
saunas 55
scale, map 4
Scotland 56
Seoul (South Korea) 83
Seven Natural Wonders of the World 48
Shiraz (Iran) 91
Sicily (Italy) 67
Silk Road 82, 92
sites, great 106–7
see also historic sites; modern sites; natural wonders; religious sites
skiing 61, 68
Skradinska Buk waterfalls (Croatia) 70
Slaibiya (Kuwait) 21
Slovakia 68–9
Slovenia 70
Snag (Yukon, Canada) 21
Sofia (Bulgaria) 73
Solomon Islands 111
South Africa 46
South America 6, 22–31
population 33
South Korea 100–1
South Pole (Antarctica) 21, 117
Southeast Asia 104–5
space travel 85
Spain 64–5
sports
All Blacks rugby team 114
baseball 15
capoeira 29
chinlone (caneball) 97
cycling 13, 59, 60
hiking 61, 68, 73
hunting 84
ice hockey 12
kendo 102
lucha libre 17
martial arts 102
mountaineering 96
Olympic Games 29
rugby 114
skiing 61, 68
soccer 29
surfing 112
tai chi 30
Tour de France 59
Tour de l'Île de Montréal 13
Sri Lanka 94, 95
steppe 98
Stockholm (Sweden) 55
subarctic regions 20
subtropical climate 20
Sudan 36
Sugar Loaf Mountain (Rio de Janeiro) 29, 48
Sultan Ahmed Mosque (Istanbul) 86
Sumatra 104
Superior, Lake (Canada/USA) 79
Sweden 52, 54–5
Switzerland 53, 61
Sydney (Australia) 33, 113
Syria 88

T

Table Mountain (South Africa) 37, 46
Taiwan 99
Tambora, Mount (Indonesia) 79
Tanzania 37
Taroko Gorge (Taiwan) 99
Tasmania (Australia) 110, 113
temperate climate 20
temperatures 21
temples, *see* religious sites
Thailand 104
Thera, Mount (Santorini, Greece) 79
thermal springs 70, 85, 86, 114, 115
Tibet 98
Tirat Tsvi (Israel) 21
Titicaca, Lake (Bolivia/Peru) 24
Tokyo (Japan) 33, 102
Tonga 111
tourist attractions
popular 107
see also historic sites; modern sites; natural wonders; religious sites
Trans-Alaska Pipeline 12
transport
cable cars 69
canals 60, 62, 66
gondolas 66
high-speed trains 103
jeepneys 105
scooters 66
treasure
Aztec ornaments 16
Bactrian gold 92
gemstones 95, 97
jewellery 90
Syrian artefacts 88
Trinidad and Tobago 19
tropical climate 20
Tugela Falls (South Africa) 49
Tunisia 38, 39
Turkey (Türkiye) 86–7
Tutendo (Colombia) 21
Tyre (Lebanon) 88

U

Ukraine 71
Uluru (Australia) 107, 110
United Kingdom 56–7
United States of America 10–11, 14–15
population 32, 33

V

Valley of the Roses (Bulgaria) 73
Vancouver (Canada) 12
Vanuatu 11
Vatican City 67, 107
vegetables, *see* produce
Venezuela 26
Venice (Italy) 66
Victoria, Lake (Africa) 79
Victoria Falls (Zambia/Zimbabwe) 45, 48
Vienna (Austria) 61
Vietnam 104
Virunga National Park (Congo) 44
volcanoes
Changbaishan Volcano (China) 79
Etna (Italy) 67
Eyjafjallajökull (Iceland) 54
Kilauea (Hawaii) 10
Mauna Loa (Hawaii) 10
most powerful erruptions 79
Mount Fuji (Japan) 103
Mount Tambora (Indonesia) 79
Mount Thera (Santorini, Greece) 79
Parícutin (Mexico) 48
Vesuvius (Italy) 67
Vostok Station (Antarctica) 21

W

Waialaeale (Hawaii) 21
Wales 56, 57
Washington, D.C. (USA) 15
waterfalls
Angel Falls (Venezuela) 26, 49
Browne Falls (New Zealand) 49
Cataratas Gocta (Peru) 49
highest 49
Iguaçu Falls (Brazil/Argentina) 29
Niagara Falls (Canada/USA) 13
Ramnefjellsfossen (Norway) 49
Skradinska Buk waterfalls (Croatia) 70
Tugela Falls (South Africa) 49
Victoria Falls (Zambia/Zimbabwe) 45, 48
West Bank 89
wildlife
alpacas 31
Alpine marmots 61
Amur tigers 85
bees 71
brown bears 77
camels 36, 40
cattle 31
cobalt blue tarantulas 97
emperor penguins 116
emperor tamarins 27
game reserves 37
giant pandas 98
giraffes 41
golden eagles 84
green lizards 87
grizzly bears 12
horses 61, 83, 99
horseshoe bats 72
jaguars 29
kangaroos 112
kiwis 114
krill 116
lemurs 47
Lipizzaner horses 61
markhors 93
marsupials 112
monarch butterflies 17
morpho butterflies 28
mountain gorillas 44
mussels 60, 115
orangutans 105
peacocks 94
polar bears 118
pygmy hippopotamuses 43
resplendent quetzals 18
salmon 85
scarlet macaws 26
southern yellow-billed hornbills 45
Spanish Riding School (Vienna) 61
striped hyenas 38
swimming pigs 19
Tasmanian devils 113
tomato frogs 47
veiled chameleons 91
wildebeest 37
yellowfin tuna 41
The World 6–7

XYZ

Yaeyama Islands (Japan) 103
Yangtze, River 78–9
Yenisei, River 78–9
Zambezi, River 45
Zambia 45
Zimbabwe 45

ACKNOWLEDGMENTS

Dorling Kindersley would like to thank the following people for their assistance in the preparation of this book: Helen Garvey and Bhagyashree Nayak for design assistance; Emma Chafer, Jolyon Goddard, Katy Lennon, and Kathleen Teece for editorial assistance; Ann Kay and Laura Gilbert for proofreading; Molly Lattin and Mohd Zishan for additional illustrations; Rituraj Singh for additional picture research.

Picture Credits:
The publisher would also like to thank the following for their kind permission to reproduce their photographs:

(Key: a-above; b-below/bottom; c-center; f-far; l-left; r-right; t-top)

10 Dorling Kindersley: Claire Cordier (br); Greg Ward / Rough Guides (cb). **11 Dorling Kindersley:** Ian Cummings / Rough Guides (cr); Rowan Greenwood (tc). **12 Corbis:** PCN (tc). **Dorling Kindersley:** Tim Draper / Rough Guides (cb); The University of Aberdeen (bl, fbl); Paul Whitfield / Rough Guides (cra). **13 Dorling Kindersley:** Tim Draper / Rough Guides (c). **14 Corbis:** Louie Psihoyos (cl). **Dorling Kindersley:** Martin Richardson / Rough Guides (tl). **16 Corbis:** AS400 DB / Bettmann (clb); Mauricio Ramos / Aurora Photos (cla). **17 Corbis:** Juan Medina / Reuters (fcr). **Dorling Kindersley:** Demetrio Carrasco / Rough Guides (c); Thomas Marent (tl). Dreamstime.com: Lunamarina (tc). **18 Dorling Kindersley:** Greg and Yvonne Dean (tl); Tim Draper / Rough Guides (tc). **19 Alamy Images:** BlueOrangeStudio (tc). **Corbis:** EPA / Alejandro Ernesto (cra). **Shutterstock.com:** pansticks (tr). **20 Dorling Kindersley:** Rowan Greenwood (cl).
24 Dorling Kindersley: Tim Draper / Rough Guides (cb); Thomas Marent (bl). **25 Corbis:** Hagenmuller / Jean-Francois / Hemis (b). **26 Alamy Images:** Maxime Dube (bc). **Corbis:** Philip Lee Harvey (tr). **27 Alamy Images:** Florian Kopp / imageBROKER (bl). **Dorling Kindersley:** Cotswold Wildlife Park & Gardens, Oxfordshire, UK (fcr); Hoa Luc (cr). **Dreamstime.com:** Yuliia Yurasova (tl). **28 Corbis:** Corbis / David Selman (tl); Robin Hanbury-Tenison / robertharding (tc). **Dorling Kindersley:** Natural History Museum, London (bc).
29 Alamy Stock Photo: Celia Mannings (bl). **Corbis:** Tim Tadder (tc); Tim Kiusalaas / Masterfile (cr). **Fotolia:** Eric Isselee (tr).
Getty Images: Grant Ordelheide / Aurora Open (bc).
30 Dorling Kindersley: Tim Draper / Rough Guides (bc). **31 Alamy Images:** Image Gap (bl). **Corbis:** Christopher Pillitz / In Pictures (cr). **Dorling Kindersley:** Tim Draper / Rough Guides (br). **33 Dorling Kindersley**: Tim Draper / Rough Guides (cr). **36 Dorling Kindersley:** Suzanne Porter / Rough Guides (b). **37 Dorling Kindersley:** Rowan Greenwood (tc); Alex Robinson / Rough Guides (cr). **Dreamstime.com:** Roman Murushkin / Romanvm (br). **38 Alamy Stock Photo:** Reuters / Shereen Talaat (clb). **Dorling Kindersley:** Suzanne Porter / Rough Guides (c, fbl). **39 Alamy Images:** blickwinkel / Irlmeier (bc). **Corbis:** Kazuyoshi Nomachi (bl). **Dreamstime.com:** Gelia (tc). **40 Alamy Stock Photo:** Reuters (clb). **Dorling Kindersley:** Bolton Metro Museum (tr).
41 Alamy Images: Andrew McConnell / robertharding (tc). **Alamy Stock Photo:** Reuters / Thomas Mukoya (crb). **42 Alamy Images:** Images Of Africa / Gallo Images (br); Paula Smith (bc). **Alamy Stock Photo:** Sipa USA / MCT / Shashank Bengali (cr). **Dorling Kindersley:** Powell-Cotton Museum, Kent (cr); University of Pennsylvania Museum of Archaeology and Anthropology (tr). **43 Alamy Images:** blickwinkel (bl). **Dorling Kindersley:** Barnabas Kindersley (cra), Roger Dixon (ca). **Dreamstime.com:** Wirestock (br). **44 Alamy Stock Photo:** Frederic Reglain (cl). **Corbis:** Dr. Richard Roscoe / Visuals Unlimited (tc); Olivier Polet (br).
45 Alamy Images: Liam West (tr). Corbis: Paul Souders (bc). **46 Alamy Stock Photo:** UK Sports Pics Ltd (br). **47 Alamy Images:** Zute Lightfoot (cra). **Corbis:** Foodfolio / the food passionates (bl). **48 Alamy Images:** Chad Ehlers (cl); Emmanuel Lattes (crb); robertharding (bl). **Dorling Kindersley:** Greg Roden / Rough Guides (tr); Tim Draper / Rough Guides (clb). **Dreamstime.com:** Bin Zhou / Dropu (br). **Fotolia:** Galyna Andrushko (bc). **PunchStock:** Digital Vision (cb). **54 Corbis:** Dave G. Houser (tc). **Dreamstime.com:** Klikk (cl). **Getty Images / iStock:** Lena_Zajchikova (br). **55 Dorling Kindersley:** Roger Norum / Rough Guides (tc); Helena Smith / Rough Guides (cr). **56 Corbis:** Iain Masterton / incamerastock (cl). **57 Alamy Stock Photo:** PA Images / Zak Hussein (tr). **58 Dorling Kindersley:** Angus Osborn / Rough Guides (cla). **Fotolia:** Zee (clb). **59 Depositphotos Inc:** karandaev (cra). **Dorling Kindersley:** Paris Tourist Office (c). **Dreamstime.com:** Madrabothair (tc). **60 Dorling Kindersley:** Greg Ward / Rough Guides (bl). **Dreamstime:** Alain Lacroix (clb); Travelpeter (br). **Shutterstock.com:** Dutch_Photos (cra). **61 Alamy Images:** Realimage (br). **Corbis:** Werner Dieterich / Westend61 (cl). **62 Alamy Images:** Hans P. Szyszka / Novarc Images (cla). **Dreamstime.com:** Markwaters (bc). **63 Corbis:** Jon Hicks (tl).
65 Corbis: Hugh Sitton (bc). **Dreamstime.com:** Netfalls (tr). **66 Corbis:** Rolf Bruderer / Blend Images (br); The Gallery Collection (tl). **Dorling Kindersley:** James McConnachie / Rough Guides (tr); Scootopia (cl). **67 Alamy Images:** amphotos (bc). **Dorling Kindersley:** Jon Cunningham / Rough Guides (c).
68 Dorling Kindersley: Jon Cunningham / Rough Guides (c); Helena Smith / Rough Guides (cl). **69 Dorling Kindersley:** Barnabas Kindersley (cra). **70 Dorling Kindersley:** Tim Draper / Rough Guides (bl, bc); Eddie Gerald / Rough Guides (tr); Michelle Grant / Rough Guides (fcrb).
71 Alamy Images: Viktor Onyshchenko (bl). **72 Dorling Kindersley:** Gregory Wrona / Rough Guides (tl, tr).
75 Dorling Kindersley: Chris Christoforou / Rough Guides (tl); Michelle Grant / Rough Guides (bc).
76 Alamy Stock Photo: Douglas Lander (cb). **77 Alamy Stock Photo:** Lisovskaya Natalia / The Picture Pantry (bl). **Alamy Stock Photo:** Iain Masterton (tl). **79 Dorling Kindersley:** Roger Norum / Rough Guides (tr). **82 Corbis:** Earl & Nazima Kowall (cl); George Steinmetz (tc); Jochen Schlenker / robertharding (bl). **83 Corbis:** Tuul & Bruno Morandi (tr); Jose Fuste Raga (cr). **Dorling Kindersley:** Tim Draper / Rough Guides (br). **84 Alamy Images:** Nurlan Kalchinov (cl). **Corbis:** Gavin Hellier / JAI (br); Jose Fuste Raga (tr). **85 Alamy Images:** NASA (t). **Corbis:** Robert Jean / Hemis (bl). **Dorling Kindersley:** Blackpool Zoo, Lancashire, UK (br). **86 Dreamstime.com:** Alexandre Fagundes De Fagundes (tr). **90 Dorling Kindersley:** University of Pennsylvania Museum of Archaeology and Anthropology (cl, cb/bull, cb/necklace, bc). **91 Alamy Images:** ArkReligion.com / Art Directors & TRIP (cr); Dario Bajurin (br). **92 Alamy Images:** Danita Delimont (clb); George Rutter (tr); Farhad Hashimi (cla). **93 Alamy Images:** Ali Mujtaba (cl). **Dreamstime.com:** Dragoneye (tr). **94 Corbis:** Philippe Lissac / Godong (cl). **Dorling Kindersley:** Dave Abram / Rough Guides (ca).
95 Alamy Stock Photo: Everett Collection, Inc. (bc). **Dorling Kindersley:** Archives du 7e Art / Ashutosh Gowariker Productions / Photos 12 (bl); Tim Draper / Rough Guides (tl); Gavin Thomas / Rough Guides (ca); Natural History Museum, London (fcr/amethyst).
96 Alamy Images: Thornton Cohen (fcr). **Dorling Kindersley:** Tim Draper / Rough Guides (tc, fcl).
97 Dorling Kindersley: Liberty's Owl, Raptor and Reptile Centre, Hampshire, UK (br). **Getty Images:** AFP (cr). **98 Alamy Stock Photo:** John Norman (cb). **Dorling Kindersley:** Karen Trist / Rough Guides (c). **Fotolia:** Eric Isselee (bl). Getty Images: Ltd, Imagemore Co. (bc). **National Geographic Creative:** O. Louis Mazzatenta (tr). **99 Corbis:** Peter Langer / Design Pics (tl). **Dorling Kindersley:** Alan Hills / The Trustees of the British Museum (tr); Brice Minnigh / Rough Guides (fcrb). **Dreamstime.com:** Dušan Zidar (cr).
100 Getty Images / iStock: narvikk (bc). **101 Dorling Kindersley:** Tim Draper / Rough Guides (tc, br). **102 Alamy Images:** Thomas Frey / imageBROKER (br); Horizon Images / Motion (cl). **Corbis:** Adam / photocuisine (tl); Jeremy Woodhouse / Masterfile (tr). **Dorling Kindersley:** Durham University Oriental Museum (cb). **103 Corbis:** Stefano Politi Markovina / JAI (bl). **Dreamstime.com:** Craig Hanson / Rssfhs (tc). **104 Dorling Kindersley:** Tim Draper / Rough Guides (ftl, fcla). **105 Dorling Kindersley:** Simon Bracken / Rough Guides (tc); Museum of the Moving Image, London (br). **106 Dorling Kindersley:** Sean Hunter Photography (cl). **107 Dorling Kindersley:** Simon Bracken / Rough Guides (crb); Sarah Cummins / Rough Guides (cl); Suzanne Porter / Rough Guides (clb); Jean-Christophe Godet / Rough Guides (bc); Tim Draper / Rough Guides (br). **111 Corbis:** Laurie Chamberlain (br); Frans Lanting (tc); Pete Oxford / Minden Pictures (tr). **113 Alamy Stock Photo:** Penny Tweedie (cra). **Dorling Kindersley:** Sydney Opera House Trust / Jamie Marshall (crb). Dreamstime.com: Callan Chesser / Ewanchesser (br); Bin Zhou / Dropu (tr). **114 Corbis:** Steve Christo / Steve Christo Photography (cla). **Dorling Kindersley:** Pitt Rivers Museum, University of Oxford (tr). **115 Alamy Images:** travellinglight (tl). Dorling Kindersley: Paul Whitfield / Rough Guides (ca, bl). **116 Dreamstime.com:** Staphy (clb). **Getty Images:** Frank Krahmer / Photographer's Choice RF (fbl). **Science Photo Library:** British Antarctic Survey (fcl). **117 Alamy Images:** Classic Image (cr). **NASA:** U.S. Antarctic Search for Meteorites (ANSMET) (tr). **118 Dorling Kindersley:** The University of Aberdeen (tl); Jerry Young (fcl). **119 Alamy:** Chad Ehlers (tr). **Dorling Kindersley:** Roger Norum / Rough Guides (cr); Pitt Rivers Museum, University of Oxford (br).

All other images © Dorling Kindersley